DESIGN FOR COMMUNICATION

DESIGN FOR COMMUNICATION
Conceptual Graphic Design Basics

Elizabeth Resnick, *Massachusetts College of Art*

WILEY

John Wiley & Sons, Inc.

Margaret Cummins, Editor
Rosanne Koneval, Senior Editorial Assistant
Diana Cisek, Senior Managing Editor

Book design by Susan and Brian Lucid
Cover Design by Elizabeth Resnick
Text type set in Scala and Scala Sans by Martin Majoor

Library of Congress Cataloging-in-Publication Data:
Resnick, Elizabeth.
   Design for communication : conceptual graphic design basics / by Elizabeth Resnick.
     p. cm.
   Includes index.
   ISBN 0-471-41829-3
1. Graphic arts—Technique.   2. Commercial art.   3. Communication in art.
I. Title.
NC1000.R47 2003
741.6—dc21
                                               2002152203

Printed in the United States of America

10 9 8 7 6 5 4 3 2

Education is the highest form of philanthropy.
– John Maeda

For Sylvia and Sy

PREFACE

A graphic designer is a creative problem solver who is trained to conceive, plan, and execute a design that communicates a direct message in an imaginative and visually arresting manner to an intended audience regardless of the medium. Effective visual communication requires a graphic designer to inform and motivate a viewer. To do so, the graphic designer develops a concept and a visual means to present an idea.

Ideas are generated through the design process, in which graphic designers research, organize, and interpret the information, define the objectives, originate ideas, and create new visual forms. New and constantly evolving computer and communication technologies further challenge the role of the graphic designer in creating clear messages for vastly different media—the Internet, film, television, print, signage, and packaging.

Design for Communication: Conceptual Graphic Design Basics offers an appreciation and understanding of visual elements and principles of design through creative assignments that encourage experimentation and the development of personal methodology. The primary objective of this book is to encourage students to develop and master the basic conceptual thinking and technical skills that distinguish graphic designers from desktop technicians.

Design for Communication: Conceptual Graphic Design Basics is a compilation of forty-two creative college-level graphic design and typography assignments that emphasize developing a conceptual approach to graphic design problem solving. Written by twenty professional educators representing colleges and universities in the United States, England, Germany, Turkey, and Korea, each assignment is illustrated with actual visual solutions developed by their students in the classroom. Student process narratives and the educator's critical analysis, revealing fundamental principles of form and content, enhance the example projects.

Design for Communication: Conceptual Graphic Design Basics offers instructors enormous flexibility in creating graphic design courses. The number and sequence of problems assigned can easily be adjusted to fit the length and needs of any course or tailored to fit an instructor's individual style. The assignments are divided into six sections: The Elements and Principles of Design, Typography as Image,

Creative Word Play, Word and Image, Grid and Visual Hierarchy, and Visual Advocacy. Within the different sections, assignments are sequenced from basic to advanced.

Design for Communication: Conceptual Graphic Design Basics can be used as a resource by both students and instructors in and out of a classroom environment, as a primary textbook, or as a source of assignment ideas and information to refer to or by which to be inspired.

ACKNOWLEDGMENTS

Now that this project has finally been realized, my deepest appreciation must go to my editor at John Wiley & Sons, Margaret Cummins, for her patience, enthusiasm, and confidence in this project from its inception, and to Rosanne Koneval, her editorial assistant, for her patience with my inability to adhere to set deadlines.

This book is truly a compilation of the many talented design educators who kindly offered their assignments and student illustrations for publication so that we can all learn from them. Thank you for your support of this project.

I owe a great debt to all my colleagues at the Massachusetts College of Art, a caring, creative community of educators. I have also been very fortunate to be inspired by many gifted educators: Harry Callahan, Marie Cosindas, Malcolm Grear, Armin Hofmann, Maryellen Mark, Philip Meggs, Tom Ockerse, Paul Rand, Douglass Scott, Mary Anne Staniszewski, Jan van Toorn, and Wolfgang Weingart.

Thank you to the MassArt graduates who supported this project with their considerable talents: Adrienne Yapo who took on the daunting task of organizing and editing the manuscript before it was submitted to the publisher; Michael Koid who adeptly illustrated the various elements and principles of design; and Ben Barstrom who scanned many of the student images not provided in digital format.

When it became obvious that I would not have the time to design my own book, I sent an SOS out to my colleague Brian Lucid. Brian and his wife, Susan, took on this challenge and provided a superb book design.

Finally, I must thank the three most important people in my life: my husband, Victor Cockburn, who has been my loving partner for so many years, and our children, Alexei and Elana; together they were my support team throughout the duration of this project. Without their love, nothing would make any sense.

CONTENTS

INTRODUCTION

What Is Graphic Design?

"What is graphic design?" I ask my students during the first class meeting of the semester. They stare back at me quite perplexed, and I have generally come to expect this kind of response. Graphic design in our culture lacks clear boundaries that give it a simple definition. I can see it will be up to me to provide an answer. I tell them, "Graphic design is the most ubiquitous of all the art forms since it can be found everywhere and anywhere—in our homes, in the restaurants we frequent, on the streets we walk, on the highways we drive, in the movies and theaters we attend, and in every shop we enter."

It takes only a few seconds for them to visualize this information, and then their expressions register understanding. I am now at the blackboard, chalk in hand, ready to make a list. "Let's list the most obvious examples of graphic design that come to mind." It doesn't take long before someone calls out, "Advertising." Everyone nods in approval. "Is there a difference between advertising and graphic design, and if so, what is it?" I venture to ask. Silence. They are all stumped, and again no one offers up an answer. They think this is a pop quiz, and no one wants to risk giving a dumb answer.

"In the old days," I begin, "when I attended art school, the definition of graphic design was the promotion of goods and services and the definition of advertising was the selling of goods and services." Ah, it was so simple then, but this is no longer the case. The boundaries between promoting and selling have totally blurred with the arrival of global branding (the promotion of lifestyle through the selling of a particular product or service). Promotion and selling have simply joined forces.

"It is no exaggeration to say that designers are engaged in nothing less than the manufacture of contemporary reality. Today, we live and breathe design. Few of the experiences we value at home, at leisure, in the city or the mall are free of its alchemical touch. We have absorbed design so deeply into ourselves that we no longer recognize the myriad ways in which it prompts, cajoles, disturbs and excites us. It's completely natural. It's just the way things are."
— Rick Poynor

A more contemporary definition of graphic design might include the "art" of communication—to inform, educate, influence, persuade, and provide a visual experience—one that combines art and technology to communicate messages vital to our daily lives. It is simply a cultural force.

What Do Graphic Designers Do?

The graphic designer conceives, plans, and executes a design that communicates a direct message to a specific audience. The term *design* refers to the planned arrangement of visual elements organized and prioritized into a cohesive whole that becomes the visual message. Graphic designers work in business and industry as well as in the cultural and educational sectors of contemporary society. Their work is mass-produced in print, film, and electronic media—books, magazines, newspapers, advertisements, corporate identity, packaging, posters, CDs and multimedia, Web sites, billboards, television and film graphics, environmental and transportation signage, maps, charts, and other forms of information design.

Basically, graphic designers develop images to represent the ideas their clients want to communicate. This is usually accomplished by combining images (photographs, film, video, art, or illustration) and words (typography) into a unified form that responds to the content and conveys a clear message.

I Want to Be a Graphic Designer—Where Do I Begin?

Many freshmen interested in graphic design at my college ask me this question, often anticipating that the answer will involve learning computer graphics software. They look surprised when they learn they need to take foundation courses in basic design principles (2-D and 3-D) and observational or life drawing first. They need to draw and develop basic visual language vocabularies in order to communicate so that others will understand.

"Visual language can convey facts and ideas in a wider and deeper range than almost any other means of communication. It can reinforce the static verbal concept with the sensory vitality of dynamic imagery."
– Gyorgy Kepes

Visual language consists of the basic elements of two- and three-dimensional design: line, shape, texture, value, color, composition, volume, mass, and space, and how they combine to create balance, unity, proportion, rhythm, and sequence. It is beyond the scope of this book to detail this information beyond the brief summary of terms I offer in section 1: The Elements and Principles of Design. For this reason I have included an extensive bibliography that lists many fine books devoted to explaining the principles of two- and three-dimensional design.

This book is a compilation of forty-two introductory graphic design and typography assignments developed and written by creative and informed graphic design educators from the United States and abroad. Each assignment offers students a challenging encounter with creative problem solving. Before undertaking any assignment in this book, students will need to understand the basic relationship between *content* and *form*. The term *content* implies the subject matter or the information to be communicated to the viewer, and *form* is the purely visual aspect. Simply stated, content is what you want to say, and form is how you choose to say it. This relationship is negotiated during the first stage of the *design process*, the term for the steps taken before arriving at a finished design solution.

The Design Process

In professional practice, the design process usually begins with the clarification of the client's objectives (the content) and continues through an analytical phase in which the objective is further clarified and detailed. The process progresses through a visualization phase in which the overall look and feel of the piece is determined (the form).

"It is common practice among designers, especially young designers, to look for inspiration for their own designs from other designers and their work. Although someone's solution to a particular communications problem may spark a unique solution to another's problem, the practice of turning to other designers' work for ideas also influences an inappropriate pursuit of style and trend that can ultimately undermine the substance and purpose of design."
– Mark Oldach

In the classroom, the design process begins with the introduction of an assignment. It is important to listen to the instructor, who emphasizes the objectives, just as a professional designer listens to the client articulate objectives. An *objective* is the desired result, or goal, of any course of action. In design, our course of action is to project a message to a specified audience in the hope of obtaining a desired response from them. A clear definition and understanding of the problem at hand are essential to a successful project.

Once you have been given the assignment, you need to define your objectives. It is too easy to get stuck on preconceived ideas that might appear brilliant at first but create blocks to future development. The most brilliant idea is quite useless if it doesn't communicate the message or reach its intended audience. Here are steps you can follow to guide you through the design process:

1. Define the Problem and Establish Your Objectives

What is the message? Who is it for? What format can best express the message? What are the budget constraints? Creative success starts with a combination of good listening skills and asking pertinent questions. It is impossible to solve a problem you don't understand.

"Design activity is often referred to as a problem or series of problems. While the word problem in this context may seem negative, it actually signifies a challenge, an opportunity to create a successful and meaningful outcome."
– John Bowers

2. Do the Research

Learn about the subject at hand. Look for parallels in other fields, subjects, time periods, and industries. Are there any key words to define the objective? The more information you collect from multiple sources, the more associations you can make between them. Your own experiences and memories can be rich sources for inspiration. In fact, inspiration can be found just about anywhere, so carry a sketchbook to record your ideas as they occur. Besides writing and sketching, you can use your sketchbook to paste in collected items for later use.

3. Develop Your Ideas by Brainstorming

Brainstorming is an idea-generating process based on free association that uses a written record of verbalized ideas that can reveal direction toward a solution. You can start by making word lists of everything that relates to your subject. These lists can help you explore the trail of thoughts influenced by your research. Also, using words is far more time-efficient because you can write a word much faster than you can draw an idea. Keep an open mind to all ideas and let the words flow out without censorship or judgment. Make associations with the word ideas; a dictionary and the thesaurus are helpful tools to facilitate your creative thinking.

Another effective method used in brainstorming is verbal diagramming or "thought mapping." This is done by placing a key word in the middle of a piece of paper and branching out in all directions as you write down other ideas that occur and are related to the initial word. You can facilitate this procedure by asking yourself questions: Why? When? Who? How? What? This particular approach lets you picture the structure of your thinking.

If the ideas do not come easily after spending a significant amount of time working on a problem, consider diverting to another activity or task to give your mind an opportunity to process and synthesize all the information you have gathered. Once you return, you will bring a fresh eye to the work.

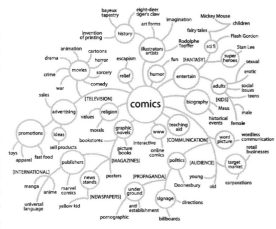

When you feel you have enough material to work from, begin visualizing your ideas by making thumbnail sketches. A *thumbnail* is a small rough sketch of a preliminary design idea. Try to generate as many of these sketches as possible because every communication problem has an infinite number of possible visual solutions. Your first ideas will probably be your most obvious ideas. Empty your mind of these and continue until it becomes increasingly difficult to think of any others. You will discover that finding unique solutions involves patience and hard work.

Thumbnails

Layouts

> "A good process keeps the mind alert. We progressively layer the material, prepare the way for connections to occur, and get ready for intuitive actions that are informed and appropriate—preventing us from jumping to conclusions prematurely. And while process is more important than result, we respect a good result from a good process."
> – Ken Hiebert

From the thumbnails you create, select at least three to develop into layout form. A *layout* is a full-size sketch of the design idea detailing its placement of type, images, and color. They are made to test whether the idea will work once it is drawn at full size. Layouts can be done with markers and a drawing pad or on the computer. Computers permit designers to accomplish numerous possibilities once a concept is identified, without the time-consuming task of having to simulate the type and image by hand. As you compose your variations in whatever media you choose to use, make it a habit to save all the layouts to later review your process.

4. Analyze Your Ideas in Terms of the Project Objectives

Critiques are the best way to articulate your ideas to others and get immediate feedback. When presenting an idea, you should be able to articulate it in one coherent sentence. During the critique, the class analyzes the individual solutions and suggests ways to increase the visual and conceptual impact of each existing idea.

In addition, a critique gives you the opportunity to scrutinize other student solutions. You can identify what works about them and what to avoid in your own work. I usually require students to present multiple solutions during the layout stage because the strongest ideas will always surface. Often you discover that what you tried to say in your layout may not always be what others read into it.

Take notes when your work is being critiqued and do not edit the responses, whether you agree with them or not. Afterward, your notes will give you insight into understanding the feedback offered about your work.

5. Implement the Final

Review your critique notes and reflect on what was said. Then ask yourself how you could combine, transform, or expand the layout that shows the most promise. Once you have determined a course of action, develop the idea into a comprehensive. A comprehensive, or *comp*, is the term used for the very detailed, polished representation of a finished design shown to the client for approval before print production. For design students working on class projects, the comp is the last stage of the design process. As a student, you will need to develop excellent manual and technical skills—a good concept poorly executed will not reveal the potential of your idea to others.

Why Bother with Such a Long Process When I Just Like to Make Things?

All too often, students mistakenly think that the design process begins by turning on a computer without first brainstorming or developing a basic concept. The computer can do much to enhance an existing concept but cannot create it. The practice of graphic design is more than the mere styling of a message.

Another common misconception students often possess is that their creative thinking will be stimulated by looking through design annuals or design magazines. At best this method can trigger an idea for a solution that has been incubating, but more often it leads students to influence and to outright plagiarism. For a solution to possess meaning or significance, it must begin with something to say. It needs content. The content is the meaning or significance contained within any visual message. If you respond with openness and sensitivity throughout the design process, your own personality will emerge and determine the look of the work.

"A creative solution always seems to be one that, when seen, appears obvious, but completely unexpected. Anyone seeing it understands it immediately. It does not require explanation. Everything fits.... You understand it more from an intuitive than from a logical thought process."
– Kit Hinrichs

Why Should I Do These Assignments?

The purpose of graphic design education is to prepare students for professional practice. Therefore, it is project-based rather than subject-based. When students engage in the process of designing they are learning by doing. Teachers create assignments to clarify visual principles and provide direct experience with certain kinds of problems or media. A good assignment will challenge a student to conceptualize and synthesize gathered information into a form that responds to the content. Good design thinking is developed through investigation, experimentation, and genuine curiosity on the part of the designer or design student. In a course, design assignments generally become more complex as students build on the visual vocabularies gained from their previous assignment experiences.

To summarize, the objective for a student of graphic design is to follow the design process to develop and present content in the form of good ideas that fit the parameters of the assignment given. What is a good idea? A good idea is an idea that requires little thought to understand but stimulates the viewer's thinking. A good idea can be expressed without having to be explained. A good idea can communicate instantly. But developing a good idea is only half of the work. To reach an audience, the good idea must be communicated visually. Class critiques help students develop a shared vocabulary for discussion. Critiques provide the opportunity for students to exchange critical and supporting ideas in a peer group setting. Students learn best from one another. To illustrate this point, only student work is used to illustrate graphic design solutions in this book.

"Whatever our goals we need a foundation—a set of guidelines to use as a reference when making basic design decisions. Such a foundation must be coherent and inclusive. It must provide us with a reference for making a multitude of design decisions, and it must simply rather than complicate the process of designing."
— Suzanne West

THE ELEMENTS AND PRINCIPLES OF DESIGN

Every assignment in this book requires a different approach, format, and concept. First and foremost, you should approach every assignment by developing a concept that will be carried throughout the design process. A *concept* is a well-developed thought, the primary idea on which your message will be based. The terms *concept* and *idea* are often synonymous and interchangeable. The word *format* here refers to the surface or substrate on which the design elements are placed. It is how you want your viewer to see your message, whether it be two-dimensional, three-dimensional, or four-dimensional. But no matter what its format or concept, every design will consist of one or more of these basic elements—*line, shape, texture, space, size,* and *value.* Successful designers organize these elements into dynamic relationships that are visually effective and understandable to a targeted audience.

The Elements of Design

Line is the element of length as a mark connecting any two points. Lines can organize, direct, separate, be expressive, suggest an emotion, or create a *rhythm.* They can join elements or divide them using a *rule,* which is a line that separates one element in a design from another.

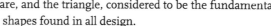

Shape refers to the external outline of a form or anything that has height and width. An example would be the three basic shapes: the circle, the square, and the triangle, considered to be the fundamental shapes found in all design.

Texture is the look and feel of a surface. In two-dimensional form, texture is essentially visual and adds richness and dimension to work. Texture can also refer to pattern, which is visual texture.

Space refers to the distance between shapes and forms, but it is best understood in design as *white space* or *negative space*— terms used to refer to the empty but often active areas that are void of visual elements.

Size is how big or small something is in scale to other objects. *Scale* refers to the process of making size relationships. Unless there is a scale of reference within a design, it is impossible to discern the relative size of objects and the meaning they represent.

Value is the relative lightness or darkness of an area or object. Value adds dimension by creating the illusion of depth in a design. With the addition of *color*, you can create and convey a mood to enhance a strong concept.

Once the concept is formally realized, it will need to be applied. The principles of design—*balance, emphasis, rhythm, unity*, and *contrast*—define the structural foundation of a design and determine how the various design elements are organized within the compositional space.

The Principles of Design

Balance occurs when all the design elements are equally distributed through the design. There are essentially two types of balance: *symmetrical* and *asymmetrical*. Symmetrical elements are arranged equally on both sides of a composition to suggest a stable or static motion. Asymmetrical elements create a deliberate imbalance to suggest variety or dynamic movement.

Emphasis indicates the most important element on the page based on the message. It's the element that stands out and gets noticed first. The most emphasized visual element in a design is called a *focal point* because it attracts the viewer's attention first. How can you create emphasis in a design? By taking an element and making it bigger, bolder, or brighter, by putting it in a contrasting color, or by surrounding it with white space.

Rhythm is a pattern created by repeating elements. Rhythm denotes the movement in the way that elements direct our gaze to scan the message for understanding or information. The term *sequence* is used to refer to the viewing order of the elements and to determine the *flow* of a multipage publication such as a magazine or book.

Unity is achieved when all the design elements relate to one another and project a sense of completeness. A viewer will always seek unity in a message. Without it, the viewer will lose interest. Designers use ideas drawn from gestalt theory to help unify their designs. Gestalt theory is the psychological process by which a viewer unites disparate design elements into a whole form that is greater than the sum of its parts. Two such ideas are *grouping* and *figure/ground*. *Grouping* happens when elements are close together and visually appear as part of a group. *Figure/ground* occurs when a viewer can identify an object (figure) as a shape distinct from its background (ground). This perception is dependent on the design principle of contrast.

"Education addresses fundamental areas of preparation: the understanding and use of the elements of visual form and syntax; the potential for the expression of meaning through form; the synthesis of form and meaning in boundaries of time, formal, the cooperation and competitiveness of the classroom, the catalytic action of the teacher and, not least, the student's own make-up, intelligence, and prior education."
– Kenneth Hiebert

Contrast stresses the visual differences in size, shape, and color between the elements to enhance the perception of a messageintended. Contrast also draws and directs the viewer's attention to specific areas of information.

The assignments in this section encourage basic exploration of both the elements and principles of design.

"Graphic design is the intersection between art and communication. Having come of age at a time when the computer was introduced and subsequently embraced as a radical new design tool and solution, I and other designers of my generation are seeing it now dominate almost every aspect of design. Design is fundamentally idea-oriented, and designers carry profound influence in their power to shape and communicate cultural concepts. The future of design lies as much in this active and critical role within society as it does in the further development of technology. Graphic design is the art of visualizing ideas, activating space, intuiting proportion. It is the result of meticulous attention to detail. Good graphic design prompts the viewer to meditate, often unconsciously, on potent word/image combinations. Good graphic design is always memorable."
– Phillippe Apeloig

Star Symbol

San Diego State University, Instructor: Susan Merritt

Everyone is familiar with the pentagram, or five-pointed star, and with its perceived meaning: outstanding, excellent, of high quality. By building on familiarity, this project helps students to understand symbolism and the role of symbols in the visual language of our culture.

The star seems at first to be a simple shape, yet it is complex and dynamic. The inherent geometry, particularly multiple instances of the golden section, provides an interesting structure, or grid, upon which students can explore and expand. Students are encouraged to work with intuition and mathematics, such as the ratio of the golden section and the Fibonacci series, to further develop the star's structure in meaningful and relevant ways. Outcomes vary tremendously even though the basis for each design is the same.

The project guides beginners through a disciplined designing process, which includes research and information gathering. At this stage students realize how ubiquitous the star actually is as they collect examples of existing symbols, such as Texaco and Carl's Jr., that include or are based on the pentagram. Additional phases of the process help students to determine criteria, investigate possibilities through sketches, and evaluate, assess, and select appropriate solutions. Once a selection is made, students develop and refine a chosen design; execute a comprehensive drawing; implement computer-generated vector art in black and white and in color, which is rendered in Illustrator; and finally make an oral presentation about the outcome of their work.

Students are encouraged to focus on visual quality by effectively applying elements and principles of design, particularly line and shape, contrast, figure/ground relationships, symmetry and asymmetry, movement, depth, repetition, radiation, pattern, rhythm, and harmony. Once the two-dimensional versions are finalized, students translate the design into a three-dimensional form, which further promotes critical thinking and problem solving and expands their ability to think and communicate visually.

Assignment Brief

Focusing on the principles of design, such as pattern, symmetry, balance, radiation, repetition, movement, and figure/ground relationship (positive and negative shapes), develop a visually dynamic symbol that evolves from the inherent geometric structure found in the five-pointed star—no letters, no pictures. As you work, prepare to describe how you have used a particular design principle.

The symbol must be designed with straight lines only. Sketches are to be done using various black markers (sixty minimum—six to a page, ten pages, based on the template created in exercise 6). T-square, triangles, and technical pens may be used to ink the final art on a high-quality 15" × 20" hot press illustration board (Letramax 2000), or it may be cut with an X-acto knife from either parapaque, rubylith, or amberlith opaque block-out films. Final art must measure 10" from point to point.

Objectives

Symbol design makes up a large part of the day-to-day activity of a graphic designer. A symbol is a visual element used to identify a company, product, or organization. The purpose of this assignment is to offer you an opportunity to understand the demands of developing and the discipline required to execute a symbol while becoming familiar with the tools and materials of graphic design. You will learn more about the perceived meaning of the five-pointed star and the dynamic structure of this shape, including the inherent golden section, through exercises, sketches, research, collected examples, and study of existing symbols. This project will also provide an opportunity to improve necessary design and technical skills as you carry your idea from the sketch stage to the final color presentation comp and camera ready art

Specifications

1. Black-and-white version inked on 15" × 20" illustration board.
2. Color version using Pantone or similar paper (one or two colors) on 15" × 20" board.
3. Notebook documenting the project, to include in this order: one-page typewritten design brief, star research (geometry on the star's structure and collected examples of existing star symbols, such as Carl's Jr., Star Systems, and Texaco, to name a few), six exercises, star practice drawings, two golden rectangle exercises, two angled-ruler exercises, sixty black-marker sketches (ten 8.5" × 11" pages, six sketches to a page), six refined sketches of the selected final sketch (one page with six sketches on a page), twelve color sketches of the final design (two 8.5" × 11" pages, six sketches to a page), 10" colored-marker comp, 10" black-and-white comp, and at least one revised comp on 15" × 20" visualizing bond. Include all additional research, sketches, or comps that you do, including Illustrator exercises to be determined. Put your name on the spine of the notebook with an Avery label.

Process

1. The star must be recognizable even if vague.
2. The design must be successful in black and white and not rely on color to be successful.
3. The color version should build on the black-and-white art, being careful not to alter the original concept and composition when assigning color.
4. Experiment with symmetry, balance, radiation, repetition, movement, and figure/ground relationship (positive and negative shapes).
5. The design must hold up when reduced. (Be careful of complexity, very fine lines that can fall apart, and small areas that can "clog up" in reduction.)

Timeline

Week One

Students research various methods to construct a five-pointed star and collect examples of existing symbols that incorporate or are based on a five-pointed star, to demonstrate wide use.

Complete exercises 1 and 2. Reduce exercise 2 so that the point-to-point measurement of the horizontal line of the star is 2½" and make six copies to be used in exercise 6.

Week Two

Material demonstrations: adhesives (rubber cement, spray mount); parapaque, rubylith, and amberlith block-out films. Complete exercises 3, 4, and 5.

Demonstrate how to divide a given space into equal parts using an angled ruler. Complete exercise 6.

Lecture on the golden section. Discuss the five-pointed star as a metaphor and review design elements and principles. Begin sixty sketches using the sketch template created in exercise 6.

Week Three

Complete all sixty sketches, and bring copies of all ten sketch pages to be cut up in class. As a group: Define categories based on the visual communication possibilities, such as simple, complex, symmetrical, asymmetrical, dynamic, static, inclusive (elements are contained within the pentagram/pentagon), expansive (elements extend outside of the pentagram/pentagon), and so on. Sort sketches into categories on the bulletin board or tape to large sheets of white paper. Each student chooses three of his or her own sketches to refine; do six refinement sketches based on each of the selected sketches, then choose one and draw a 10" point-to-point comprehensive using black marker on visualizing bond.

Week Four

Lecture on communicating with color, and introduction of the Pantone Matching System. Critique the 10" black-marker comprehensives in small groups of no more than five students. Complete a revised 10" marker comprehensive based on feedback from critique and twelve colored-marker or colored-pencil sketches using one or two "flat" colors based on final design.

Week Five

Complete the 10" colored-marker comprehensive.

Demonstrate cutting and mounting colored paper.

Complete the final camera-ready art using technical pen and ink, parapaque, amberlith, or rubylith (red opaque block-out films recommended).

Demonstrate Adobe Illustrator (Mac interface; Illustrator tutorial; pen tool [open and closed paths; fill and stroke]); complete exercises 1, 2, 3, and 6 in Illustrator. Based on the final 10" camera-ready art, re-create the star symbol in Illustrator.

Due for presentation: three-ring binder documenting the design and production processes, including Illustrator exercises and laser output of final design; final camera-ready art on 15" × 20" hot press illustration board; color comprehensive using cut paper mounted on 15" × 20" hot press illustration board; and high resolution output of black-and-white and color star symbol mounted on 15" × 20" board.

Exercise 1
Draw non-repro blue guidelines. Ink, as shown, using technical pen point #00 on 8.5" x 11" Letramax 2000 illustration board. (10 horizontal, 16 vertical lines). Extend lines and retouch using embibed eraser and eraser shield. Cover with tracing paper.

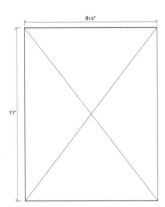

Exercise 2: Step 1
Find the center of the 8.5" x 11" Letramax board by drawing blue guidelines from corner to corner. The two lines intersect at the center point.

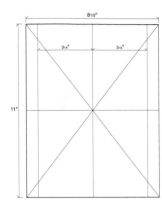

Exercise 2: Step 2
Draw a vertical and horizontal non-repro blue guideline through the center point using t-square and triangle. Measure out from the vertical center guide 3.5" to the right and 3.5" to the left. Draw two blue guidelines to represent a distance of 7".

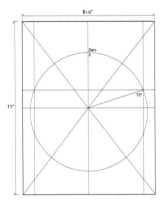

Exercise 2: Step 3
Use a protractor to mark off a 72° increment with zero at the top (360° divided by 5 points of the star equals 72°). Draw a non-repro blue line connecting the center and the point at 72° that intersects the vertical guide on the right side. Draw a circle using this angled line as the radius.

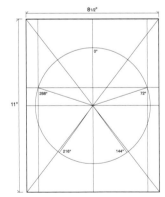

Exercise 2: Step 4
Draw the remaining lines at 72° increments using non-repro blue. These lines are the center spines of the points of the star. The points of the star touch the circle. Beginning with the horizontal segment, connect the five points to define the star.

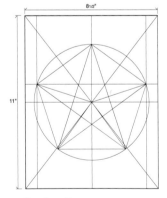

Exercise 2: Step 5
In non-repro blue, connect all the outer points to create the star. Connect all the star's points to define the pentagon. Draw the lines carefully. Be exact.

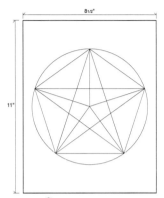

Exercise 2: Step 6
Using technical pen #1 with a compass and universal adapter, ink the circle. Carefully ink the spines of the star's points and the outer lines of the star. Carefully ink the pentagon.

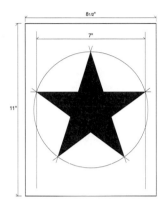

Exercise 3
Draw guidelines with non-repro blue, then ink on Letramax 2000 using #1 technical pen point, criss-cross all outer points as shown, then retouch with eraser and eraser shield/white out to get sharp points. Cover with tracing paper.

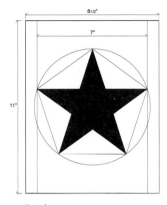

Exercise 4
Draw guidelines with non-repro blue on 8.5" x 11" Letramax 2000 board, place a piece of Parapaque (red opaque film) over the star, then cut along the star's outer edges. Remove film on the outside of the star, leaving a red star. Cover with tracing paper.

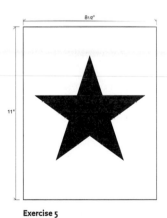

Exercise 5
Draw guidelines with non-repro blue on Letramax 2000 board. Using white drafting tape, attach an amberlith or rubylith overlay to the top edge of the board. Cut along the star's outer edges; remove the film leaving the opaque star. Cover with tracing paper.

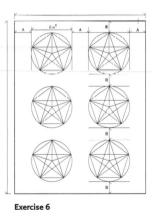

Exercise 6
Reduce exercise #2 to 2.5" point-to-point on a copy machine. Make six copies of the small star. Draw guide-lines with non-repro blue and paste-up stars spacing them equally as shown on 8.5" x 11" Letramax 2000 to create a template for the sketches. Cover with tracing paper.

Critiques

A variety of star designs are included here to demonstrate the range of solutions. Since these projects have been collected over a series of semesters, the students were not readily available to offer their comments. However, as a result of suggestions from students, as well as my observations of their work and their reactions to the project, I have modified the assignment over time to improve the learning experience. For example, I assign a specific number of sketches because students never do enough on their own and thus limit their potential to develop an interesting solution. I restrict the process to only allow straight lines in order to focus students on principles of design and the structure of the star instead of the addition of unrelated shapes and images. I include a three-dimensional component since graphic design students tend to think very two-dimensionally and apply two-dimensional thinking to three-dimensional forms. Working with paper, foam core, or clay, students explore the potential for expanding the flat shape into a form.

Sometimes students grumble about the project being too structured and limiting their creativity when, in fact, the limitations sharpen their problem-solving abilities. Later, many students come back to express their appreciation for an environment in which they were able to establish a disciplined working process.

Here are some additional observations for teaching this project: Students should avoid a fine-pointed marker when sketching because it allows them to work in too detailed a manner. Also, avoid sketching with a pencil since it displays the concepts in gray, not black. Often students struggle to create a design that is asymmetrical because they have learned that asymmetry is more interesting than symmetry. However, the star is inherently symmetrical and full of repetition. Students should work with these attributes, especially since a goal of the assignment is to build on the structure and geometry of the pentagram. The center of the star tends to be the most challenging and demands much attention to resolve. Carry the thematic concept throughout the design and provide a sense of relationship between the outermost parts to the center.

Figure 1-1.1: **Robert Hernandez**

Figure 1-1.2: **Arturo Gonzalez**

Figure 1-1.3: **Jonathan Cayabyab**

Figure 1-1.4: **Berenice Limon**

Figure 1-1.5: **Sheila David**

Figure 1-1.6: **Jessica Schieber**

Figure 1-1.7: **Michael Novido**

Figure 1-1.8: **Rosalina Damicog**

Figure 1-1.9: **Sylvia Wagner**

Figure 1-1.10: **Allan Manzano**

Object Semantics
North Carolina State University, Instructor: Kermit Bailey

Assignment Brief
Select an object from one of the following categories:
– Fruits and/or vegetables
– Carpenter's tools
– Musical instruments
– Kitchen tools

Some general guides for your choice:
– Easily recognizable
– Interesting but simple in form, though not too simple
– Smaller rather than bigger
– Handheld
– Common, not novelty
– Object that has articulated nuances, accent points of difference
– If fruit or vegetable, won't rot in three days
– Has potential expressive value

Objectives
– Development of a critical eye necessary for the design of letter forms, fonts, logo, page design, and so on.
– Understanding of the usefulness and necessity of process in design
– Understanding and analysis of semantics as related to form-generative techniques
– Expansion of approaches to drawing, interpretation as a means of illustration
– Introductory software mastery, technical training

Process
Bring interesting examples of your object to class. These can be photos of the object, but it is best to have the actual object to study from multiple views. Consider how the object looks, what it is made of, how it reflects light, and what the essential features are for recognition. This object/subject will be explored in multiple iterative situations over four to five weeks.

Timeline
Week One
Create a series of black-and-white line drawings (gestures) using brush and ink or any other mark-making tool. This will be reproduced and eventually digitally scanned. At this point in the process, stay loose in your drawing technique and your approach to suggesting or describing the object. Vary your drawing style. Some

drawing iterations may have very little detail, while others will have more. Produce some drawings very fast, others with more deliberation. Consider the potential expressive value of the object relative to its meaning (semantics), functionality, and/or materiality. Maintain object recognition even when the form becomes more abstracted. Initially, you may want to bring a couple of objects into class and draw them until you discern better the goals of the project, but try to avoid flip-flopping—most common objects are adequate. Find beauty in the commonplace and simplify the complex.

Weeks Two and Three

Use the original gesture as a starting point, a base drawing. Based on the following methodology, develop and draw a series of studies in Adobe Illustrator or Macromedia Freehand.

Target qualities:
– Original gesture of the object derived from paintbrush or other mark-making tools
– Painterly: system of thick and thin strokes, calligraphic, closest to the original gestural expression
– Graphical: system of uniformity in stroke or rectilinear in general, distinctively evolved from its brush stroke origin
– Radical: extreme deviation or abstraction from the original form/gesture, bizarre
– Nirvana: selection of best expression or form considering all the methodologies; possible hybridized form; form that feels right or best

Weeks Four and Five

Develop a documentation book whose form and semantics are inspired by the object. The book should reveal the process and iterative studies (five unique iterations and predevelopments), compositional studies utilizing form elements and extrapolations from the object, color studies, and an object study in the context of communication such as a poster.

Critiques

Object Semantics: "Dustpan Studies," *Emily Jones,* Figure 1-2.1

Instructor's Evaluation

Emily's choice of object for the study, a dustpan, is an interesting one in that it definitely fits the criteria of being commonplace but not novelty, simple but not too simple. As I see it, her challenge and eventual success lie in finding the beauty in the commonplace object and uncovering its potential for expressive value.

Emily brought the actual object to class. After drawing the object from multiple perspectives, she decided relatively early in the process that the mostly flat, full frontal view would create the highest level of object recognition. I believe that this was an especially important decision by the student. For the dustpan, the front reveals its essence, or object language, and gives the greatest possibilities for departure and variation while still maintaining relative recognition.

Figure 1-2.1

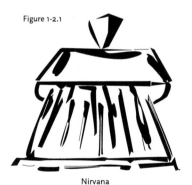

Nirvana

Radical

Graphical

Painterly

Gesture

Student Statement

Starting with india ink and brush, the first step was to generate hundreds of quick gestural drawings, trying to capture the essence of the dustpan. After scanning the most successful sketch, the creation of the four formal compositions began: painterly, graphical, radical, and nirvana. A system of line weights and shapes was used to create each concept. Once the final compositions were created, they were examined and dissected for the creation of other compositions, ending with the series of posters.

In considering its success, the dustpan series is a careful, expressive articulation of difference. As should be expected and accepted, the categories within the series may share formal overlapping characteristics. As such, one could have an iteration that is seemingly both graphical and radical—a hybrid expression. Emily takes effective advantage of these possibilities and discoveries. In improving the series, I might suggest an increased distinction between the painterly studies and the graphical studies at the first-glance optical/perceptual level. Otherwise, I believe that the series is an outstanding example that honors the process and shows a critical eye.

Object Semantics: "Trumpet Studies," *Jennifer Newnam,* Figure 1-2.2

Instructor's Evaluation

Jennifer's selection of a trumpet as the object of study was a particularly good choice. The trumpet meets many of the suggested guidelines in that it is easily recognizable and has potential expressive value. As an object, the trumpet also presents possible contradictions that lend themselves favorably to the problem. It may be perceived as both simple and complex in form, organic or geometric. In addition, the trumpet cannot be divorced from its social context, that of music—jazz, R and B, classical, and so on. I believe that Jennifer's studies are a negotiation of these issues and contexts through formal changes and associated cultural meanings.

Jennifer did not draw with the benefit of actually studying a three-dimensional trumpet in the classroom. Initially, she made drawings based on photographs, all done in a loose fashion consistent with the gestural requirement as the base drawing. Perhaps more important, she made drawings based on memory, impressions, and experience with the object. The consequence of not having the object at hand, I believe, served as a useful, maybe even serendipitous, way to distill the image (object) into a simpler form.

The trumpet iterations successfully negotiate difference (form and expressive value) as an important criterion to meet. Although different, a formal kinship is clear throughout the series from the original gesture to the more exaggerated radical state. Jennifer drew, redrew, and tweaked literally tens of trumpet iterations, each maintaining a high level of technical and expressive clarity. In further enhancing her series, I would suggest at least one more iterative development to even further radicalize the far end of the series, making it even more bizarre. Otherwise her series serves as an outstanding example, and I believe it will be instructive to her as she considers more applied graphic design problems (logo design, font, etc.) later.

Figure 1-2.2

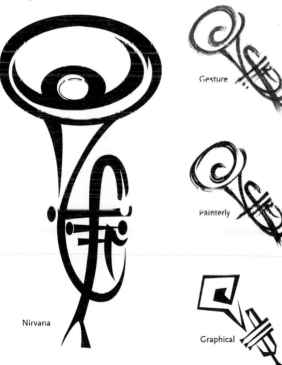

Nirvana

Gesture

Painterly

Graphical

Radical

Student Statement

I felt that the most crucial part of the project was the original gesture drawing, because it served as the template for the other renderings. I acquired the gesture drawing after doing pages of sketches. The more familiar my hand became with the instrument, the quicker I drew it; the quicker I drew it, the more fluid the strokes became.

Symbol Design

Iowa State University, Instructor: Lisa Fontaine

Assignment Brief

You will create a symbol design using simplified graphic forms, exploring their potential to impart meaning. Your design decisions (about line quality, mass, orientation of forms, etc.) will help to enhance and clarify the specific intended meaning to be communicated by your symbolic form.

Select a word from the list of industries or disciplines:

agriculture	conservation
hydroelectricity	mediation
hotel (or hostel)	navigation
optics	manufacturing
international trade	telecommunications
engineering	animal protection service

Create a distinct symbol for the selected word. The success of your symbol will be based on both formal and conceptual criteria.

Conceptual criteria: The symbol must communicate a clear message about the industry or phenomenon by incorporating symbolic visual references that suggest some of its inherent qualities and attributes.

To begin, consider the attributes of the industry you are trying to convey. How can these attributes be conveyed? Consider fundamental questions about your industry: Why does it exist? What does it contribute? How is the world different because of it (or what would the world be like without it)? What are the contributing "ingredients" to your industry? Are there historical or mythological references? Are there metaphors or analogies that could be considered?

For example, if your industry was biotechnology (not one of your choices), you might consider the following:

— Attributes: control, precision, duplication, exaggeration, uniformity, predictability, growth, enlargement
— Why it exists: to control the quality, quantity, or durability of living things
— Ingredients: sun, soil, test tubes, DNA strips, double helix, sheep
— Historical references: Dolly (the first cloned sheep)
— Mythological references: any of the creation stories from mythology
— Metaphorical references: playing God, acting as the creator

Formal criteria: The symbol must create a synthesis of forms by successfully applying the design principles.

Consider which of the design principles seem appropriate to your topic:

direction	anomaly
concentration	focal point
repetition	contrast of line/mass
radiation	contrast of organic/geometric
similarity	contrast of few/many
confrontation	contrast of small/large

Objectives

– To become familiar with the formal and conceptual aspects of symbol design
– To explore form reduction as a methodology

Specifications

Develop the final symbol in black and white. The final symbol should be 6" in its longest dimension. You may complete your drawing on the computer or render it by hand, as long as it is clean and well crafted. This submission will be made as a quality printout that is included in the front of your process notebook. Include all of your ideation and process sketches (with explanations of the decision making) in this notebook. Identify your objectives on each sketch.

Process

Collect related imagery, including historical engravings or other references. Collect existing symbols that relate to similar topics. What makes them successful or unsuccessful? Begin the ideation process with sketches that explore the conceptual attributes and ingredients you've already identified. Create several rough sketches. Select the strongest and most unique ideas to develop further. Refine your ideas by exploring formal variations in contrast, focal point, dominance, repetition, similarity, and so on. Develop one of these symbol variations to a final design.

Your symbol should communicate its meaning clearly with a minimal amount of detail.

Figure 1-3.1

Student Statement
In this symbol, my goal was to communicate both the product and the process of international trade. The tilted square in the center represents a package, or product, which can go in any direction from its source. The rotating arrows represent the continuous movement of goods around the globe.

Critiques

International Trade Symbol, *Maritas Algones,* Figure 1-3.1

Instructor's Evaluation

In this symbol for international trade, the designer employs the principles of contrast, repetition, and direction to great advantage. The rotation of the globe is suggested through the orbiting forms of two arrows moving in contrasting directions. These arrows, which can also be seen as the lowercase letter t for trade, are visually dominant in the symbol. This dominance is achieved through the contrast of linear and massive form. Conceptually, this emphasizes the importance of the trading activity. By placing the two arrows in exactly opposite directions, the designer calls to mind the dichotomy of import and export. The area enclosed by the two arrowheads forms a "package"—an object to be bought or sold in the trading process (and hence the focal point of the concept). The central location of the package is an intriguing choice, since symmetry tends to stabilize a form and reduce its sense of movement. This contradiction of symmetrical form and dynamic movement within the symbol is intentional—through it we can see the continuous flow of goods, stopped momentarily for the exchange that occurs as the package passes between buyer and seller. The 45-degree tilt to the globe and its arrows helps to avoid misinterpretations about the symbol's meaning. For example, a horizontal emphasis of the arrows might seem to address only east-west exchange, while a vertical placement might refer to north and south. By keeping the two arrows equal in dominance yet tilted in axis, it more effectively represents all global traders, without focusing on who sells to whom.

Figure 1-3.2

Agriculture, *Zach King,* Figure 1-3.2

Instructor's Evaluation

In this symbol, the designer employs the design principles of repetition, similarity, radiation, direction, and contrast to embody many of the attributes of agriculture. Some visual references are immediately recognizable, while others are more subtle. For example, it is easy to see the leaf forms as they sprout from the curving branch. Other forms are less direct: an implied water drop in the negative space, for example, or the sense of outward growth as organic forms radiate from the center to emerge larger and stronger. The sense of radiation also calls to mind the energy of the sun, an integral

Student Statement
While agriculture is dependent on machinery, it has its origins in the natural process of plant growth. By emphasizing the organic forms, this symbol is able to make reference to the plants, the seeds, the sun, and the cycle of growth. Similarity of the forms helps to create a sense that all of these forces are working together in harmony.

player in the process of agriculture. While the crescent forms move outward in a radiating gesture, they can also provide a protective enclosure for the fragile leaf forms. This identifies the farmer (and the agricultural process) as a nurturing, protective force in the life of the plant. The circular rotation of the symbol also alludes to the cyclical nature of crop growth. The leaf forms are intentionally generic, so as not to represent a specific agricultural crop. Their simple shape allows them to also be interpreted as seeds.

Through the integration of these concepts, the designer is able to communicate all of the elements inherent in the agricultural process: seed, plant, water, sun, growing cycle, and the nurturing hand of the farmer. That the complexity of the agricultural process can be suggested in such a visually reduced form is a testament to the designer's creative process.

Telecommunications, *Budi Sutomo,* Figure 1-3.3
Instructor's Evaluation

Figure 1-3.3

In this symbol, the designer uses extreme simplicity of form to refer to the essence of telecommunication, which is the transmission of information and communication through electronic means. The principles of contrast, similarity, direction, gradation, and radiation are used to bring formal interest and conceptual clarity to the symbol. The designer chose the most immediately recognizable forms that relate to the topic: sound waves and electrical energy. Each is represented by a linear element—

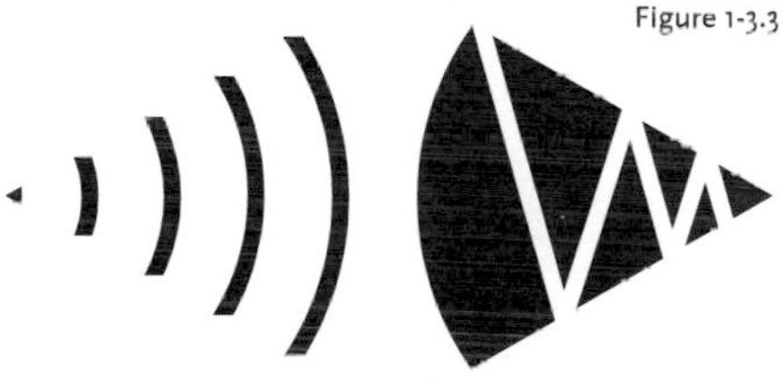

Student Statement
Telecommunications involves a process where information is being transmitted electronically from one end to another. Dynamic movement is represented in this symbol by the radiating curves and the gradating zigzag lines. Presenting the sound waves in curves and the electric waves in sharp angular lines gives contrast and interest within the symbol. The play on negative space also helps in creating tension and a focal point.

the radiating curved lines and the gradating zigzag form. These lines can also be interpreted as information, or messages, moving through space.

These two forms, while contrasting in their curving versus angular lines, are made similar through their containment within cone shapes. Each seems to move toward the other, creating a "charged" field of energy in the negative space between them. This energy field remains undefined, yet is clearly suggestive of a result or effect of the convergence of audio and electronic signals. While the two forms are seen mostly as moving inward toward each other, the cone shapes themselves point outward, referring to the ultimate purpose of telecommunications, which is not to merely bring these two elements together, but to do so for the purpose of both outgoing and incoming communication.

Optics, *David Young,* Figure 1-3.4

Instructor's Evaluation

In this symbol, the designer chose to present the human eye as an example of all optical phenomena. In any optical device, the natural phenomenon of light is controlled, focused, and directed through a lens (or lenses) so that it can be converted into something specific by the user. By focusing on the human eye, the designer calls on the viewers' intimate appreciation for this optical manipulation of light. Since vision is considered one of the vital senses required in so much of human endeavor, the eye becomes an ideal metaphor to communicate the significance of the optical process, whether it is mechanical or human in nature.

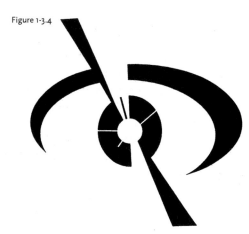

Figure 1-3.4

The decision to use the human eye brings depth to the concept while ensuring simplicity of form. It seems unnecessary to show the technical process by which light is converted, since the viewer is encouraged to apply his or her background knowledge about human eyesight to the topic. The designer has effectively used the principles of similarity, direction, contrast, and radiation to create a simple and clear symbol.

Student Statement
In designing a symbol to represent optics, my intention was to keep it simple without being too simple. I constructed an eye using basic geometric forms that resulted in an easily understood optical representation. Shapes representing light added dynamic quality.

Lettermark
San Diego State University, Instructor: Susan Merritt

Armin Hofmann assigned this project at the Basel School of Design when I was a graduate student there. I found it to be a challenging and rewarding learning experience, so I passed it along to my beginning students when I started teaching. Most beginning students take the alphabet and its individual letterforms for granted. This project requires that they examine the characteristic shape and structure of the two letters in their initials and determine how the two forms can be integrated into a unified whole to create a mark in which each letter is integral to the other. It demands attention to all of the details of letterform design, including stroke, weight and contrast, serif style, case, and especially positive and negative space. Using a student's initials allows it to be personal, and if it is well designed, the mark can be used later in the student's stationery layout.

Assignment Brief
Focusing on contrast and figure/ground relationship (positive and negative shapes), design a visually interesting logotype that integrates the initials of your first and last names (two letters) into a unified whole. The letters should be based initially on these five typefaces: Garamond, Baskerville, Bodoni, Century Expanded, and Helvetica. The lettermark must contain curves and the letters must "read" in consecutive order: first initial first, then the last initial. You may incorporate either serif or sans serif, uppercase or lowercase, roman or italic, condensed or expanded, bold or light, or a combination of any two.

Sketches are to be done using various black markers (sixty minimum—six to a page, ten pages). French curve, T-square, triangles, circle template, and technical pens must be used to ink the final art on a high-quality hot press illustration board or Mylar. The final design should measure 10" in height on 15" x 20" hot press illustration board, such as Letramax 2000. The width of the logotype will vary based on your design.

Objectives
The purpose of this assignment is to offer students an opportunity to understand the demands of developing and executing a mark that is based on letterforms and incorporates curves. Students learn about the structure of certain letterforms and type styles as they research and study existing typefaces, as well as other marks that incorporate letters. This project will also provide an opportunity to improve necessary design and technical skills as ideas are carried from the early sketch stage to the final color presentation comprehensive and camera-ready art.

Specifications

1. Black-and-white version on 15" × 20" illustration board.
2. Color version using Pantone paper (one or two colors) or comparable paper.
3. Notebook documenting the project, to include in this order: one-page typewritten statement, logotype research (collected examples of existing logos, such as Bank of America, IBM, and 3M, to name a few), six exercises, any additional in-class exercises or computer exercises, 60 black-marker sketches (ten 8.5" × 11" pages, six sketches to a page), at least one page of additional refinement sketches, twelve color sketches (two 8.5" × 11" pages, six sketches to a page), 10" black-and-white comp, and at least one revised comprehensive on visualizing bond. Notebooks should be identified by student's name on white tape or an Avery label.

Process

1. The solution must be successful in black and white. It cannot rely on color to be successful.
2. The color version should build on the black-and-white art; be careful not to alter the original by applying color.
3. Experiment with balance, movement, symmetry/asymmetry, interesting positive/negative space relationships, and other principles of design.
4. The work must hold up when reduced. (Be careful of very fine lines that can fall apart and small areas that can "clog up" in reduction.)

Timeline

Week One

Begin logo research: Students research different letterform styles and collect examples of existing logotypes and wordmarks, especially those that integrate two or more letters to create a new mark. This allows for discussion and critique of existing solutions, demonstrates widespread use, shows possibilities, establishes guidelines on what is successful and what isn't, and builds a database for what has already been done. Complete exercises 1, 2 and 3.

Week Two

Complete ten shape studies based upon the sixteen-dot grid of exercise 3 following the guidelines for exercise 4. Complete ten shape studies based on the sixteen-dot grid of exercise 3 following the guidelines for exercise 5. Material demonstration: Mylar. Complete exercise 4 and 5.

Week Three

Tool demonstration: French curve. Complete exercise 6. Lecture on the letterform design and grid of Albrecht Dürer. Complete exercises 7 and 8. Complete twenty-four of the sixty sketches (four pages, six sketches to a page).

Week Four

Complete all sixty sketches—bring copies of all sixty sketch pages to be cut up in class. As a group: Define categories based on the visual communication possibilities, such as simple, complex, symmetrical, asymmetrical, dynamic, static, connected on the side, connected on the top or bottom, well integrated, use of positive and negative space, figure/ground relationship. Sort sketches into categories on the bulletin board or tape to large sheets of white paper. Each student chooses three of his or her own sketches to refine; do six refinement sketches based on each of the selected sketches, then choose one and draw a 10" comprehensive using black marker on visualizing bond.

Critique 10" black-marker comprehensive in small groups of no more than five students.

Complete a revised 10" marker comprehensive based on feedback from critique and twelve colored-marker or colored-pencil sketches using one or two "flat" colors based on final design.

Complete the 10" colored marker comprehensive.

Demonstrate cutting curves out of colored paper.

Complete final camera-ready art using technical pen and ink.

Week Five

Demonstrate creating Bezier curves in Adobe Illustrator; complete exercises 1–5 in Illustrator. Based on the final 10" camera-ready art, re-create the mark in Illustrator.

Due for presentation: three-ring binder documenting the design and production processes, including Illustrator exercises and laser output of final design; final camera-ready art on 15" × 20" hot press illustration board; color comprehensive using cut paper mounted on 15" × 20" hot press illustration board; and high-resolution output of black-and-white and color star symbol mounted on 15" × 20" hot press illustration board.

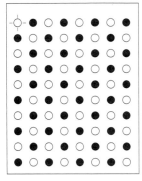

Exercise 1
On Letramax 2000, draw guidelines with non-repro blue, then use technical pen #0 for outlined circles and #1 for filled-in circles. Fill-in solid circles with black ink. Cover with tracing paper.

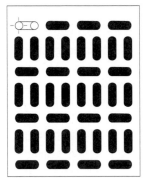

Exercise 2
Draw guidelines with non-repro blue, then use technical pen #1 to create two circles and two lines connecting them so they look like a single shape. Fill in shapes with black ink on Letramax 2000.

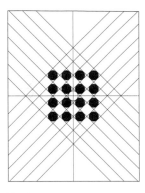

Exercise 3
On Letramax 2000 board, draw guidelines with non-repro blue, then draw sixteen ⅝"-circles to form a grid of four rows of dots centered on the board. All circles should be tangent to (touching) blue guidelines drawn at 45° angles as shown. Fill in the sixteen circles with black ink.

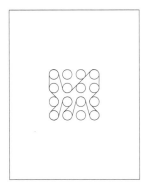

Exercise 4: Step 1
Create 10 shapes by connecting the dots with straight lines at various angles as needed. The lines should not touch or cross each other. Select one of the shapes. Ink on Letramax 2000 board using circle template, technical pens, and straight edge.

Exercise 4: Step 2
Ink the outline. Leave circles non-repro blue. Shape to be filled in with black ink.

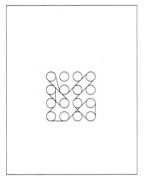

Exercise 5: Step 1
Create 10 more shapes by connecting the dots with straight lines at various angles as needed. In this exercise the lines must touch or cross at least once.

Exercise 5: Step 2
Attach a mylar overlay to the top of the board with white tape, Recreate the shape on mylar using circle template, technical pens, and tools.

Exercise 6
Spray mount letterform onto Letramax 2000 board. Tape mylar to the top of board. Recreate the letterform using ink, technical pens, t-square, triangles, and french curves.

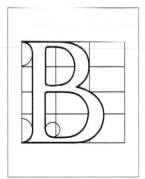

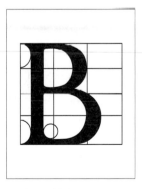

Exercise 7 and 8: Step 1
On two different Letramax 2000 boards, in non-repro blue draw the first letter of your first and last names 7" in height based on the structure of Albrect Dürer's letterforms.

Exercise 7 and 8: Step 2
Use technical pen #1 to ink the outline, then fill in with black ink. Use compass and/or circle template to create the curves. Cover with tracing paper.

Figure 1-4.1: **Karen Jacobs**

Critiques

A variety of lettermark designs are included here to demonstrate the range of solutions. Since these projects have been collected over a series of semesters, the students were not readily available to offer their comments. However, as a result of suggestions from students, as well as my observations of their work and their reactions to the project, I have modified the assignment over time to improve the learning experience. For example, I assign a specific number of sketches because students never do enough on their own and thus limit their potential for developing more unique solutions. To complement the star project, which I assign

Figure 1-4.2: **Michelle Taylor**

first and which only allows straight lines to be used, I require the lettermark solution to include curves. Students are introduced to curve-making tools and engage in exercises to help them learn how to work with these tools.

Figure 1-4.3: **Sheila Franks**

If your graphic design curriculum does not include letterform design, instructors need to demonstrate methods of constructing letterforms. Historical reference and research materials, such as the Albrecht Dürer diagrams, are helpful and ensure that students maintain the structural integrity of the letters. The exercises also offer experience with constructing the forms, particularly with transitions from straight strokes into curves.

Some observations for teaching this project: Beginning students should avoid sketching with a pencil since it displays the design in gray, not black, and minimizes the contrast between positive and negative shapes. Encourage students to explore a wide range of possibilities and to develop their ideas. Experimentation is important. Try the two forms in different

Figure 1-4.4: **Jeff Guerra**

relationships: one above the other, one below the other, side by side, and overlapping. Explore one letter as a positive shape and the other as a negative shape. Examine the parts that make up the letters. What parts are necessary for recognition of the letter and what parts can be defined with implied line and shape?

Figure 1-4.5: **Stephanie Stearns**

Vinyletteror

Old Dominion University, Instructor: Ken Fitzgerald

The primary elements of design—text and image—are usually assigned strict and separate roles. In addition to the content of the words, meaning in text can come from the typography: the fonts chosen and the arrangement of the letterforms. Imagery usually is illustrative of the text and is primarily photographic. Illustration (drawing, painting, collage) is frequently realistic or representative.

All the birds turn to words
All the words float in sequence
No one knows what they mean
Everyone just ignores them
—Brian Eno, "Sky Saw"

Since the introduction of the computer as the means to realize text, letterforms have (arguably) been regarded and handled more abstractly as imagery. Designers engage in form making to create meaning, usually stylizing provided text and commissioning (or acquiring by various other means) imagery. They may also extend this role to be image makers, fusing the roles of text and image.

Assignment Brief

Make an abstract composition with vinyl lettering, as is commonly used for sign making. This project should not be considered a sign and should not be readable as such. While you are beginning with recognizable letterforms, they should be rendered in whatever manner(s) as to make them unrecognizable. How far must you go in distorting the characters to eliminate their recognition as letterforms? How does direct manipulation of letters affect (if at all) your relationship with computer-generated characters?

Specifications

1. Size: 11" × 17" horizontal or vertical orientation.
2. Color: Black vinyl lettering on white background. A minimal use of red vinyl may be used for emphasis.

Process

- Create an abstract composition derived from letterforms but which shows little or no remnant of their origin.
- Make your composition as unexpected and engaging as possible.
- Design the entire page.
- Consider the potential of letterforms that are unavailable in computer-generated and printed characters.
- Make maximum use of the specific characteristics of vinyl letters: flexibility, dimensionality, directness, and the negative space of the sheet. Push these to the limits: bend, twist, layer, rip, and cut.

Figure 1-5.1

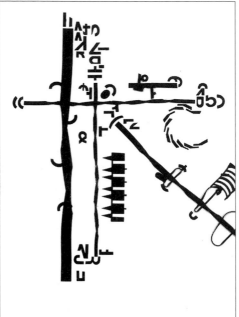

Student Statement
*There is much more to vinyl letters than the individual letters.
I portrayed this idea by using the entire vinyl sheet (edges,
spaces between letters, etc.) and wanted the completed abstract
form to be both symmetrical and chaotic.*

Critiques

Vinyletteror, *Jimmy Brown,* Figure 1-5.1

Instructor's Evaluation

Jimmy's work makes good use of the vinyl's 3-D aspect, an element that is obviously lost in this reproduction. While exactingly crafted, the composition doesn't become overwrought; it remains surprising—and abstract—across its entire surface. Jimmy's work is rare in that it's unexpected—and recognizable—across the page. There are references to diagrams which remain enough in the area of abstraction not to be overt and interrupt the purely formal qualities.

Vinyletteror, *Kevin Combes,* Figure 1-5.2

Instructor's Evaluation

This work is delightfully surprising because it uses the "wrong" vinyl lettering. Kevin took another kind of adhesive letters that have the letterform printed in black on white plastic. With these he was able to build up textures that wouldn't have been possible with the lettering that's usually used. As with most of these projects, the strength of the compositions lies in the tension between the barely recognizable letterforms and their abstraction. I would have liked to see the black letterforms combined into larger shapes.

Student Statement
*Our instructions were to work fast
with the vinyl letters and without thinking create an abstract composition
that did not include recognizable letter
forms or words. I found this initially
hard to do, but after I finished I began
to appreciate its inherent textures,
interesting shapes and forms, and wide
range of values. The artificial handicap
of not being permitted to rely upon
my training to date opened me up to
a broader understanding of what is
possible in design.*

Figure 1-5.2

Figure 1-5.3

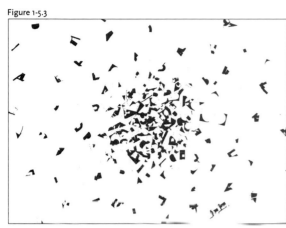

Student Statement

I wanted to use the vinyl letters in an unrecognizable way. I started by randomly cutting up the vinyl letters so that they would not be recognizable. Then I began to place each piece in the middle of the paper. I packed the letters on thick in the middle of the page and then less and less moving toward the edges. My intent was for the letter pieces to appear as though they were falling or flying out from the center.

Vinyletteror, *Lauren Duffy*, Figure 1-5.3

Instructor's Evaluation

With few exceptions, students use a strict additive process in making their works. Elements are added until a desirable point is reached. Lauren's work technically is additive but is ultimately subtractive, as she cuts away portions of letterforms and also layers white vinyl letters on top. The slight variation in the making results in a unique kind of mark across the work's surface. Often with this project, students make very dense and busy works, and this is refreshingly sparse and restrained.

Vinyletteror, *Tricia Querol*, Figure 1-5.4

Instructor's Evaluation

This piece dissolves and obliterates the letterforms to create this ambience of language. At every point across its surface, a letterform will almost resolve itself but will be subsumed into the overall "hum." Crafting this required both control and abandon. The blend of curvilinear and angular forms keeps the work in suspension, and more engaging than alphabetic wallpaper.

Figure 1-5.4

Student Statement

I cut up the letters until they lost their letter characteristics and became basic forms. Then I started in the middle with red and integrated black letters and randomly set them in place. The finished product was not planned out; it was the result of repeatedly placing the forms randomly.

Figure 1-5.5

Student Statement
I focused on speed, rhythm, movement, and space to create a piece that is pure chaos. Formally, the piece can be described as an abstract expression, but contentwise the piece reflects the tormented feelings of living alone in a new place, capturing my feelings during fall 2001.

Vinyletteror, *Diego Rioja,* Figure 1-5.5

Instructor's Evaluation

Diego's work is another that uses the letters three-dimensionally to great effect and to generate unexpected 2-D forms. Diego uses the "negative" vinyl within and surrounding the letterforms well. His composition seems musical in its horizontal structures above blending into improvised shapes below. A reading of torment in the forms is possible; however, I could as readily see its opposite.

Letterform as Shape
State University of New York at Fredonia, Instructor: Jan Conradi

If type (letterform) is understood as a basic design element, in terms of shape and form, the user of type will be more sensitive in manipulating it when it is used to convey a message. All letterforms were originally signs, and all signs were once images. The alphabet is a source...

Assignment Brief
Exploring letterforms in an abstract sense enables students to achieve greater confidence and diversity in their communicative typographic solutions. The series of four panels created in this assignment expands thinking and approaches to visual problem solving; the four panels are not required to act as a visually related series. Each panel focuses upon a different approach, emphasizing negative space, texture, size contrast, and fracturing. The problem reinforces the use of design vocabulary, and it also develops comping and presentation skills and critiquing ability. The final solutions are hand-generated (although it would be easy to adapt this to computer output).

The project requires problem solving, from thumbnails and initial visual research through refinements and the comping of final solutions. You will learn the value of pushing beyond your initial comfort zone and sense of visual organization and learn to set limits to maintain control throughout the design process. Integration of color and values are possible, and the visual impact of each additional element must be carefully considered. The project also requires thinking about relationships between 2-D and 3-D forms. The 3-D aspect of the assignment provides groundwork for packaging and applied dimensional work in subsequent courses.

Objectives
– To understand letterforms in an elemental way rather than as a vehicle for conveying written information.
– To begin to develop a discerning eye for the subtlety of typographic forms and the creative potential within these forms.
– To continue gaining finesse with craft and presentation.

Process
You will be assigned a letter at random. You may choose to work with either Univers 65 or Caslon Bold type. Before beginning to sketch possibilities for the following compositions, accurately render your letter in both fonts, both uppercase and lowercase, to be sure you are familiar with its form. Stay with the same font for all compositions, but you can alternate between uppercase and lowercase forms of the letter if you wish. You will choose a single geometric shape (circle, square, or triangle)

to incorporate, and you can also incorporate a straight line. Working in a 5" square format, construct the following compositions:

First image—negative space of letterform is visually dominant, each element is used once, cropping is allowed. The comp is drawn.

Second image—use letterform, line, and shape in the composition once only. Incorporate type texture from magazines to enhance the composition by using implied texture for added visual interest. The comp can be photocopies, magazine cutouts, and drawn.

Third image—emphasize scale and size contrast; elements can be used more than once. The comp is drawn.

Fourth image—use your geometric shape or line to create multiple fractures in the letterform. The letterform can be cropped but should still remain recognizable, with elements repeated as needed. This could emphasize motion/kinetic flow through the composition. Comp is drawn and/or photocopied.

Fifth image—create a three-dimensional composition using the elements and ideas you have explored in the first four flat solutions. This will be a simple cube; the form and the surface treatments should work as a complementary unified whole. Use media as appropriate; chipboard or mat board is an inexpensive base, although other possibilities could be tested. Size should be no larger than about 5" in any dimension.

If photocopies have been used, you may want to recopy if necessary to remove unwanted edges. Make sure all elements are glued securely. You can draw back into a photocopy if desired to create the intended visual effect.

Mount four final comps on a single board. Cover the board with black presentation flap, labeled on bottom right corner.

The dimensional solution will be presented as directed in class.

Critiques

Letterform as Shape, *Heidi Abel,* Figure 1-6.1

Instructor's Evaluation

From her initial sketches, Heidi explored diverse possibilities and didn't get locked into a particular approach. She also demonstrated understanding of how to effectively use the design process and thumbnails to explore tangents and dig the potential out of rough sketches while refining her ideas. I think part of her boldness in trying different things grew out of effective visual research; she included wildly varied examples from known designers as part of her background inspiration.

I did not warn her about the KKK danger and was glad when she discovered it without being prompted. Smart thinking allowed her to avoid pitfalls, which was a good lesson for the whole class: Design is as much a mental process as a visual one. Compositionally, her second and fourth compositions are the most eloquent in using space and controlling visual flow. The third composition sits awkwardly in its format; it feels forced into the square. The first needs a bit more adjustment: I'd consider pushing the whole composition slightly to the left for a stronger visual balance. I also think using a single small K rather than the series in the upper section would provide a more interesting sense of rhythm and counterpoint to the grouping at the bottom.

Figure 1-6.1A

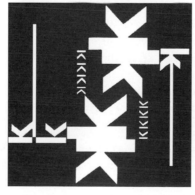

Student Statement

We take the beauty of letters for granted when we see them as part of everyday written messages. The letter K is an interesting and dynamic shape. Considering its historically negative use (KKK), I had to be extra sensitive when developing my ideas and compositions. I was careful to use the letterform alone or in groups of more than three. Using a pink hue for the additional color also helped avoid any ominous meaning. The cube was very frustrating to construct, but I was pleased with the compositional balance; no one side dominates over another.

Figure 1-6.1B

Heidi's adaptation of her designs to a cube has great visual energy. The use of diagonals leading viewers around the edges make this otherwise stable form dynamic. Pink has never been a favorite color of mine, but her reasoning for choosing the color is sound, as is the particular hue she chooses, which has enough saturation to balance against strong black and white. Controlling the placement and quantity of pink allows it to accent rather than overwhelm the composition. Craft and accuracy in rendering letterforms is an area that she can continue refining, but her problem-solving ability and communication skills already show that Heidi has the potential to be a strong designer.

Letterform as Shape, *Michael Ruberto,* Figure 1-6.2

Instructor's Evaluation

Too often designers approach a problem by adding complexity. One thing that is refreshing about Mike's solutions is the pared-down quality that he has maintained on each of the four panels, which provide a sense of unity (although that wasn't necessarily required by the project statement). There are really no extraneous elements in any of these compositions. I also appreciate his restraint in working with black and white, although the project did allow for consideration of hue and/or value as appropriate. Too often graphic designers use color as a crutch; he's made a valuable discovery about the possibility for striking communication through economical means.

Of the flat panels, the fourth is the weakest because any immediate recognition of the letterform is lost. The diagonal bar dropping into the center is a bit too dominant and starts to overwhelm the rest of the composition. Panels one and three have the curved strokes of the letterform to effectively relieve the sharpness of the geometry. In panel two he crops bold display text to remove readability, allowing the found text to create a counterpoint to the lowercase e below it. Mike's explorations of type as texture showed him how to control the inherent complexity of using found type to not overwhelm other design elements.

I required the final solutions to be rendered by hand because I believe that solid hand skills are always an asset and lead to a more critical eye when a student is later working on the computer.

Figure 1-6.2A

Mike was more comfortable with this than some of his classmates, and I think that gave him the gumption to propose a more complex dimensional form for the final part of the project. Even as a beginning designer, he has already begun to understand the importance of keeping focused and attentive to details. Allowing the dimensional form to grow from the letter was a smart move conceptually, and the playfulness of creating individual drawers that pull out from the arms is a nice way to add an element of surprise and interactivity.

Figure 1-6.2B

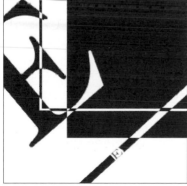
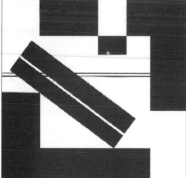

Student Statement

I chose the rectangle as a reflection of the upper-case E; I used the fonts Univers 55 and Caslon Bold. Each font is linear, but the Caslon E has greater delicacy and variation in line weight and form. Through the design process I found that my solutions were stronger if I kept my designs less complex. Cropping the forms helped in my search for simplicity, but generally I kept the letterforms readable and recognizable. I felt especially good about my three-dimensional solution because most people stayed with a basic cube and I was able to use my letterform to define the shape instead.

Concert Poster
California State University, Fullerton, Instructor: Arnold Holland

Rectilinear describes shapes with hard, straight edges and angular corners. The regular and precise nature of rectilinear shapes suggests geometry and hence appears artificial and manufactured. The opposite of rectilinear is curvilinear. We think of *curvilinear* shapes as natural, reflecting the soft, flowing shapes found in nature. The term biomorphic is sometimes used to describe this same idea.

Of course, these are very broad conclusions. Geometric shapes abound in nature, especially in the microscopic structure of elements, and people often design objects with irregular, free-form shapes. Most art combines both types.

When using the two types of shapes, one way to achieve a successful composition is to stress one type and use the other sparingly, as a counterpoint of emphasis.

The Visual Elements
All visual art comprises combinations and permutations of the visual elements, the basic building blocks of design. All visual idioms—drawing, painting, printmaking, sculpture, architecture, and applied design—are founded on the following factors:

Point	Value
Line	Texture
Shape	Color

These visual elements are animated by the principles of organization and the creativity of the artist. In concert, these elements help the designer to turn dots, squiggles, and shapes into organized and meaningful structures and images.

Assignment Brief
Design two variations of a concert poster, one in color and one in black and white. Using the text provided, design two poster compositions that visually structure the information based on the given instruction and lecture. Think about font selection, image proportion, positive/negative space relationships, and typographic hierarchies.

Process
Select a composer from the following list:
– Antonio Vivaldi (1678–1741)
– Wolfgang Amadeus Mozart (1756–1791)
– Ludwig van Beethoven (1770–1827)
– Johannes Brahms (1833–1897)
– Igor Stravinsky (1882–1971)

Select a musical work composed by the artist. Collect images of the particular instrument used primarily by the composer and related objects. Choose images for your design on three grounds: the quality of the print, the merit of the design, and the strength of the communication. Watch for contrast between darks and lights, a full tonal range, sharp focus (where appropriate), and lack of scratches, dust spots, and other imperfections.

Poster Text

The [insert name of composer] Festival is sponsored by the Jerome L. Greene Foundation and the Peter Jay Sharp Foundation.
California State University, Fullerton
School of Fine Arts, Department of Music
Performing Arts Recital Hall
Saturday, April 12, 2001
8:00 P.M.
Free Admission
Contact Information
Telephone: 714-255-7525
E-mail: csufperformancearts@fullerton.edu
Web: www.fullerton.edu/~classicalconcert/

Timeline

Weeks One and Two

— Research discussion and evaluation
— Fifteen 5" × 5" reductive sketches of instruments
— Image scans

Week Three

— Individual critiques
— Rough sketches
— Four full-size sketches
— Four full-size sketches with text

Weeks Four and Five

— Critique by each group
— Comprehensive sketch
— Two full-size sketches of each poster

Week Six
– Class critique
– Comprehensive sketches
– Two-full-size sketches of each poster

Week Seven
– Final photocopy
– One bound process book, with all portions of process and notes labeled.

Critiques

Beethoven Poster, *Emma Ekblad,* Figure 1-7.1

Instructor's Evaluation

Image creations and combinations constitute 90 percent of the design process required for this project. Emma combines her images to accentuate their sophisticated and additive characteristics. The poster ground, composed of subtle yet complex lines, represents piano strings, and the darkly colored, contemporary flat shapes represent piano keys; the black planes modulate the space well. Simple geometric shapes combined with inorganic elements create rhythm. The combined images convey inside, outside, interior, sight, and sound. The title interrupts the design, although not arbitrarily, and the piano shape acts as a focal point.

The elliptical marks, the piano strings, have the strongest presence. The depth of the ellipse that surrounds them signifies more to the viewer than the actual image of the piano to the lower right. While Emma has created a mostly geometric poster, she succeeds in creating a dynamic design. This project is memorable because the elements are engaging and make the viewer participate.

Figure 1-7.1

Student Statement
The concept behind this Beethoven poster was to highlight the piano's traditional simplicity and boldness. The background's grid structure is related to the piano's interior. The text was organized in blocks to enhance the form of piano keys.

Figure 1-7.2

Student Statement
I wanted to reflect the geometrical shapes of the violin throughout the design by dividing the space organically. I found it visually dynamic to use curvilinear and rectangular shapes to create the grid structure. The placement of typographic elements is related to the surrounding planes of colors. The colors were chosen from research, relative to the violin and the composer. The elements mentioned above combine to create an organized and meaningful composition for a musical poster.

Stravinsky Poster, *Susie Halim,* Figure 1-7.2

Instructor's Evaluation

While at first glance the composition appears fragmented, further observation reveals a purposeful positioning of elements. The alignment of the edges of the shapes and flowing text provides an orderly structured appearance.

After Susie's intense exploration process, her goal was to communicate illusion and reflection. Through Photoshop, she explored ten different combinations of the same two images. Then she took the elements from different permutations and combined them into one. Susie's poster makes one aware of musical structures that contain forms consisting of melody, harmony color, shape, texture, and, most important, rhythm, which Susie interpreted in her own way. A harmonious relationship between progressive circles and circular motion is realized. The circles of differing weight intensify the concept of progression and motion by following organic arcs.

Tchaikovsky Poster, *Domingo Roma,* Figure 1-7.3

Instructor's Evaluation

The objective of this project was to pique curiosity and inform viewers musically. This particular poster focuses on the piano music of Tchaikovsky. Domingo's objective was to resemble the internal string structure of a grand piano, but he wanted to avoid the cliché of piano keys. To make things semantically connect, he added an inverted image of a piano. By layering the piano beneath the strings, he creates a balance between figure and ground. The simple positioning of the type animates the grid panels and the inversion of letters and change of weights still permits recognition of the type. Additionally, irregular visual rhythms are expressed through the text by varying circular arrangements.

Student Statement
This poster was designed to target young adults. In achieving this goal, I combined two grid systems to create the layout of the composition, which gave the design a modern, techno look. One of the grid systems came from the actual structure of the piano. The second grid system was created to give the illusion of depth.

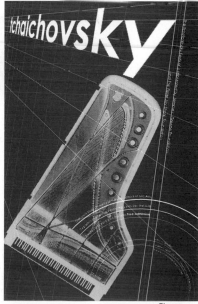

Figure 1-7.3

Beethoven Poster, *Samuel Yap,* Figure 1-7.4

Instructor's Evaluation

Sam's use of graphic elements is an ideal project example. The points, lines, and planes do not carry specific messages but make a major contribution to the effectiveness of the design. The dotted lines modulate the less active space and guide the reader's eye through the poster. The gradients and overlapping shapes organize the typography, structuring and balancing the main image, and create a musical rhythm that elicits an emotional response.

Figure 1-7.4

The formal qualities of the images and elements establish structure for the type. The slanting text emphasizes direction and visual flow. However, the positioning of the second-tier type near the center slightly discourages balance and disrupts a potentially restful space.

Student Statement

I did not have a preconceived idea of how the poster should look, but I did know the feelings that I wanted to convey. My color choices and composition are visually lyrical and reflect the passions and movement in Beethoven's music.

Design History Chair
Portfolio Center, Atlanta, Instructor: Hank Richardson

Assignment Brief

The late designer Dan Friedman noted his proclivity for understanding the condition of "radical modernism" as an ideology of a progressive force and attitude—one full of passion, humor, and value—and of being a catalyst to explore critical relationships of culture. He noted, "It is important to find comfort in the past only so long as it might expand insight into the future and not just for the sake of nostalgia."

With this intent, you as a neophyte designer will begin to explore the relationship of design history and design criticism as a catalyst for new ideas. The priority of this instruction will suggest much more than a physical deliverable product or a reflection of style. Rather, it will mirror a revivalism for interpretation of manifestos born by the contrast of personal ethos from designers who believed *steadfastly that they had a responsibility to improve the world in which we live*. Each transient period has become known as a "graphic style." Each, moreover, is a narrative for history representing a reappropriated and specific moniker of characteristic attitudes and taste, which expresses a *philosophy of life* positioned during a time of the disorderly, often tumultuous twentieth century. These times shaped the shifting currents and concepts of our modern world. The celebration of the designs will become a tribute to the seminal thinking and beliefs construed from this origin and offer a visual metaphor for understanding these periods in history that transformed our societies and the world in which we live. Your conceptions will be a reinterpretation and a reaffirmation that design is a catalyst for life; therefore, it is culture.

Objectives

The chair is a true denomination of culture. It is genderless, unless you make it gendered; its statue is unassuming, or not. Chairs are a reminder of modernist principles and of form, function, and beauty. The chair is perhaps the most immediate piece of equipment affecting worker performance in an office setting. Make your project alive, make it exciting, and make it sensory. This assignment is about the contrast of creating brand awareness, and the exploration of the varieties of and motivations for using historical sources to positively transform design.

Process

From a random drawing, select two choices of graphic styles. After researching and understanding your particular creative movements, prepare a research paper, no more than two to three pages, on both styles, and prepare yourself to present a summary of the movement that you have chosen.

Subsequently, design a chair from your own appropriation and interpretation, and then name your chair and create a brand awareness for your new chair, appropriating the style of your selection. As you are doing this, consider that you are using historical comparison, taking into account that the transformation through historical comparison might employ a set of values different from the manifesto of the original movement.

The appropriation of your selected style for this project should reflect content and substance and priority of logic. In order that this might occur, you will need to unite contemporary influences of culture, taking into consideration social and economic climates of today. As you go about this, look for the relationship of revival.

The designer is concerned with self-consciousness about what it means to appropriate influence. It's about understanding that good design history offers alternative solutions and is a catalyst for ideas. It underscores a reference that this is how someone thought about an idea then and this is how that work fits into culture.

Critiques
Design History Chair: Vienna Secession, *Meg Dreyer*, Figure 1-8.1

Figure 1-8.1

Student Statement

Internal conflict was evident everywhere in Vienna at the turn of the century: Gustav Mahler, Arnold Schoenberg, and Richard Strauss were overturning the hallowed musical tradition of Mozart and Beethoven with the surging emotion of their works. The Vienna Secession was rebelling against the grand Baroque style, introducing increasingly abstract forms, geometric pattern, and exuberant color to the city's architecture and interiors. The eroticism of the paintings of Egon Schiele and Gustav Klimt was exploding from the city's art galleries into its conservative streets. The city's response to such tumultuous changes was a pervasive anxiety, in particular a bourgeois discomfort with the encroaching erotic.

The young Sigmund Freud began his probing of the nature of the unconscious mind and published The Interpretation of Dreams, *in which he formulates his theories of the conflicting ego and id. These ideas were the inspiration for my Idego chair.*

According to Freud, the id is the part of the unconscious representing the primitive drives and emotions. The id is primal, instinctual, unrestrained. The ego is the part of the id that has been modified by its perception and integration of the external. The ego attempts to impose sober reality upon the id's unrestrained pursuit of pleasure.

The Idego chair is a rocking chair based upon the relationship between the ego and the id. The id is represented by a curve of dark mahogany that swells beneath the ego, the lighter-colored pine seat, much as passion swells beneath reason, sometimes uplifting it, sometimes upsetting it.

Figure 1-8.2

Design History Chair: Art Deco, *Scott McBride,* Figure 1-8.2

Student Statement

After researching the Art Deco period and being inspired by the architecture, geometric and curved shapes, and highly polished look, I created a chair that was welcoming like a doorway or entrance to new things (out with the old and in with the decorative and new). From the back my chair looks like a building, from the front a chair.

Figure 1-8.3

Design History Chair: De Stijl, *Eric Miller,* Figure 1-8.3

Student Statement

The 2017 chair sought to expand the De Stijl concept of transparent, movable planes through the marriage of typography and structure. The cantilever foundation and overall simplistic lines create a unique space within. A closer look at the 2017 chair reveals two typographic forms that pay homage to De Stijl and illustrates that poststructural design can bring forth new ways of communicating older ideas.

Figure 1-8.4

Design History Chair: American Modern, *Ally Weiner,* Figure 1-8.4

Student Statement

American Modern emphasized designing spaces that were pragmatic, informal, and intuitive in nature. Thus my chair had to be simple yet inventive. I decided on a chair that would serve a functional role—the challenge was to build a structure that would house four persons at one time. The solution was a skeletal version of a cube, in three tiers. Each side of the square allows a person to sit at a different level; therefore each seat has a unique vantage point. Additionally, the top tier can be rotated, changing the arrangement of all four seats with each turn. The chair is constructed of maple, with 120 custom joints, and is designed to look best in a gallery or museum space. I call it one2three.

TYPOGRAPHY AS IMAGE

Typography is the art of designing with type. *Type* is the term used for the letters in the alphabet, the numbers, and the punctuation marks that make words, sentences, and blocks of text. The term *typeface* refers to the design of all the characters mentioned above, unified by common visual elements.

In class, I use a metaphor to explain the essential nature of typography to my students when I compare typography to architecture.* I describe typography as two-dimensional architecture upon which a foundation of visual communication can be built. Letterforms become the building blocks that create the structure to convey an idea or deliver a message.

Like architecture, typography has both form and function—it is a graphic as well as a readable element in a design. The assignments in this section explore the notion of typography as image. Letterforms can be altered and manipulated to become both the image and a message. Typography is a visual graphic language when it is used creatively and expressively and a verbal written language when it is combined with an image. As a form, type contains the design elements of line, shape, texture, size, and value, and can be arranged into graphic compositions. As a function, type contains content—it is the message or information to be communicated.

"Typography is the mechanical notation and arrangement of language that is used to make multiple copies whether by printed or electronic means."
– Phil Baines

Type can enhance the meaning of the message by translating or transforming it. Different typefaces have different personalities and varied usages. Some typefaces are very formal and elegant, while others are casual and relaxed. Some typefaces evoke nostalgia for times past, and others suggest a modern attitude. The typeface you choose as well as the size, leading, kerning, and shape of the text block can all influence the tone of a message and directly affects how a viewer will perceive and interpret it.

"Typographic design is both process and product—a creative combination of the communication practice and aesthetic theory. It begins with the selection and arrangement of typographic elements to communicate a message, and it ends with the composition in two-dimensional space."
– Willi Kunz

At the very core of good typographic design is the graphic designer's critical interpretation of the message—the more astute the interpretation, the more effective the message. How can students get their ideas across more effectively? By building a solid foundation of typographic principles to use as a framework for reference.

---

* A *metaphor* is a figure of speech in which a word or phrase is substituted for a dissimilar subject to suggest a likeness or link between them. The original word or phrase then takes on the qualities of the linked subject, increasing understanding.

Shaping Words

Art Institute of California, San Diego, Instructor: Richard Ybarra

Assignment Brief

Every day we are blasted with words, either aurally or in printed form through advertisements, newspapers, books, or other words with a visual concept. Remove words and there is no communication; remove communication and there are no ideas or dreams or visuals.

In this assignment you will shape an object with words. The words (copy) will consist of information about your shape (object). At the bottom of your copy shape will be a statement (quote) to add a finishing touch to your visual copy image. Keep in mind your use of type style—script, block, shadow, initial capital letters, and so on—in your statement. Your statement should be stylized in a nice typographical style.

Objectives

- To achieve good organizational skills
- To introduce type as an artistic form and to use typography as the primary element
- To create typography that communicates a special idea or message and to emphasize typographic design skills while maintaining visual continuity
- To introduce layout and format design, and working with body copy
- To show relationships of negative/positive spaces
- To explore computer-aided design possibilities
- To produce effective presentations

Specifications

1. Paper size: 8.5" × 11" (white).
2. Mounted: Black mat board, 16" × 20".
3. Color: One color, black—gray percentage screen allowed.
4. Presentation: Tissue overlay.

Process

Remember to think, to plan, and replan. Most of all, have fun.

Critiques

Shaping Word: Vince Lombardi Trophy, *David Reyes,* Figure 2-1.1

Instructor's Evaluation

David's project reflects a bold, tight copy statement and shape in type. The gray-screen lines give the symbolic trophy form and accent. David shows control of the project as well as relating with an image with which we all can associate.

Figure 2-1.1

Student Statement

The Vince Lombardi Trophy, a trophy awarded through the National Football League, is a goal for which every NFL team player works hard. Accordingly, the concept behind my project is "In everything you do, on any level, give it your all."

Figure 2-1.2

```
        PASS        IT ON:        WHAT
           YOUR   HANDS      DO,   IT IS
      YOUR OWN EYES THAT'VE  SEEN. SO WONT
       YOU JUDGE YOUR ACTIONS TO MAKE SURE
     THE RESULTS ARE CLEAN? IT'S YOUR OWN CONSCIENCE
    THAT IS GONNA REMIND  YOU  THAT IT'S YOUR HEART AND
   NOBODY ELSES'S  THAT IS GONNA JUDGE.   BE NOT SELFESH IN
    YOUR DOINGS: PASS IT ON,    PASS IT ON CHILDREN.  HELP YOUR
  BROTHERS,HELP THEM IN THIER NEEDS. PASS IT ON, PASS    IT ON
 LIVE FOR YOURSELF AND YOU WILL LIVE IN VAIN. LIVE        FOR
 OTHERS, YOU WILL LIVE AGIAN.  IN THE KINGDOM OF JAH
 MAN SHALL REIN,   PASS IT ON,   PASS IT ON,   PASS IT ON.
 WHAT'S    IN THE DARKNESS      MUST BE REVEALED TO
 LIGHT    WE'ER NOT HERE TO      JUDGE WHATS GOOD
 FROM   BAD,   BUT TO DO         THINGS THAT ARE RIGHT
 ON     A HOT,  SUNNY DAY,       FOLLOW THE SHADOWS
        FOR RESCUE.  BUT AS      THE DAY GROWS OLD  I
 KNOW THE SUN IS GONNA           FIND YOU. BE NOT SELFISH
 IN YOUR DOINGS   PASS IT        ON. HELP YOUR BROTHERS
 IN THERE NEEDS   PASS           IT ON. LIVE FOR  YOURSELF
 AND YOU          WILL           LIVE IN          VEIN
      LIVE FOR    OTHERS         YOU WILL         LIVE
      AGAIN IN    THE            KINGDOM          OF
      PASS IT     SHALL          REIN
      PA00 IT     ON PASS        IT ON
        PASS      IT ON          IT ON
                  IT             PA33
              -Robert Nesta
                 Marley
```

Student Statement

My image represents Bob Marley, who took his personal lessons and exposed them to the world, inspiring millions of people. As he grew, so did his locks, thus resulting in a metaphor between his words of wisdom and his natty dreads. My concept statement is "As you mature, you carry with you lessons and experiences that help you to understand life and to grow wise."

Shaping Words: Bob Marley, *Brandon Hirzel*, Figure 2-1.2

Instructor's Evaluation

Brandon's well-styled and humorous illustration of Bob Marley's dreadlocks in type shows his control of this project. The gray screen on his face is a good contrast to the bold-type hair. Using the bold sans-serif type to capitalize on the weight of the hair also captures the overall quality look of this illustrative artwork with words.

Shaping Words: Helmet, *Robert Kimball*, Figure 2-1.3

Instructor's Evaluation

The creative word-shape helmet lends a bold feeling to the overall content of the project. The thick gray lines define the contrast of the face-plate on the helmet. Readability is achieved successfully in this well-done project.

Student Statement

Inspiration for this concept stemmed from my personal experiences in a Renaissance reenactment group.

Figure 2-1.3

Newspaper Stories—A Typographic Workshop
Fachhochschule Augsburg, Germany, Instructor: Jürgen Hefele

Assignment Brief

In this assignment, you will design a visual typographic story. The "newspaper stories" workshop is aimed at sharpening visual and typographic senses, while at the same time encouraging you to disconnect in form and content from the material presented and to develop individual pieces. You will be given foreign newspapers and, by cutting out typography and images from them, will be asked to form a visual story using eight sheets of A5 ($8\frac{1}{4}$" × $5\frac{3}{4}$") paper.

Set at the beginning of the lecture without advance notice, the idea is to encourage you to work intuitively. You will present your work at the end of the workshop.

Objectives

The intention of this assignment is to give students an opportunity for playful problem solving, which can add witty solutions for the graphic vocabulary of a designer without using a computer.

Specifications

Supplied material: foreign newspapers (Chinese, Italian, English, Turkish). Use of photocopier, scissors, glue, and Scotch tape is allowed. No computer use or additional drawing is allowed.

Process

Work with typography and images found in the newspapers, visualizing your typographic story on eight pages in A5 ($8\frac{1}{4}$" × $5\frac{3}{4}$") format, made out of two folded A4 papers ($11\frac{1}{2}$" × $8\frac{1}{4}$").

Timeline

Working time is approximately one hour. After the workshop, present your work and the idea behind it.

Figure 2-2.1

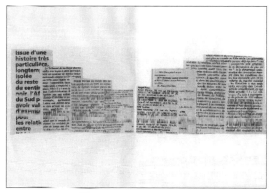

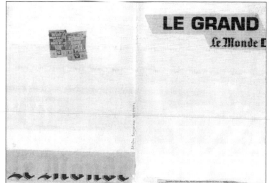

Student Statement

I concentrated my work on the particularities and contrasts of the French newspaper Le Monde. For instance, the black-letter typeface of the Le Monde header contrasts with the sans-serif type of the articles, and the articles differ in size and type style. I have overlapped parts of the articles to create a skyline of blocks with various gray tones. The main focus of this Le Monde issue was the war in Afghanistan and the demonstrations against it. The original photographs include many people with banners; I recombined these banners without the people to emphasize their typographic impact.

Critiques

All of the students put a great deal of work into the project, even if some were unable to find and develop an exciting visual story in the limited time available.

Le Monde, *Stefan Bergmeier,* Figure 2-2.1

Instructor's Evaluation

This design is marked by its exciting composition and use of contrasts. American intervention in Afghanistan had led to the fall of the Taliban but also fueled criticism. Stefan decided to use articles on this subject to create his story.

Figure 2-2.2

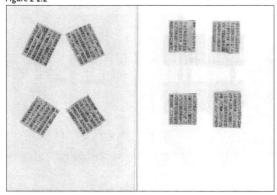

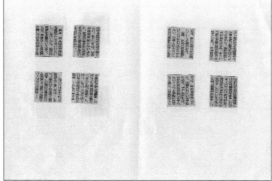

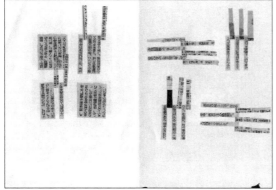

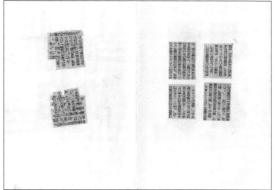

Student Statement

I considered the Japanese newspaper to be most useful for this assignment, as I neither understood the meaning of the words nor associated anything with the letters. The uniform layout (accurately split up into columns and gathered to square paragraphs that recur again and again) reminded me of texture. This was my incentive to select some of the paragraphs, to dissolve them step by step, and to create new wickerwork out of it, in order to tell a short "typographic" story of my own, changing the message of the original text.

Japanese Fabric, *Romana Fichtner,* Figure 2-2.2

Instructor's Evaluation

This was the best piece of work from the workshop. Having managed to disconnect herself from the content of the Japanese text, she worked with the character shapes instead. Kanji, hiragana, and katakana characters are based on a square grid. In contrast to the way in which letters are combined in the West, each character shape stands alone. Romana made an excellent job of transforming the character structures into a story: four moving and interweaving text blocks. Cuts enable the characters to be folded out and layered into a typographical "network," a fabric made from characters.

Figure 2-2.3

Student Statement

It always seems to me as if newspapers provide overwhelming information, which is how I got the idea to place one letter on top of another to express the dense mass of information. Traditionally, newspapers are designed with letters set side by side or one below the other. In order to break with tradition, I cut letters out of different newspapers and glued them on top of each other. New signs were created which no longer provide concrete information but are free for individual interpretation. The two one-way signs on the cover page seemingly point in different directions to indicate to the reader that he could turn the book around and have a look at it from a different point of view.

Letter Layers, *Eva Hanser,* Figure 2-2.3

Instructor's Evaluation

By overlapping, this piece of work creates a new code out of different characters. The result is interesting shape combinations and compositions. While this piece is successful because of the way in which the idea has been resolutely executed, the story lacks a sense of building excitement.

Figure 2-2.4

Student Statement
*I concentrated on the letter S
for two reasons—it has a
balanced shape and it appears
in newspaper text very often.
I looked for different font sizes
and fonts in order to tell a
story about the letter S growing
from a small to a very big size.*

The Letter S, *Philipp Hubert*, Figure 2-2.4

Instructor's Evaluation

The way in which the characters have been arranged into groups is successful, and
a story has been developed to the end. If the exciting design of the inside pages is
persuasive, the design of the title and back pages is less successful: The large S on
the back page is too isolated. The text on the title page forms a general statement
without any formal reference to the inside pages.

Baby Shark, *Ulrike Hütte,* Figure 2-2.5

Instructor's Evaluation

The second best piece is a proper picture book. The story of a baby shark that meets other sea creatures while searching for its mother is developed wonderfully from the title page through to the happy ending. The design has been kept to a minimum and the idea is communicated well: Each of the differing sea creatures has its own typographical texture and identity. To this end, the term "type family" is explained in a fun way.

Student Statement

The concept behind my work derives from the expression "type family." A human family generally consists of parents, children, and other relatives. The members of a family have their own individual look but still maintain a visual familiarity between them (as an existing German idiom says, "As the father does, the son does"). Type families are much the same: Type styles of one family have the same shape, but the individuality shows itself in the different weights, such as regular, italic, bold. The small shark in my work and his mother belong to the same type family, so they have the same shape, whereas the other sea animals belong to different type families and have different shapes.

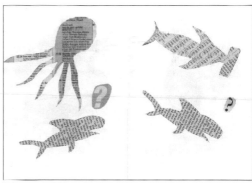

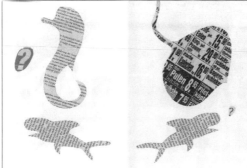

Figure 2-2.5

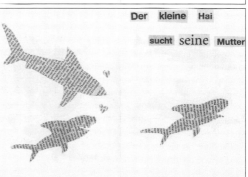

Der kleine Hai

sucht seine Mutter

Typographic Self-Portrait
Mimar Sinan University, Instructor: Esen Karol

Assignment Brief

Your assignment is to draw, paint, or make a self-portrait using typographic characters.

Use the letters—which represent sounds—to illustrate your face, thinking about how your design reflects you as a designer. Think about identity—your own identity—and study your face and its characteristics. Examine the forms of typographic elements closely to determine what will represent you best.

Objectives

– To create an awareness of the image of typography

Process

Letters, numbers, and analphabetic symbols such as parentheses are allowed, as are combinations of different typefaces. You may not manipulate or deform the letterforms. Your design should be black and white, although you may use a different background color if you wish.

Critiques

I was having a hard time explaining the importance of the relationship between the image of typography and the actual content to students. They were very concerned with do's and don'ts of typography and felt threatened by the difficulties of the craft. I decided to come up with a light and fun project, where the students would be self-expressive by definition, even if not by choice. Also I thought that if the initial aim was to create an image, they would easily understand the power of the image of typography. In this case, a self-generated—but typographic—image was indeed worth a thousand words.

I was surprised by the quality of the outcome. Students—with no exception—enjoyed the project and some of them experienced the joy of being proud of one's work for the first time.

They approached the project in multiple ways. It was not easy to select the best work, as they were all successful in different ways and represented the identities of the creators quite precisely.

Figure 2-3.1

Student Statement
Considering how plain and simple the typographic elements are that I have used, I was very surprised and glad to see that they could be so expressive and tell so much about me.

Typographic Self-Portrait, *Melike Erecekler,*
Figure 2-3.1

Instructor's Evaluation

Melike chose to work simply, using a single sans-serif typeface without deforming the basic forms of the letters.

Typographic Self-Portrait, *Murat Göven,* Figure 2-3.2

Instructor's Evaluation

Murat's work is unique. He decided not to use the computer. His collage is a successful solution to the problem. However, in some parts of his work he has used texts as textures and simply cut forms out of it, something that was not acceptable according to the assignment brief. Creating a texture with type was fine, but cutting the letters into pieces was forbidden in the "game."

Figure 2-3.2

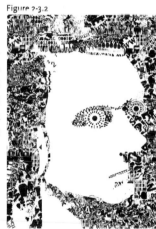

Student Statement
My work is a collage that refers to the punk movement. My intention was to approach typography and its content as one inseparable entity.

Student Statement
In order to express myself perfectly, I wanted to keep it simple and use as few and as basic elements as possible. I approached the problem as if it was a logo design project. I was careful about adding unnecessary elements to avoid turning my self-portrait in a pictorial representation rather than a graphic representation.

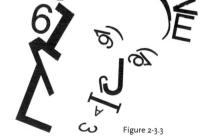

Figure 2-3.3

Typographic Self-Portrait, *Boran Erem,* Figure 2-3.3

Instructor's Evaluation

Boran's work is one of the most successful among the assignment's outcomes. Very few students actually have managed to solve the problem with so few elements.

Figure 2-3.4

Student Statement
When approaching this assignment, I didn't think about the forms of the individual letters. I built sentences with them and realized that they look like lines drawn with a pencil. To create my facial features, I composed sentences that reflected my feelings at that moment. All of the sentences create lines and shapes, with which I built my self-portrait.

Typographic Self-Portrait, *Seher Kis,* Figure 2-3.4

Instructor's Evaluation

Seher's work is a good example of the use of actual text. What looks like a composition of lines is a text about her, written by her. I think that students were so satisfied with their self-portraits that most of them weren't interested in adding a background color. At the final stage of the project—although it wasn't an essential part—we discussed the role of color in constructing identity.

Typographic Self-Portrait,
Bahadir Pacacioglu, Figure 2-3.5

Instructor's Evaluation

In Bahadir's work, he overmanipulated the forms of the letters to be able to create the chin in his portrait. Although some of the rules were broken throughout the process, I find this work to be successful.

Student Statement
When I began working on this project, I tried to visualize my internal characteristic qualities, but then I realized that I should focus on my physical appearance—working with a photo proved to be useful. I preferred to use roman typefaces to reflect my characteristic features. In some instances I have deformed the letters to be able to "draw" more precisely, but generally I've maintained the original letter shapes.

Figure 2-3.5

Typographic Self-Portrait
Massachusetts College of Art, Instructor: Elizabeth Resnick

At the time I received Esen Karol's *Typographic Self-Portrait* assignment submission in the fall of 2001, I had been experiencing the same problems in my classroom that she had grumbled about in her own class—that it had become increasingly challenging to articulate to students the importance of using typographic form in expressing content.

My first-semester sophomore graphic design students seemed uninspired by the first two assignments they had completed for me, and it showed in the results of their work. With Esen's permission, I give the same Typographic Self-Portrait assignment to my students. In one week, the results were nothing short of amazing. Working with their own name or short chosen text, not only were they successful in capturing the essence of their physical likeness, but also the work demonstrated that they understood typography could be both the form and the content.

Assignment Brief
The self portrait assignment has a very long history and tradition in art school. Some reasons for this popularity are:
– An accommodating model, one who is committed to the success of the work, is always immediately available.
– There is no need to flatter the subject or make him or her look better; the student is free to experiment with unconventional modes of representation.
– The self-portrait has always been used as a vehicle to express an artist's inner feeling and emotions, and as a way to show this to the outside world.

Your assignment is to "draw" a self-portrait using only typographic characters (letterforms, punctuation, and numbers). As your "content," use the letters that spell your name or construct a short text to describe how you see yourself, or how you would like others to see you.

Objectives
– To experiment with typographic form as mark making
– To explore positive and negative shape relationships in a design composition
– To experiment with the design element value in a black-and-white composition

Specifications
1. Size: 14" × 17", vertical preferred; black typographic forms on white background.
2. Media: You can generate the letterforms or texts on the computer, cut them from magazines, or hand-draw them. You can create your collage by hand or on the computer.

Process

The first step is to decide on your content—what text you will be using. If it is your name, write the letters out on a piece of paper and carefully examine their formal structure. If you are using a short text, do the same and look for form and shape relationships. Next, begin by making sketches of yourself using a mirror or photographs. As you sketch, your mind will generate ideas as to how to represent yourself in the composition. Sketching is a visual thinking tool. Never bypass this step.

When you've achieved the likeness and gesture that you want, start thinking about the shape of the letterforms and how they express and define the different parts of your face or body. Try incorporating hand-drawn letterforms into your working sketches.

If you are creating a collage, generate the components and begin to compose the composition. If you are using the computer, identify which software program you will use, and work closely from your sketches. Both methods, hand and computer, require much trial and error, so leave enough time for experimentation.

Timeline

Create your sketches, select the best one to work on, and make the final composition. For your presentation board, secure the composition on an 18" × 22" black mount board (2" on top and sides, 3" on bottom). Bring your sketches with you to class as well. Be prepared to present the concept behind the self-portrait.

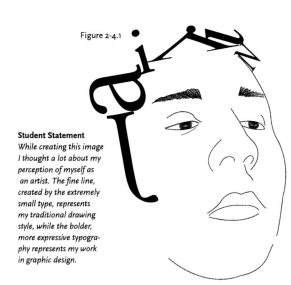

Figure 2-4.1

Student Statement
While creating this image I thought a lot about my perception of myself as an artist. The fine line, created by the extremely small type, represents my traditional drawing style, while the bolder, more expressive typography represents my work in graphic design.

Critiques

Typographic Self-Portrait, *Jaivin Anzalota,* Figure 2-4.1

Instructor's Evaluation

Jaivin employs an intuitive understanding of the principles of visual language by his use of extreme size contrast to express his self-perception through the self-portrait assignment. Typographic information is set in hair-thin lines that delineate his facial features. His stoic expression reveals this very serious and intelligent young man, who is intensively focused on his design projects. The white flatness of his face resembles a tribal mask adorned with a slippery letterform headdress. The j and a combination create a very strong focal point that I fear is far too dominant and overbearing for such a delicate line drawing. The "hair" headdress threatens to drip down his face and creates a tension that takes the focus off the expressive line drawing. Perhaps this is the effect Jaivin strives for in visually exploring the possible tension between drawing and graphic design in his life?

Regardless, I would still suggest rethinking the shape and position of the large type that forms his name, Jaivin. It could use more definition as a shape.

Typographic Self-Portrait, *Clint Durfee*, Figure 2-4.2
Instructor's Evaluation

In limiting himself to the five letters of his first name, Clint set challenging parameters for himself. With the exception of the curvature of the c and n, all the other letters in his name are made from straight lines. The l, i, and t, when combined, deliver a visual geometric response. In person, Clint projects an informal presence coupled with a relaxed sense of humor. He is the kind of person with whom you'd feel comfortable hanging out.

In contrast, the self-portrait conveys a vacant "cool" cartoon quality. Its visual zeitgeist suggests a Beat personality.

Figure 2-4.2

Nonetheless, Clint chooses his type forms well, combining both serif and sans serif into a fluid rhythm of patterns to define and shape areas of his head and shoulders. Way cool!

Typographic Self-Portrait, *Joshua Keay*, Figure 2-4.3
Instructor's Evaluation

Josh possesses what I would describe as an "in-your-face" personality. He engages, challenges, and tests you with keen intellect and intense, laserlike eye contact. Josh knows this and he seems quite comfortable with who he is. He captures this personality trait very successfully in his self-portrait, and I laughed out loud when I first saw it in class. The thick heavy strokes of the type forms create a strong contrast to the white space that defines the shape of his face. He makes good use of an asymmetrical frontal cropping of his face that allows him to add texture and value, which defines the background. The contrast between the face and the background pushes the portrait up against the foreground, to engage the viewer directly.

Student Statement
My concept for the self-portrait was to restrict myself to the five characters of my first name, Clint. I found this both challenging and fun. The result was a simplistic, nonrealistic, and somewhat abstract portrait of me. I wear glasses and have a goatee, and after I showed this portrait to a number of classmates, they all said that I look like a beatnik!

Figure 2-4.3

Student Statement
My goal was to create a stylized self-portrait, one that would convey emotion and energy rather than realism. In the font that I used, I thought the stroke weights of the characters were reminiscent of the style of brush cartoons. I cropped the composition tightly, making use of the heavy black border, which caused the image to jump out at the viewer.

Figure 2-4.4

Student Statement

My idea was to depict myself as distant and intimidating, which is often the first impression that many people have when they meet me. Using the letters of my name, I constructed lines that followed the contours of my face and hair. These contours were simple yet gave enough information to create a likeness. For the background I wanted to create a sense of depth. Since the assignment parameters allowed only the use of type forms, I used bold letters to create a shading effect.

Typographic Self-Portrait, *Bryant Ross,* Figure 2-4.4

Instructor's Evaluation

Here again, in Bryant's self-portrait, there is an interesting juxtaposition between how he visually represents himself and the friendly, accessible personality I see in the classroom.

Bryant is a very tall, engaging young man. Besides his height, his most defining feature is his bleached hair, gelled and combed to stand up in spiked tufts. As Bryant wears all black clothing, I could understand that a casual observer might think that he is an intimidating presence.

In his self-portrait, Bryant depicts a serious young man defiantly engaging the viewer. He chooses the letters of his first name to create the linear marks that collectively serve as a uniformed textured line. He reserves the bold-weight letterforms for his B marks, which, when placed in rows like uniformed soldiers, march rhythmically in straight regimented lines across the picture plane. The weight of the bold face suggests a darker receding value, thereby pushing the portrait into the foreground in direct confrontation with the viewer.

Typographic Self-Portrait, *Li Xiao*, Figure 2-4.5

Instructor's Evaluation

Li is a transfer student from the People's Republic of China. In class she is attentive, quiet, and reserved. Although she is still acquiring her English-language skills, she is very talented and possesses an innate facility for visual language. As a young Chinese woman, she has suffered many restrictions, both culturally and politically.

In her self-portrait, she projects herself as an independent and outward-moving personality. Perhaps this is who she wishes to become in a new, more open culture? For the initial assignment, Li drew the letterforms by hand. This enabled her to express the fluidity of the mood and gesture she describes in her statement. For publication, I asked her to redraw the work in a digital format. She accomplished this without any loss of the original portrait's grace or spirit.

Figure 2-4.5

Student Statement

My self-portrait is taken from a photograph. I was facing into the wind on the deck of a boat and feeling very alive. All of the letterforms I selected to use have no specific meanings individually; they were chosen because they were suitable shapes to re-create the pose. I manipulated the letterforms and organized them into this composition to tell people who I am, a girl full of freedom, casual, and with a love of life.

Typeface Poster
Samsung Art and Design Institute, Seoul, Instructor: Hyunmee Kim

Assignment Brief
Design a poster that advertises a specific typeface. The poster should strongly communicate the characteristics of the typeface that is chosen.

Objectives
– To experience the design process, which starts from research, analyzing, and thinking about the subject matter to finding form to communicate the concept
– To develop the skill to use visual principles to communicate effectively through the poster medium

Specifications
1. Size: A2 (23⅜" × 16½").
2. Color: Black and white.
3. Include the name of the typeface, the whole font of the typeface, and other words to help strengthen the concept.

Process
Visual concept can be derived from
– The formal/structural characteristics of a typeface
– The historical context that gave birth to that specific typeface
– How and for what subject matter that specific typeface has been used
– Other characteristics of the typeface with which one can associate

Timeline
Week One
Research your typeface and be prepared to present your ideas to class. Make your presentation as visual as possible. You should come up with five sketches in approximately A4 size (11½" × 8¼") and the proportions of a poster.

Week Two
Based on the critique, choose one or two conceptually and formally strong ideas and develop those into at least two full-size sketches.

Week Three
Select and refine the poster and present it on foam core.

Figure 2-5.1

Helvetica comes from the Latin word for Switzerland, which was used on 1961's Swiss postage stamps. I have presented the font Helvetica using the form of a postage stamp.

Student Statement
Helvetica comes from the Latin word for Switzerland, which was used on 1961's Swiss postage stamps. I have presented the font Helvetica using the form of a postage stamp.

Critiques

Helvetica, *Hyun Kim*, Figure 2-5.1

Instructor's Evaluation

Coming from the idea that the typeface is of Swiss origin, this student took not only the form of a Swiss postage stamp but also the style of Swiss international typographic style as an organizing method. Her understanding of Swiss style appears in the poster as steep angled composition and perpendicular grid lines. There were arguments on the use of unnecessary grid lines merely as a style. I greatly appreciated many of her decisions, such as the decision to use lowercase a and i, which are distinctively Helvetica.

Optima, *Jihae Kim*, Figure 2-5.2

Instructor's Evaluation

The student's discovery of the similarity between the shape of the letter stroke in Optima and that of bamboo made a strong and interesting concept. In the course of crafting, she studied and tried to imbue the poster with the formal and mental tradition in Oriental painting, which is to represent the essence of the subject matter with a minimum number of strokes and its harmony with the empty space. Every decision, whether on the size of the type, the space between letters, or the position of the lines of type, was made to reflect the spirit of Oriental painting. She worked very hard in her process to reach the design that she had in mind.

Figure 2-5.2

Student Statement
Optima has characters with flared terminals. I found the shape of the stroke similar to that of bamboo, which has long been the loved subject of sumukwha (drawing in China). Accordingly, I wanted this poster to be perceived as sumukwha.

Figure 2-5.3

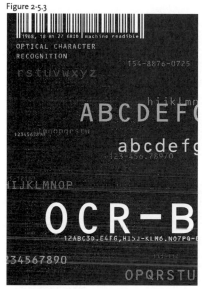

OCR-B, *Hyunjoo Lee,* Figure 2-5.3

Instructor's Evaluation

This student's poster communicates the mechanical image of the fixed-width font through the visual of the complexly layered information on the DOS-operated computer screen. Her successful use of different type sizes and gray value made the text information float deep in space. Bleeding out the information on the edges contributed to the motion and dynamism of the poster. There was argument on the communicative function of the bar code in the upper left corner.

OCR-A, *Jihee Lee,* Figure 2-5.4

Instructor's Evaluation

Jihee's OCR-A poster effectively communicates the formal characteristic of the typeface by showing the letters on the actual grid that was used for designing them. Although the student began with a strong concept, the initial draft was rigid and flat. When

Figure 2-5.4

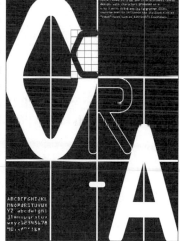

Student Statement

Even though something cannot be seen in daily life, it can still exist and control the world. OCR-B (optical character recognition B) is the information connection between human and machine. OCR-B is used in bar codes, computers, and input systems of complex machines. People work every day with OCR-B, even though we may not recognize this typeface.

she started to play with different sizes and visualizing methods, she began to perceive the given space as one with great depth. The student learned that the visual principle of contrast and variation should fully act to achieve effective visual organization. Through her work, other students got an understanding of the role of the grid, which gives order and unity to the composition of the different visual elements.

Student Statement

OCR-A characters are designed on a four-by-seven grid system. My design accentuates how the typeface works within a grid. Each letter of OCR-A is prominently displayed, and I used different sizes, colors, and strokes for contrast.

Directions Poster
Philadelphia University, Instructor: Frank Baseman

Assignment Brief

The assignment is to design a poster with traveling directions from the student's home to school (or vice versa). Since this project is part of an Introduction to Typography course, students are asked to solve this problem strictly typographically (no use of photography or illustration), utilizing basic typographic principles covered in exercises from the beginning of the semester. Students are encouraged to design within the limited typographic palette of earlier assignments (Bodoni, Garamond, Kunstler Script, Rockwell, and Univers) but may explore outside of this palette if they desire. For written information, students are to write the actual directions one would travel from point A to point B (in this case from their home to school or vice versa). Once the information has been written in clear, concise language, students are then asked to design a poster using these same directions as the information. The emphasis is on typography and typographical elements; of course, the information should be clear and easy to understand. In other words, the designer must be able to communicate the basic information to the audience. Beyond that, the design should be visually interesting and grab the viewer's attention.

Objectives

– Conceptually driven idea based on typographic principles
– The poster must function (the reader must be able to understand the written directions and use them to travel from point A to point B)

Specifications

1. Size: 18" × 24".
2. Color: Full color, no limitations
3. Outcome: Full-size color output, inkjet or fiery, flush-mounted to illustration board or foam core

Process

Very often in the "real world" designers are given text written by someone else. Sometimes this text is well written, sometimes not. Nonetheless, the designer must work with it. In this assignment the designer has the distinct advantage (and challenge) of being both the designer and writer, which leaves no room for complaining about poorly written text. Begin by writing good copy. Be descriptive, even flavorful, in your writing. Visualize some of the scenes as you are reviewing your text, and imagine visual ideas or treatments that could come out of this text. Ultimately, in this situation, the design is only going to be as good as the text written for the assignment.

Timeline

Week One

Begin by writing out the directions you take to travel from your home to school. Use clear, concise language; write in a way that people could easily understand. Be descriptive: describe the landscape, landmarks, mileage driven, routes taken, and so on. Once you have the directions written, edit your own writing, proofread, and make sure your directions make sense. Review your directions with another classmate. Look for some interesting parts of the text to emphasize. Is there a hierarchy that could be displayed within this information? Is there an idea that you can make the viewer understand about your travels, even if the idea is somewhat abstract? You will need to do a minimum of ten thumbnail sketches for your poster. These should be done in pencil, pen, and/or markers before you begin to work on the computer. Make your thumbnail sketches clearly understood, crisp, and detailed. Do not work on the computer until your thumbnail sketches have been approved for direction. Bring these thumbnail sketches to class for critique.

Week Two

Based on the feedback that you received in the last classroom critique, choose two of your idea sketches and develop them further to laser-print sketches, printing them out at half size (50 percent). Make variations on a theme if necessary by adjusting the same idea slightly, and then redo it but change something else. Continue to refine your sketches until you are satisfied that you have strong results, and bring all of your work to class for critique.

Week Three

Based on the feedback that you received in the last classroom critique, continue to refine your laser-print sketches. Make adjustments to the typographic elements, and if necessary to the writing itself (since you are both the designer and author). Keep refining your ideas, and print out at full size so that you can check your type treatments at actual size. Bring all of your work, including your earlier sketches, to class for critique.

Week Four

Based on the feedback that you received in the last classroom critique, it's time to go to a finish on your chosen design direction. You may still make further design refinements, adjusting minute details of your design and perfecting it. Once you are pleased with your final design, load up all of your files (working document, all graphics, all fonts used) and collect for output; make sure to take along a clean,

Figure 2-6.1

Student Statement
To visually articulate driving directions from my home to school in Philadelphia, I emphasized the length of the drive using long angular lines of text. The viewer can read the poster as a visual map.

accurate laser print of your design. Go to a service bureau and request color full-size color output, inkjet or fiery, for your poster. Flush-mount to illustration board or foam core.

Critiques

Directions Poster, *Lindsay Crissman*, Figure 2-6.1

Instructor's Evaluation

I love the movement in Lindsay Crissman's poster. I love the activity of the texture of type that describes the actual directions, moving from really small type in the upper left corner, cascading, zigzagging down the page, crossing from one edge to another, doubling back and getting progressively larger as the directions continue. The shape that is created by the lines is an abstraction of a map of her journey from New York State to Philadelphia. Intermittently she has cleverly used larger type for the names of routes in a different color as buzzwords to help anchor the context and to add visual interest. I asked Lindsay about her color choices, and she told me that coming to school makes her think of the fall season, thus she used fall colors. Fair enough.

Figure 2-6.2

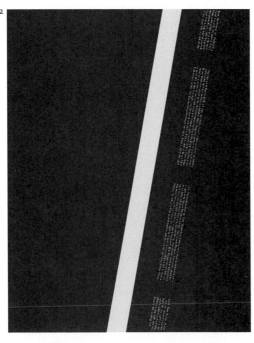

Student Statement
I took a literal approach to this project but conveyed my message by using just type and a thick rule. The type and the rule form a street pattern that I commonly see in my journeys. Although the pattern is not quite exact to its real counterpart, my goal was to allude to the lines and patterns in the street. The text is simple to read and engaging in the slanted manner I presented, which gives this poster a sense of motion.

Directions Poster, *Charles DiSantis*, Figure 2-6.2

Instructor's Evaluation

What I love about this poster is its sheer simplicity. Numerous times when I see a student approaching a project with a simple, bold solution, I have found myself saying to that student, "I wonder if you can be brave enough to be so simple." In this case, Charles was brave, very brave, for you don't get much simpler than this. From afar this poster looks like the stripes from a road or a street. On closer inspection, the viewer finds that the pattern of white type is actually made up of tiny words—the verbal description of how to get to Charles's house. I really like the angles that are used for the yellow stripe and the stripe of type, and I love the way that it is positioned on the page: off center on purpose with a great use of the overall black background. It's simple, and the craftsmanship is right on. It is very well done, proving once again that sometimes simpler is best.

Figure 2-6.3

Student Statement
This poster serves as the blueprint of travel from Long Island to Philadelphia, with letters arranged to form texture and movement.

Directions Poster, *Chris Holub*, Figure 2-6.3

Instructor's Evaluation

The strength of Chris Holub's poster is in the simple yet important typographic details. Overall, the viewer is taken by the use of the oversize numbers 1, 2, and 4. At first, one might wonder why not 1, 2, and 3, as if she was telling the viewer to go in a particular order. Soon enough, one realizes that the 4 is actually part of 476, with the 76 turned on its side, and then on a deeper read I understand this to mean 476 South, an interstate highway. The type is strong and simple, and the use of color helps me to understand what she is doing with the large numbers. The use of the smaller, subordinate body copy text in a consistently narrow treatment, all in white, makes for a nice touch on what is an overall effective poster.

Figure 2-6.4

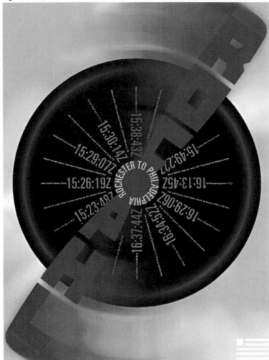

Student Statement
*When most of my peers took to the streets with their
directional poster, I took to the skies, relaying aviation
directions from Rochester International Airport to
Philadelphia International Airport. Forming the three-
character abbreviations for these cities into literal
prop blades, I then proceeded to illustratively organize
the copy so that the composition resembles a propeller
and its engine fuselage.*

Directions Poster, *David Reed Monroe,* Figure 2-6.4

Instructor's Evaluation

From the get-go David's solution was going to be off the charts, because while most
other students were writing their own directions in order to travel via car, David needed
to write his directions via airplane, as that was the way he traveled to and from
school (his dad is a pilot for USAir, thus the USAir logo at the bottom of the poster).

David's directions were written as if the pilot was speaking to the air traffic
controller. Editorially it was different, and I highly commend him for choosing this
very creative approach. In addition, the overall look of his poster as a solution was
far and away different from the other students' in that his solution is much more
illustrative. I love the swooping propeller, the blur of color that it leaves. I love the
important typographic details in this piece: the ROC for Rochester and the PHL for
Philadelphia; the use of the smaller type, "Philadelphia to Rochester" in white in
the circular form; the circular pattern created by the military time; the use of the
additional pattern of the tiny type in between the military times. The simplicity of
using the same typeface adds to the success of this piece. Overall, this is a highly
sophisticated, well-executed solution to this project, and quite a pleasant surprise.

Poetry in Motion*

Massachusetts College of Art, Instructors: Elizabeth Resnick, Glenn Berger

Assignment Brief

Merriam-Webster's Collegiate Dictionary defines poetry as *"writing that formulates a concentrated imaginative awareness of experience in language chosen and arranged to create a specific emotional response through meaning, sound, and rhythm."* Poetry enables our society to express and reveal personal and universal aspects of the human experience. As such, poetry can evoke vivid images and strong emotions, making it the perfect content for expressive typographic experimentation.

Your assignment is to choose a short poem or an excerpt from a poem (ten to fifteen words) and give it interpretive visual expression using only type, value, and color. The goal is to use typography as a form language to express your interpretation of the meaning or message of the poem.

Objectives

– Exploring typography as a form language to express ideas and concepts

Specifications

1. Size: Either a rectangle (11" high × 28" wide) or a square (22" high × 21" wide) (tile to print).
2. Color: Two-color (spot).
3 Copy: Name of poem and author.
4. Credits: Poetry in Motion® (note: include ® mark as shown), name of poem, author, and © date (only if given).

Process

Once you've made your poem choice, read it aloud, and then have someone read it to you—you'll be amazed at how an auditory reading can influence or alter your poem's meaning. Listen to how the individual words sound out loud and how those sounds might influence your perception. Close your eyes and imagine how the words sound.

For the design, you may repeat lines to achieve a visual layered or rhythmic effect, but you may not alter or change any of the words. You can choose a poem that you feel an emotional connection to, or one that intrigues you by the images it evokes. Choose a poem you understand so that you can communicate this understanding to others.

---

* This assignment is based on the national Poetry in Motion project, which is a collaboration between the Poetry Society of America (PSA), various urban mass transit authorities, and the American Institute of Graphic Arts (AIGA). Inspired by a similar program in the London Underground, the Poetry in Motion program places poem-placards (small posters) in the spaces usually reserved for advertisements in subway cars and buses. Since its founding more than ten years ago, the program has expanded to many cities across the country, with a committee from the PSA and local transit authorities meeting periodically to agree upon the poems for the series.

Timeline

Week One

Make thumbnail sketches conceptualizing at least three distinct ideas for possible placards. Select the idea that you think might work best and draw it up at half size. Once you have a layout that works for you, develop it on the computer. You can either flow text in from the digital Microsoft Word file provided by your instructor or type it in yourself.

When you are satisfied with each version that you create, print it out to fit on 8.5" × 11" paper. Save each version so that you can return to it if necessary. Select the best from among your versions and print them out for presentation at 100 percent tiled. Black and white is fine for the first critique, along with your pencil sketches and the scaled-down print. When presenting your work, be prepared to share your personal feelings about your poem and how those feelings influenced your visual interpretation.

Week Two

Based on the feedback from class critique, continue working on your placard. Follow the same procedures as outlined above, except the final output should be in color. Tile your final composition and mount it centered for presentation on a 32" × 40" black mount board (cut the board down to 15" × 32" for the rectangular format and 30" × 30" for the square format). Add a protective cover sheet (heavyweight tracing paper or brown kraft paper work best) cut flush with the board and hinged at the top with tape.

Critiques

"A Man Said to the Universe," *Michael Koid,* Figure 2-7.1

Instructor's Evaluation

The strength of Michael's visual response to Stephen Crane's short poem "A Man Said to the Universe" is in its simplicity and use of negative space. Employing the design principle of contrast to differentiate between the words man and universe enables Michael to suggest man's small place within the vastness of the universe.

Michael molds a half sphere with the words of the poem and positions it at the top edge of the composition. The vastness of empty or negative space contributes an illusion of depth. This placement also suggests that there's another half of the sphere hidden beyond the top edge and the universe continues on beyond the edge.

Although the composition possesses a monumental quality, it is also rather static because of the symmetrical placement of the large half sphere at the top of the page. I had suggested to Michael during one of the critique sessions to position the large shape off center, possibly toward the top right-hand corner, to create more dynamism. After considering this, Michael felt that it would be too difficult to achieve a balance given his attempts to make this position work.

Figure 2-7.1

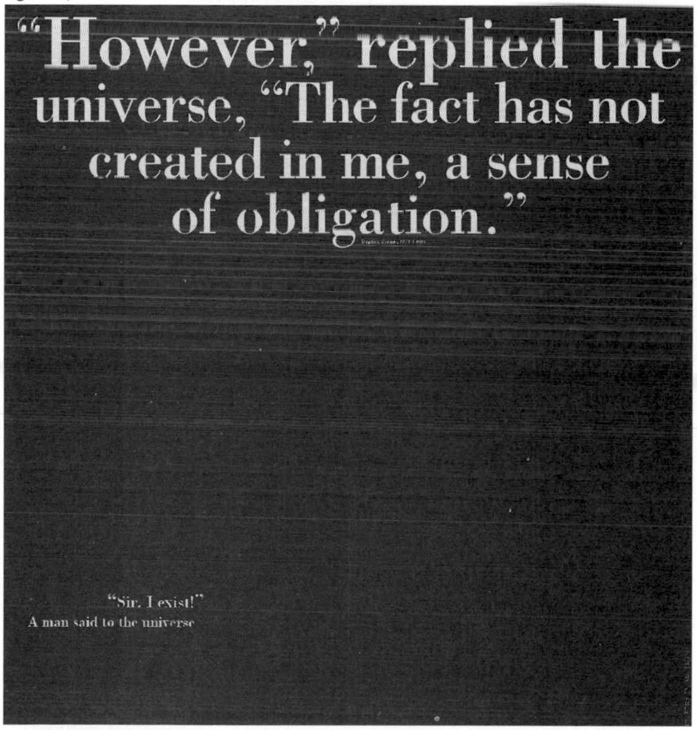

"However," replied the universe, "The fact has not created in me, a sense of obligation."

"Sir, I exist!"
A man said to the universe

A Man Said to the Universe
A man said to the universe:
"Sir, I exist!"
"However," replied the universe,
"The fact has not created
A sense of obligation."
– Stephen Crane

Student Statement

I chose this poem by Stephen Crane because it reminds me of the enormity of the universe and the arrogance of mankind. Instead of nurturing this tiny and fragile planet we call home, we wage wars against each other and irresponsibly consume huge amounts of natural resources that pollute the earth with toxic waste. Do we not realize what we extract from Mother Earth is finite? Do we not realize that the pollution we create today will ultimately consume us in the end? Why do we arrogantly proclaim to the universe that we exist when we will eventually drive ourselves toward extinction?

Figure 2-7.2

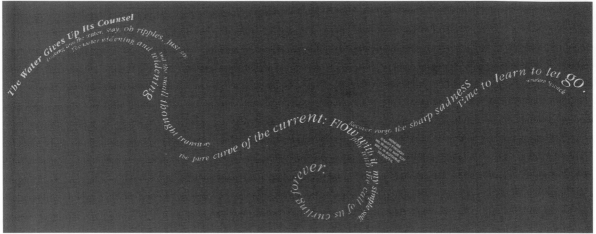

Student Statement

The poster serves as a visual analogy of Kathleen Spivack's poem "The Water Gives Up Its Counsel." The design concept was to reinforce the visual qualities of water and emulate the introspection that the author expresses in her poem. The challenge was to typographically manipulate the words so that they visually capture the feeling and emotion of gently flowing water. The idea came quickly given the visual richness of the poet's words; however, resolving the execution of the concept took some time.

The Water Gives Up Its Counsel

Looking into the water,
stay, oh ripples, just so:
the water widening and widening
and the small thought transitory.
The pure curve of the current:
flow with it, my simple self, flow
with the call of its curling
forever. Recover. Forgo
the sharp sadness.
How we grasp, though we wish it not so!
Will is nothing to water. Time
to learn to let go.

– Kathleen Spivack

"The Water Gives Up Its Counsel," *Sam Montague,* Figure 2-7.2

Instructor's Evaluation

Sam's challenge was to re-create the motion of water and waves, expressing the rhythm and flow of the words in the poem. The composition also possesses balance and unity and a sense of symmetry created by how the negative space dividing the flow of the words moving across the picture plane. The graduated type sizes add depth to the definition of the water. A nice interplay between the flowing and feminine serif typeface evokes a moving current of water and the sans-serif solidity of the rock divides the water current.

Unfortuately, the small reproduction renders the composition almost illegible. But when reproduced at the fill size, 11" × 22", it is easily read and comprehensible.

Figure 2-7.3

Student Statement
I wanted to communicate the feeling of floating down into the mist of the sky. The words are meant to feel like clouds lost in the large horizon. It was challenging for me to find the way that I wanted the words to cascade toward the horizon line.

Bright Sky
bright sky
and the skeleton of trees
I want
to be pure process
not the act itself,
stopped
like a birdcall suddenly
silenced;
cascades of water falling
flow of
time like slanting
yellow
light, the beech
trees hammered gold
medallions
drifting luminescent hair:
oh let me blow down
like these leaves
heedless in the misty
air, shattering
the clear
outlines of moment.

– Kathleen Spivack

"Bright Sky," *Kristina Rivers,* Figure 2-7.3
Instructor's Evaluation

In her composition for Kathleen Spivack's poem "Bright Sky," Kristina suggests a land-scape-like interplay between three design elements: the square sky, the rectangular sea, and the typographic clouds forming the message as it recedes into the distance.

Her design lends itself to a square format for the depth that it needs. She chooses the typeface Meta, designed by Erik Spiekermann, for its clarity of expression and contemporary tone, and ease of shaping the type into clouds.

The poem celebrates nature, and Kristina illustrates a blue landscape with white clouds. Overall, the composition possesses balance and unity and evokes serenity. In this small reproduction, it is difficult to read the words, although there is no problem with legibility when the poster is full size at 21" × 22".

CREATIVE WORDPLAY

Type is a visual element—it is first and foremost pure shape. You can alter the shape of a letterform by adding or deleting parts. You can stretch, bend, or manipulate letter shapes to reinforce the meaning of the message that you are creating. Type not only organizes the message, it helps to express it. In the hands of a graphic designer, type becomes a magic tool capable of expressing any subject matter or emotion, be it humorous, factual, dramatic, inquisitive, direct, or illustrative. The range of expressions and emotions that can be conveyed through typographic forms is limited only by the creative ability and imagination of the person designing with them.

Expressive typography is a term used to describe the technique of reshaping a word or text block into an illustration reflecting its own content. Type has a voice—it can shout or it can whisper. When you choose a typeface, be consistent with the message that you are trying to deliver. A typeface's visual personality can enhance or detract from its goal to reach a specific audience.

"Type as art—whole words, individual letterforms, or physical shape of the text—can be used to amplify the meaning of the words, create a mood or metaphor, form a decorative pattern, or become a visual pun."
– Kit Hinrichs

How Can I Create Expressive Typography?

The focus of this section's assignments is creative word play. In each assignment you still must develop an idea or concept that establishes the framework for your design decisions. Once you have completed the research and brainstorming phases of the design process, consider the following strategies to convey your message:

– Substitute one or more letters of a word or phrase with an object or image. This adds an amusing and clever element to the typography and expands on the meaning of the visual message.
– Word ideas can imitate sounds associated with certain actions or objects. Manipulate the letters to visualize the sound and you can create a visual experience for your viewer.
– Letterforms can be constructed from most any image.
– A *typograph* is a graphic image comprised of letterforms or words. A *logotype* is a good example of a typograph. A logotype is a word set in a particular typeface

and designed to be a cohesive graphic unit. It functions as a graphic identity for a product, company, or service.

– New ideas are often derived from old ideas. A cliché is an expression or idea that has become overly familiar or commonplace. Clichés provide us with a common language upon which to expand in new or different ways.

– Use contrast for emphasis. Contrasting elements function as reference points in a design. They help to establish a visual hierarchy and therefore clarify the message.

– Using an overly distinctive display face to illustrate a concept will not communicate your message as effectively or originally as applying your own personality through exploring different typographic possibilities. Students often spend too much time searching for that "perfect" typeface to solve a problem, when in fact, it is the idea applied to a typeface that communicates the message.

"In printed communication, when the text clearly conveys the message, design can afford to, in fact often should, strive for novelty and visual vigor."
– Edward Gottschall

"The only way to break typographic rules was to know them."
– Wolfgang Weingart

Descriptive Pairs

Massachusetts College of Art, Instructor: Elizabeth Resnick

Assignment Brief

Some words can inspire their own visual solution, while others need more thought to bring about the ideas inherent in their meaning. When grouping two different words together to form a *descriptive pair*, each word still retains its individual meaning. But once the words are "paired," we read the unit meaning of the grouping. An example of a descriptive pair would be "time flies." Each word has a different meaning—time, as a noun, refers to a measured period of time, and flies, used as a verb, can mean "to fade and disappear," but together they metaphorically suggest a quick passage of time.

Your assignment is to select two words that form a descriptive pair, and visually interpret the pair using only letterforms and punctuation as illustration. The resulting pictorial representation should parallel the common verbal meaning.

Objectives

– To explore and interpret typographic form to express meaning

Process

When you begin, first experiment by illustrating a single word. Pick a word and consider the following strategies to communicate its meaning:

– Your ideas could express a literal and descriptive approach to a word's visual meaning.
– You could take a more playful approach in the expressing the word's meaning.
– You might try to express sound associated with meaning.

Whatever your approach, the effective solution will result from careful reflection on the word's meaning—its symbolism in present-day language and close observation of its formal elements and shape. Once you have experimented with single-word ideas, you can begin this assignment by making a list of ten descriptive pairs. Create several quick thumbnail sketch ideas for each pair on the list. Visual research implies trying out visual alternatives—two or three for each pair. Review your sketches for ideas that are the simplest and yet most compelling.

Timeline

Week One

Begin the process as described above. Choose one of your thumbnail sketches and draw it full-size on tracing paper. Situate the drawing in the middle of 15" × 20" illustration board with ample white space on all four sides. Transfer the image to illustration board using graphite paper. Select black ink, black gouache, or black color-aid paper as your media. Render the finished project and bring both of your thumbnail sketches and the finished project to class for critique.

Week Two

Based on the feedback that you received in critique, revise your concept by redrawing it on tracing paper, but this time render your idea digitally and bring your 11" × 17" printouts for class critique.

Figure 3-1.1

Student Statement

After a long process of conceptual trial and error I became frustrated with my lack of creative energy. When good ideas are elusive in my work, I feel a crushing mass of pressure. I used this stress as an advantage for this assignment and was able to internalize and visual this pressure in my concept.

Critiques

Work Load, *Jaivin Anzalota,* Figure 3-1.1

Instructor's Evaluation

The expression workload often refers to the amount of working time expected of or assigned to a person. This is an abstract concept because it has no physical, concrete form. In order to visually express the pressure he felt from his own workload, Jaivin had to imagine and visually describe this pressure he felt.

He visualizes a crushing heavy mass of work weighing down load (himself). He is successful in communicating the word load being crushed by the sheer weight of work. The visual impact of the message could be further enhanced by altering the letter spacing of the word load to be tighter in order to form a more impactful unit. The large amount of white space between the letterforms lightens the load visually.

Figure 3-1.2

Student Statement

My concept was derived from how a person interacts with a scratch ticket. The words are illustrated to reflect what the words represent. The unit cleverly mimics the search-and-discovery process a person experiences as they scratch their ticket.

Scratch Ticket, *Matthew Berube,* Figure 3-1.2

Instructor's Evaluation

"Scratch ticket" is common vernacular for an instant lottery ticket. You uncover whether you have won by scratching off the opaque metallic coating to see what's underneath. Matthew's concept is to visually simulate the experience a person would have engaging with the scratch ticket. Matthew's depiction is clever, easy to read, and utilizes the design principle of contrast to illustrate the idea. It's obvious he has carefully examined these tickets (visual research) because most scratch tickets use a display-sized sans-serif typeface for its boldness and legibility. The large word scratch is visualized with a bold gothiclike typeface stacked tightly together that creates straight-edge boundaries to suggest the shape of the rectangular ticket. The act of scratching then reveals the answer, ticket, which is used as a stand-in for the prize sought.

Figure 3-1.3

Student Statement
In this project, I chose to emulate how the digital clock shows its function through its own display. I constructed the words "digital clock" using the same units and proportions used to display digital time, and drew the letters of the two words within these units. Some characteristics inherent to each letter had to be compromised in order to adhere to the project restrictions.

Digital Clock, *Bryant Ross,* Figure 3-1.3

Instructor's Evaluation

The goal of this assignment is to visually and conceptually interpret an existing form or abstract concept into an expressive typographic message that adds a layer of meaning to the word combination. Bryant's use of the word digital refers to the readout in numerical digits. The word clock means a device by which time is measured. Together they describe a common object found in homes and offices: a digital clock.

Bryant cleverly employs the visual vocabulary associated with the LED digital displays commonly found in digital clocks. He set his design parameters to stay within the spirit of this language only to be challenged by the geometric unit structure within the LED display, especially when it came to the k in the word clock. There is no convention to create a diagonal line in the LED display, and he had to create an h shape in place of the k. But the viewer is not fooled and the readability of the object remains intact.

Student Statement
My idea was to conceptually interpret and visually communicate the meaning of the descriptive pair "broken glass." I visualized what glass looks like when it is broken—many sharp cracks and sometimes missing pieces.

Figure 3-1.4

Broken Glass, *Aleksandra Zarkhi,* Figure 3-1.4

Instructor's Evaluation

The term "broken glass" is another common objective description. Aleksandra's concept is to visually interpret and communicate the physical idea of broken glass. When describing the aftermath of an action, it is helpful, whenever possible, to work from a life model or a picture. I am not sure whether Aleksandra did this (broke a proportional pane of glass) or whether she imagined it based on previous experiences of seeing broken glass.

The project does, however, articulate its message by presenting the letters in a fragmentary manner. A few of the letters, such as the last s in glass, are not as believable and could use some revisualizing. I am also left wondering why the other s in glass survives intact. Perhaps there is a story behind this.

Letters as Image

Samsung Art and Design Institute, Seoul, Korea, Instructor: Hyunmee Kim

Assignment Brief

Choose three words in Korean characters, Chinese characters, and the Roman alphabet, respectively. It could be one word of the same meaning in three different alphabet systems, or three different words of different meaning depending on your interests and intention of study. Design three different panels that visually represent the meaning, the feeling, the sound, and other aspects that you can associate with the words.

Objectives

– To discover the realm of typography that represents and amplifies the semantics of written language.
– To explore the poetic quality of visual language, which is to experience the content.

Specifications

1. Size: 20 cm × 20 cm square (7.8" × 7.8").
2. Color: Four-color, spot color, or black and white.

Process

You can insert, substitute, omit, and/or exaggerate the type to achieve the desired semantic. You are responsible for the designing the type and its placement within the square format.

Timeline

Week One

Present three full-size sketch ideas in each language.

Week Two

Based on the critique in class, select and develop the sketches that are conceptually and formally strongest. Prepare at least one full-size sketch in each language.

Week Three

Develop and refine the final ideas and present them on foam core.

Figure 3-2.1

**s
st
sta
stair
stairw
stairwa
stairway**

Student Statement
My goals was to represent aspects of stairway by the typeface and the structure I chose. Reading the letters, I hope that the viewer will experience the word.

Critiques

Stairway, *Eunjin Kim*, Figure 3-2.1

Instructor's Evaluation

Through careful selection of the typeface and the well-thought-out construction of typography, the word stairway is communicated and experienced. The diagonal patterns composed of the same letters add aesthetics and stability to the stairway.

Figure 3-2.2

Maple Tree, *Hyun Kim*, Figure 3-2.2

Instructor's Evaluation

The student's understanding and perception of the maple tree makes this typographic representation very successful. The red color of maple trees deepens as it becomes colder and windier. The subtle difference in reds in the image broadens the viewer's perception of time and space.

Student Statement
In Chinese characters, when the trees meet the cold wind, they become maple trees. I tried to express what Chinese characters express about the nature of the maple tree.

Figure 3-2.3A

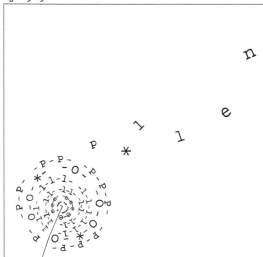

Student Statement
*When the wind blows, pollen flies with
the wind. The seeds of the dandelion also
fly with the wind. I tried to express the
form of the dandelion through concentric
circles made up of type.*

Pollen, *Kynchang Shin,* Figure 3-2.3A

Instructor's Evaluation

The light nature of pollen is well expressed through the
selection of Courier and the overall typographic construction. The student utilized not only type but also punctuation
marks to describe the form.

Kite, *Kynchang Shin,* Figure 3-2.3B

Instructor's Evaluation

The student's typographic communication of the Chinese character for "kite" is
witty and exquisite. Through the discovery that the character for "kite" is based
on the character for "bird," the student created an image of birds and kites

flying together. Through
his process, he improved
the character for "kite" to
make it appear as though
freely flying.

Student Statement
*In Chinese characters, new meaning
is created through the transformation
of an existing character, which was
the basic concept of my work. Each of
the characters in the upper right
corner means "bird." The character
for "kite" is based on the character
for "bird."*

Figure 3-2.3B

Concrete Poetry
Old Dominion University, Instructor: Kenneth Fitzgerald

Assignment Brief
Create two "concrete poems" of original typographic compositions. A major aspect of the designer's work is typography—arranging the provided text to make it engaging and commodious to the reader, and reflecting, emphasizing, and expanding the meaning of the text. This is accomplished through the styling and choice of typefaces.

Objectives
– Explore the expressive potential of type forms and their arrangement
– Explore the interaction/relationship of the meaning of text and the meaning created by its arrangement
– Investigate the inherent nature of the computer in representing and handling type

Specifications
1. Size: 8.5" × 11" vertical orientation.
2. For poem one: letterforms cut from printed materials.
3. For poem two: computer-generated black-and-white type on white background.

Process
Currently, type is almost exclusively generated and manipulated on the computer. However, many arrangements are not possible (or are exceedingly difficult) to create using this technology. Rather than increasing possibilities, the computer may close off various approaches.

Text for extended reading (known as *body copy*, used for articles and stories) and brief readings (signage, headlines, and posters) share concerns but function in distinctly different ways. What might these differences be?

In both poems, consider the specific attributes and possibilities of the medium. Many of the original concrete poems were about the typewriter and exploited its particular capabilities. What effects are unique to publishing software?

When selecting characters from printed material, consider the font, the color of the letterforms, and the surrounding area. In both, keep your poem simple; concrete poems often feature one word. Your poem could consist of one character and be about the various fonts that you found the character in.

Figure 3-3.1

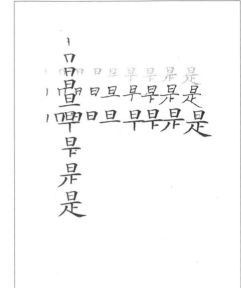

Student Statement

In this concrete poem, the Chinese character progressing stroke by stroke into existence is the character for the verb "to be." In this design, my intent was to express the meaning of the word visually, so that even someone who cannot read Chinese might be able to decipher its meaning. The character is constructed stroke by stroke from left to right in the order that it would actually be written. Likewise, in the horizontal lines, the character moves from a shadowy trace of the character to a hand-written version and then to a more concrete, consistent typeface. The character for "to be" is literally coming into being on the page, creating both a visually and intellectually stimulating design.

Critiques

Concrete Poetry: To Be, *Lisa Catron,* Figure 3-3.1

Instructor's Evaluation

Out of a few tens of students who have been given this project, only two have chosen to use a language other than English. That Lisa chose these characters is a reminder of the many other descriptive systems of language. They also demonstrate an additional layer of signification that Roman characters lack. The sequential building of the characters horizontally and vertically is both dynamic and static at the same time. Such an arrangement with a recognizable Roman character wouldn't have the same impact. At the least, there is a mystery and an implied process of meaning. Another unique aspect to this poem is the grayed series of characters at the top. When acquiring letterforms from another source, students rarely modify them: They are pasted down exactly as printed. That Lisa has introduced this screened-back effect (which is frequently seen when students do the computer version of this assignment) is another impressive subtle effect.

Figure 3-3.2

Student Statement

The underlying theme of this work is crossword puzzles. Crosswords are a sequence of unrelated words connected by common letters. I played with the idea of letters being disconnected, by virtue of being woven into a background image. The image just happened to be on the opposite page of the magazine from which I cut the text, but I think it's too distracting. A more advanced draft would have lines of text woven into plain gray or black paper.

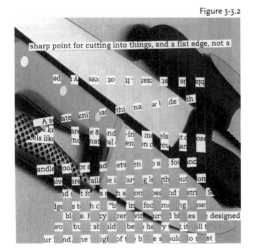

Concrete Poetry: Crossword Puzzle, *Martina Doblin,* Figure 3-3.2

Instructor's Evaluation

This work's appeal is in its meticulous crafting and the subtle "strange-making" of both the text and image. Taken separately, the two elements are literally representative:

Student Statement
*I chose the word catatonic for my poem. To be catatonic is
to be unresponsive or marked by a lack of movement,
usually from a psychological disturbance. The collection of
forms made by these letters self-illustrates a feeling of suspension, as if they became interrupted for an unknown reason.*

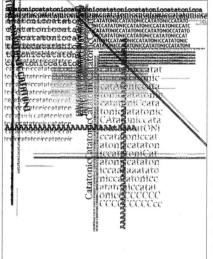

Figure 3-3.3A

the image of knives are sliced, the text describes the knives.
However, the weaving together of the two and the progression from legible words to fragments is direct and formally
engaging. The image also moves back and forth from abstract
pattern to recognizable image.

Concrete Poetry: Catatonic, *Karye LaRose,* Figure 3-3.3A

Instructor's Evaluation

The "catatonic" poem (composed on the computer) is engaging in that it utilizes a number of simple treatments (layers,
diagonal, repetition) but orchestrates them well. The composition hovers between being on a single surface and having
dimensionality. More than the definition of the word, it is the
combination of letter shapes that make up the word—the
repetition of C, A, and T—that directs this piece.

Concrete Poetry: Think, *Karye LaRose,*

Figure 3-3.3B

Instructor's Evaluation

The think poem makes good use of an aspect of
printed letters that few students exploit —making
the space surrounding the letterforms an essential
part of the composition. Another strength of the
composition is the architectural reference in
the stacking of letters, which never overpowers
the composition.

Student Statement
*The idea behind the think design came after some slight frustration—
I felt like I was unable to think creatively for the assigment. I went
through several ideas and finally ended up cutting my original idea (a
square of different versions of the word think) and creating a form
that had direction or that built up into something—like a final thought.*

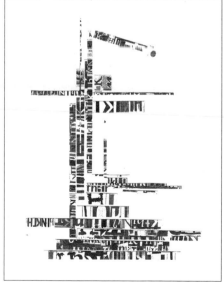

Figure 3-3.3B

Student Statement

Sound travels via waves that are not divided by anything but space. A decision that I made at the beginning of the project—a black streak dividing the two parts of the wave scope in half, lengthwise—gave rise to my design. The lines that reach out represent peaks of sound. The irregularity of the lines reflects my connection to rock music. My project was inspired by music—not by a particular song but by the changes or evolution of music, which has its ups and downs.

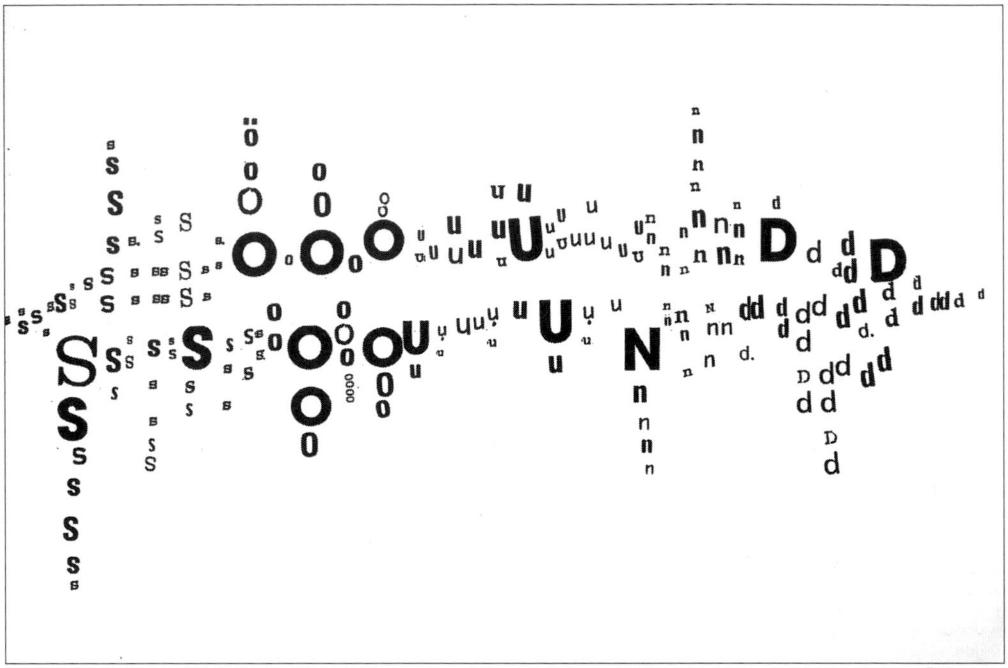

Figure 3-3.4

Concrete Poetry: Sound, *Diego Rioja,* Figure 3-3.4

Instructor's Evaluation

This work is a simple yet dynamic representation of the single word sound. In many ways, it refers to the established form-language for music. The strongest element is the O letterform, and I wonder if the use of all caps might improve the piece.

Arthur Murray Dance Advertisement
Philadelphia University, Instructor: Frank Baseman

Assignment Brief

Using boilerplate advertising copy, design an 8.5" × 11" black and white advertisement for the Arthur Murray Dance Studios. You must solve this problem strictly typographically (no use of photography or illustration), utilizing basic typographic principles covered in exercises from the beginning of the semester.

In this assignment, you will rely on basic design principles, including a thorough study of contrast as well as the concept of hierarchy of information. Work within a limited palette of typefaces to concentrate on the uses of these typefaces rather than getting bogged down with an enormous selection of fonts. The type families available are Bodoni, Garamond, Kunstler Script, Rockwell, and Univers.

Objectives

- To explore concepts using typography and hierarchy of information
- To encourage students to think editorially (what word or words to emphasize when, and why)

Specifications

1. Size: 8.5" × 11".
2. Color: Black and white only.
3. Outcome: Black-and-white linotronic output, flush-mounted to illustration board or foam core.
4. Required copy: The designer must use the entire amount of copy, and must use it in the order it has been written. If the designer would like to use additional copy, the text may be repeated as long as it is used in its entirety at least once.

Teach me.

It's easy and fun the Arthur Murray way.

Personalized dance lessons. Learn at your own speed. And only at Arthur Murray do you receive authentic instruction by professionally trained teachers.

Personalized lessons. Class and group practice. Dance parties and studio get-togethers.

Swing, Freestyle, Fox Trot, Newest Latin Steps, Mambo, Country Western, Popular Ballroom

Phone now for your complimentary private lesson.

Singles and couples welcome.

Arthur Murray Franchised Dance Studios   2417 Welsh Road
Monday – Friday, 1 P.M. to 10 P.M.   Philadelphia, PA 19103
Saturday, noon to 5 P.M.   215.698.9781

Process

Design a compelling page that will grab the viewer's attention. Give typographic emphasis to the word dance. The emphasis is on an experimental, nontraditional approach to typography. Research well-designed magazine ads in existing publications. Make copies of at least six ads to evaluate their typographic landscape. How will your visual space be perceived? What is the tone of this piece? Develop a hierarchy that includes clarity and legibility. Begin with thumbnail studies and half-size roughs before implementing your design on the computer.

Timeline

Week One

Do your typographic research as outlined above. Bring your typographic examples to class and be prepared to discuss them. Why do they resonate with you? What makes these designs strong? You will need to do a minimum of twenty thumbnail sketches of your dance ad. These should be done in pencil, pen, and/or markers before you begin to work on the computer. Make your thumbnail sketches clearly understood, crisp, and detailed. Do not work on the computer until your thumbnail sketches have been approved for direction. Bring these thumbnail sketches to class for critique.

Week Two

Based on the feedback that you received in the last classroom critique, choose two of your idea sketches and develop them to laser-print sketches. Make variations on a theme if necessary by adjusting the same idea slightly, and then redo by changing something else. Continue to refine your sketches until you are satisfied that you have strong results, and bring all of your work to class for critique.

Week Three

Based on the feedback that you received in the last classroom critique, it's time to go to a finish on your chosen design direction. You may still make further design refinements, adjusting minute details of your design and perfecting it. Once you are pleased with your final design, load up all of your files (working document, all graphics, all fonts used) and collect for output. Make sure to take along a clean, accurate laser print of your design. Go to a service bureau and request linotronic output of your dance ad. Flush-mount to illustration board or foam core.

Figure 3-4.1

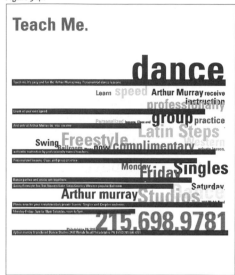

Student Statement

My concept in creating this dance ad centered on the notion of typographic movement as related to dance. I used several black bars as design devices that jut into chaos of words in various shapes, sizes, and values emphasizing the rhythm of the words.

Critiques

Arthur Murray Dance Advertisement, *Lindsay Crissman,*
Figure 3-4.1

Instructor's Evaluation

Visual interest in Lindsay Crissman's Arthur Murray Dance Ad project derives from simple elements of contrast, since all of the typography is from the same type family (a version of Univers). Lindsay is using size as contrast (some type is big, some small, some in-between) and value as contrast (some type is full-strength, solid black, some type is screened back to very light, and some is in between), and some type overlaps (but never so much that we can't read it). While all of this texture and play with words and letterforms occurs, hugging and clustering the flush-right side of the page, from the flush-left side are a series of same-weight bars that jut out at different lengths, extending and prodding the active type on the right. Lindsay has wisely repeated all of the text as a texture of simple white type knocking out of the jutting bars to make what I think is a beautifully layered, active, sophisticated solution.

Figure 3-4.2

Arthur Murray Dance Advertisement, *Charles DiSantis,*
Figure 3-4.2

Instructor's Evaluation

This solution utilizes type running slightly askew on a strange yet interesting angle to create impact. The all-lowercase use of Univers is simple yet direct, and interesting in its stepping quality and the way in which it touches the edges of the page. However, what really makes this solution work is the very simple contrast to the smaller, subordinate type. It is still Univers, but aggressively small, perhaps 8-point type. All of the subordinate

Student Statement

My intent behind this project was to emphasize the word dance without letting the other text suffer. I incorporated the rest of the copy by creating text resembling a waterfall that leads its way to the N in dance, then falls through the opening of the letter and trails off. I treated the types of dances as random drops of rain. I achieved this by angling the words and placing them to feel random. Combining all of these elements created an advertisement with just the right amount of variety to make the reader want to read every bit of information on it.

type is the same style, but some (like the names of the dance steps themselves) float like rain on the same angle, which makes the type hold together like a pattern. Interrupted just a few times by longer line length is type set on a much harsher angle, with a very different feel than the raining type.

Figure 3-4.3

Student Statement
My goal was to deliberately design an ad that closely resembles propaganda. In this instance, typographic treatment provides the visual persuasion.

Arthur Murray Dance Advertisement, *Chris Holub*, Figure 3-4.3

Instructor's Evaluation

In Chris Holub's solution to the Arthur Murray Dance Ad project, the strength lies in the small yet important typographic details. First, the use of all-lowercase Univers Bold Italic for the headline is cropped off the edges of the page, yet readable enough for the viewer to make out the words Arthur and dance. The simple position of these strong words on the spatial page, with dance hovering near the bottom and Arthur just above center, is the beginning of a strong solution. Chris then uses hierarchy and direction using the words "Teach me. It's easy" as a bold lead-in and underline to the a in Arthur. She reiterates this use again as an overline above the ce in the word dance.

After this, she turns the rest of the subordinate type on a 90-degree angle and lets the irregular line lengths dance in the open negative space between her two dominant headline words. Overall, this is a very strong solution using the most basic of contrasting forms.

Arthur Murray Dance Advertisement, *David Reed Monroe,* Figure 3-4.4

Instructor's Evaluation

I love the use of handwriting as type in this solution. In this case, the scrap of paper works to remind us of the typical phone numbers we jot down and shove in our pocket or purse (or what we think that scrap of paper would look like). The scan of the piece of paper is very well done, and the shadow makes it appear as though it's lying on a surface. And the subordinate type is handled in a very delicate, sophisticated way: understated but with just enough visual interest, such as centering the contact info just under the name of the company and then picking up that same style and size of type as a lead-in to the rest of the body copy.

Figure 3-4.4

Arthur Murray Franchised Dance Studios
7617 Welsh Road Philadelphia, PA 19105

It's *easy* and *fun* the Arthur Murray way. Learn at your own speed with personalized dance lessons, class and group practices, dance parties and studio get-togethers. And only at Arthur Murray do you receive authentic instruction by professionally trained teachers. Teach me Swing, Freestyle, Fox Trot, Newest Latin Steps, Mambo, Country Western and Popular Ballroom. Phone now for your complementary private lesson, singles and couples welcome. Monday–Friday, 1pm to 10pm Saturday, Noon to 5pm.

Student Statement
I tried to keep the advertisement simple by emphasizing the bare minimum amount of copy (name and number) and downplaying all the rest. I then treated this display copy as a reminder note by hand-writing out the information, crumpling up the piece of paper in my pocket, and scanning it in.

CD Cover: Typographic Music
Washington University, Instructor: Heather Corcoran

Assignment Brief

Choose a song (with lyrics) and create a typographic interpretation. Consider the structure of the music itself, the lyrics, the context in which the music was made, the instruments, voices, and overall quality of the music. Create a CD package for your song by applying your typographic interpretation to a four-page folding booklet of appropriate size. You may generate letterforms in any way that you wish. The words of the song must be contained somewhere within the four pages in a clear, legible way.

Objectives

– To explore the interpretative power of typography
– To explore typography as it relates to sound
– To apply type informationally
– To affirm typesetting skills
– To refine Quark, Photoshop, and Illustrator skills

Process

Each package must be presented in a hard plastic CD case.

Each package must contain a physical CD that lists the song and artist and is visually related to the packaging.

CD packages must contain the name of the song, the name of the artist, the lyrics, the producer, the copyright, and other information that you deem appropriate.

The CD design must be composed of typographic forms.

Final CD packages must be produced in Quark.

Figure 3-5.1

Student Statement

Buju Banton is successful in the reggae community due to his lyrical skills and social consciousness and remains ingrained in people's minds because of his strong visual presence. I chose to display this concept by utilizing Buju's unmistakable dreadlocks and filling his image with the letters of his name, creating an interesting micro/macro effect. The overall density of the letterforms create Buju's image, which draws the viewer's attention. Upon closer inspection the complexity of the letters portrays the lyrical bombardment of his music.

Critiques

Typographic Music CD, *Anna Dole,* Figure 3-5.1

Instructor's Evaluation

The strength of this project is in the inventive use of type to create an image. The shift in scale of the letterforms, as well as the use of the color red, helps to make a compelling icon of the head. From a distance, the composition reads as an image; closer up, the forms become visible as letters.

The title and artist type on the cover could perhaps be better integrated into the image type. In addition, the interior spread doesn't connect to the cover as well as it might. I question the use of the curve for the type and the composition as whole, which feels a bit static. Perhaps the interior could borrow something from the strength of the cover.

Figure 3-5.2

Student Statement
The aim of my CD design was to portray a metamorphosis. I designed the type to morph into a variety of visual elements, which were intended to depict not only the music per se but also the instruments used to make the music and the atmosphere created by the music.

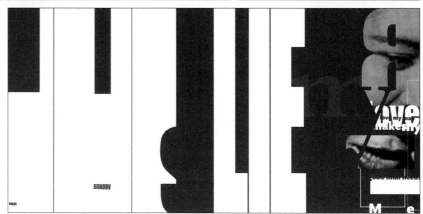

Typographic Music CD, *Anna Kardaleva,* Figure 3-5.2

Instructor Evaluation

The interior spread, back cover, and disc all work well in this package. What is striking is the way that Anna has created letterforms in a variety of ways and then integrated them into a cohesive whole. Her use of photography and simple line drawings in the letterforms is especially successful. The deep purple feels appropriate to the music, and dramatic scale shifts give the package energy.

The idea for the cover is nice, but its composition is a bit static at the moment. I am unconvinced by the black bar that appears at the top and the typeface and position of holiday, which runs vertically down the page.

Typographic Music CD, *Casey Krimmel,* Figure 3-5.3

Instructor's Evaluation

Painted letterforms seem particularly appropriate for the soft, melodic quality of this song. The scale and position of the letterforms seem right for the size of the package. The textured quality of the ground is well integrated and adds richness. The repetition of the artist's name in type makes sense, as it helps the viewer to make sense of the painted letters. The color is also a good choice for the music and gives the cover some snap. Casey's investigation and willingness to get off the computer and use her hands is at the heart of why this solution works.

While the form of the inside spread is intriguing, it is slightly difficult to tell where the lyrics begin and end. I think the position of the type on the spread could be rethought, and perhaps given more weight within the whole.

Figure 3-5.3

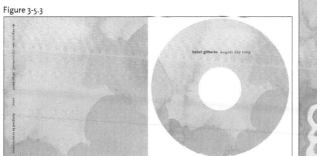

Student Statement

"August Day Song" is a mellow song with English and Portuguese lyrics that speak of daydreaming during a rainstorm. The plucking of guitar strings and other light percussive sounds also bring raindrops to mind. I tried to reflect the idea of falling rain in different ways both on the cover and inside of the booklet, and used watercolor to give my letterforms a soft and watery quality. I chose warm colors to reflect the title and the tone of the voices.

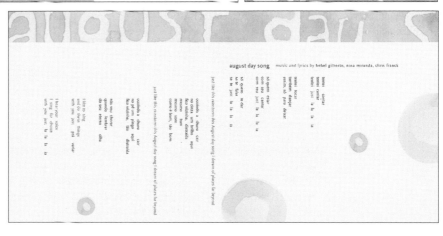

Figure 3-5.4

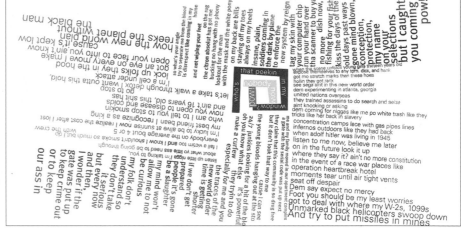

Student Statement

This cover reflects a gloomy, paranoid song, based on a mechanical beat—like the gears of a clock—that also has an eerie quality. Shape and viewing direction are important to the design; the lyrics on the inside spread of the package sprawl outward from the center, which contains the chorus. The lyrics become more intense and isolated as the song progresses; the jumbled letters on the cover are meant to address this.

Typographic Music CD, *David Kroll,* Figure 3-5.4

Instructor's Evaluation

The interior spread of this solution does an especially good job of reflecting the slow but energized beat of this song. The palette feels appropriate and the type remains legible even when turned at various angles. Subtle weight and size shifts seem well considered and add to the whole.

The cover is interesting, but I would encourage more investigation. Not only is the white type hard to read, but the cover as a whole could perhaps be better integrated with the inside spread. The large curved letterforms on the cover are at odds with the more angular text blocks on the inside. It would be nice if there could be a stronger relationship between the shapes.

Typographic Music CD, *Ellen Sitkin*, Figure 3-5.5

Instructor's Evaluation

This solution seems especially appropriate to the quality of the music and the lyrics of the song. The semidegraded type and the reddish brown palette with white knocking out are strong choices. The relationship of the cover to the interior spread also seems appropriate. The two are closely connected, with the inside spread more aggressive (a reference to the progression of the song).

In this project, I wonder if the composition of the interior spread couldn't be more dynamic. The shape and position of the two blocks of supporting white text create symmetry, which is static. I'd like to see that shaken up somehow.

Figure 3-5.5

Student Statement

The booklet contains a mini-narrative that begins on the cover with the initial breaking through and culminates on the "other side" with the type fully broken through. Inspired by the context in which the song was written and the culture surrounding the artists, my process involved experimentation with generating type. The typographic image on both the front cover and the inside of the booklet began as charcoal written and smeared on slightly textured paper. I then brought the image into the computer, wrote over it several times, and finally set a crude, rough font over it. The lyrics, divided by stanza, are set in irregular, tilted lines to emphasize the wild nature of the "other side" but still remain legible.

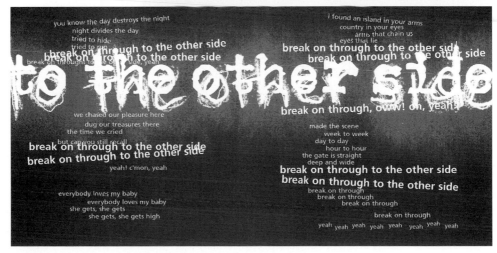

WORD AND IMAGE

The focus of this section's assignments is the integration of words and images. Just as the letters of the alphabet can be combined in numerous ways to form words and convey meanings, so can visual elements be joined in innumerable ways, with each particular relationship generating alternative solutions. Often words carry more specific meaning than images, but images can extend and intensify the meaning of words. For this reason, words and images should act as equal partners in the forming of a message. Although a designer's first instinct is to focus on the visual aspects of the message, a successful concept is formed within the interrelationship of words and the images.

How Can a Concept Be Communicated in Visual Terms?

A concept can be defined as a well-developed thought or idea. To successfully transmit an idea, the viewer's attention must be gained. Visual communication depends upon order, and the viewer will look for a system or structure to help him or her understand the meaning of the message. Designers use *visual hierarchy* to arrange the visual elements according to their importance within the design. Each element in a design contributes to the information being presented—words carry the message, and the images explain or enhance the meaning. An image with no meaning is like a sentence that makes no sense; therefore images should be as carefully chosen as the words to construct a coherent sentence. If there is no apparent hierarchy in a message, the relative importance of each piece of information becomes subjective and open to viewer interpretation. This creates an ambiguity in the message, making it unclear and possibly unreadable.

"When graphic designers bring word and image together to create visual-verbal messages, two problems must be resolved. First, visual organization is a problem, for two totally unlike systems of communication—language signs and pictorial images—must be merged into a cohesive whole. The second problem involves message making: How can these two unlike communication systems come together to reinforce and extend one another?"
– Philip B. Meggs

How Can I Make My Messages Memorable?

Here are a few strategies to consider:

– When you think in opposites you impose a different point of view on any idea or word. Irony is a twist of perspective or the opposite of the literal meaning of the subject.

– The use of contrast in either your subject matter or design elements can provide an effective context for conveying meaning. The arrangement and ordering of shape, color, and form into patterns can suggest or evoke the content or message.

– Abstract ideas can give physical characteristics to inanimate objects or ideas, bringing them to life.

– Metaphors describe abstract concepts in concrete terms or explain something complicated in simple terms.

– Visual puns exist within a juxtaposition of two possibilities and give funny twists to simple ideas. The purpose is to create understanding through the visual comparison of opposites. In the same way that letters are combined to create words, symbols can be put together to create messages. A pun is created when symbols (letters are symbols as well) are used in a context to suggest a dual meaning. A good example of this would be Milton Glaser's promotional design for New York City, "I ♥ NY."

– Defamiliarize the familiar by distortion or by transposing the usual way we think of the subject.

– Reducing something to its most elemental visual components makes the idea easily accessible. A pictogram is the visual essence of an object or thing. An example of a pictogram is a telephone handset to communicate the idea of a telephone booth.

No matter what the assignment, a creative person can always make something unique out of what is given by following the design process. Never perceive the parameters of any assignment as a limitation to your creativity. A problem with no constraints is really not a problem, as there is nothing to solve.

"Clichés may be the most under-valued tools of our profession, as they represent our culture's commonly accepted ideas and images of itself. For the designer, it is crucial to understand clichés and know when to twist them in new and interesting ways."
– Kit Hinrichs

Word and Image
Massachusetts College of Art, Instructor: Elizabeth Resnick

Word and Image Relationship

A visual idea can be described as a pictorial response to an abstract thought or problem. By merging words (type) and images (pictures), a designer can create articulate messages to engage a viewer or convey information. This can be accomplished by skillful manipulation, interpretation, and possibly juxtaposition of words and images, literally or figuratively, to suggest or imply a specific or desired meaning.

The use of symbolism, analogy, metaphor, or pun may further expand your visual vocabulary.

Symbolism is the term used to describe the art or practice of using symbols. A symbol is a thing standing for or representing something else, especially a material thing taken to represent an immaterial or abstract concept. An example of a symbol is the American flag (a material object) that stands for a united group of people—a country (an abstract concept).

Analogy is the term for a description derived from a process of reasoning from parallel or similar cases explaining what unlike things share in common. An example of an analogy is to describe a hand that "feels as smooth as silk."

Metaphor is a figure of speech in which one thing is compared to another to suggest a likeness or analogy between them. An example of a metaphor is "all the world's a stage." In visual terms, one image is used to suggest another, often in collaboration with words or other images. An example is Yusaku Kamekura's magnificent *Hiroshima Appeals* poster (1983), depicting falling butterflies on fire to express the horrors of war.

A *pun* is the humorous use of a word or image to suggest alternative meanings, a play on words with more than one meaning. A visual example is an image of a chess piece given human attributes playing a game of chess—a chess piece playing chess.

Assignment Brief

Your assignment is to select one of the words listed below and convey a conceptual message by the integration or juxtaposition of type and image, possibly in a new or unexpected way. The challenge here is to add another layer of meaning born from the combination of the word and image (1 + 1 = 3).

culture	recycle	revive
vote	exercise	labor
consume	diverse	community

Specifications

1. Size: 11" × 17" horizontal or vertical.
2. Media: Collage, drawing, painting, computer illustration (without using the computer, the word can be traced, enlarged by photocopying, then rendered by hand or cut out of paper).
3. Copy: Use the selected word only.

Process

To understand all possible multiple meanings, definitions, and interpretations of your selected word, look it up in the dictionary and thesaurus and write them all down. Brainstorm by making an exhaustive list of ideas, both verbal and visual, of the word's multiple meanings. A second list can be generated to record the opposite meanings of the word. A thesaurus is a very helpful reference source for doing this.

Student Statement

The fist crushing the word consume symbolizes the destructive aspects of consumption in American society. It can also be read as a statement to take control of what you consume and to not be the pawn of corporations.

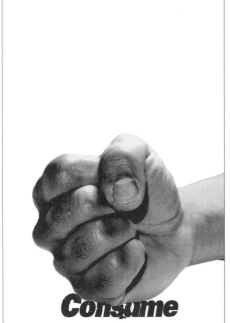

Figure 4-1.1

Timeline

Week One

Start your design process by using the dictionary and thesaurus to make lists as described above. It is best to focus on one word. From the lists that you generate, pick three concepts with different meanings and produce thumbnail sketches articulating visual solutions for each of the three possible meanings. Once you have made enough sketches, select three possibilities to develop into three full-size color layouts due for class critique.

Week Two

Based on the feedback that you receive in class on the three layouts, choose the most articulate idea and work it into a finished poster mounted on black or gray board, with a 2" margin on top and sides and 3" on the bottom. Bring it to class for critique.

Critiques

Consume, *Jaivin Anzalota,* Figure 4-1.1

Instructor's Evaluation

Jaivin explores the meaning of the word consume by advocating for a policy reversal on current American attitudes toward consumerism. He creates a classic activist statement, one that is powerful and persuasive—he argues against consumption rather than literally describing the meaning of the word consume.

The positioning of the fist in the composition supports the message. By positioning the fist at the bottom, crushing the word consume, the viewer can visualize the action of the fist coming down to pound the word. This implied action adds to the forcefulness of the visual message. The student photographed his own hand for the illustration, investing himself as part of the content, making the message that much more of a personal statement.

Figure 4-1.a

Student Statement
A visual idea conveys the meaning of an abstract thought without using words. This assignment forced me to find alternative meanings that different word and image combinations create. The concept of the assignment is that the world gets smaller every day. New technology makes it easier to talk to people on the other side of the world, and to go there too. This immediacy has created a new culture and a new way of thinking. I chose to use the World Wide Web to symbolize this new culture and technology.

Culture, *Chikage Imai Cote,* Figure 4-1.2

Instructor's Evaluation
Chikage employs a popular vernacular metaphor, the World Wide Web, for culture. The planet Earth is symbolized by the globe drawn as a spherical spiderweb, suggesting a network of gridded intersections creating connections. The image of the spider completes the meaning.

The image and word are flowing in the middle of space. The darkness of the background (midnight blue in color) adds to an implied sense of alienation. The curvature of the baseline of the serif type echoes the shape of the sphere, directing the viewer's eye across the picture plane and increasing the expanse. There is a sense of delicacy in the drawing of the spider.

Figure 4-1.3

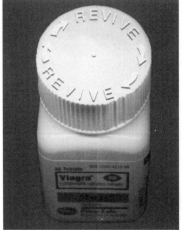

Student Statement
One definition of the word revive is "to bring back from a dead or unconscious state." Having an offbeat sense of humor, I instantly made the visual connection of dead or unconscious to the word flaccid. So how does one revive a flaccid penis? Pop a Viagra one hour before intercourse.

Revive, *John Dennis,* Figure 4-1.3

Instructor's Evaluation

John's visual response to this assignment is a good example of a pun—a humorous concept with more than one meaning. The image featured is a bottle for the drug *Viagra*, advertised and prescribed to men who wish to revive their sexual prowess.

The word revive is embossed on the plastic cap in place of the customary opening directions. The concept is very tongue-in-cheek—a play on words.

The composition is symmetrical, with the bottle situated in the center, filling up most of the picture plane. The dark red, vibrant background creates a value contrast with the white bottle and suggests that the foreshortened perspective is the focal point of the message. But what is the meaning of the message? Is this a serious jab at contemporary society's foibles or an innocent pro-drug advertisement? It makes us think about it.

Revival, *Timothy J. Welch,* Figure 4-1.4

Instructor's Evaluation

Many of the students who do this project often create messages that can be considered design for the public good. This is an excellent example. Although T.J. stretched the parameters of the assignment by changing the verb revive (bring back to life) to the noun revival (rebirth), I don't think it makes much difference which form he uses, as the message remains consistent—quit smoking cigarettes.

T.J. employs a vernacular visual language by creating the cigarette butt from cut-paper collage and spray-painting the typography using a hand-cut stencil for the letterforms. The warm beige background color is the perfect value for the white of the butt and the black of the typography. Both the image and the type are equal partners here, with one design element relying on the other for the combined meaning in the message.

Figure 4-1.4

Student Statement
I felt that this assignment was the perfect opportunity to make an antismoking statement. The assigned word was revive, but somehow I got it confused with revival, which worked best with the image of a snuffed-out cigarette butt.

Book Cover Design: The Interpretation of Dreams *by Sigmund Freud*
Massachusetts College of Art, Instructor: Elizabeth Resnick

Assignment Brief

A book cover design requires the creation of an appealing graphic—a mini-poster—that encourages the consumer to pick up the book and look through it. The cover graphic can set a mood or hint at what the reader might experience inside its covers. After reading the book, manuscript, or summary provided by the editorial staff, the designer interprets and translates the work into visual ideas.

Your assignment is to design a book cover for the paperback edition of *The Interpretation of Dreams* by Sigmund Freud.

The following copy was taken from the back of the paperback edition: "This groundbreaking work, which Freud considered his most valuable, forever changed the way we think about our dreams. In it, Freud made this century's startling discoveries about why we dream, what we dream about, and what dreams really mean."

Objectives

— To create a conceptual idea based on your own original imagery
— To integrate type and imagery into a cohesive narrative inspired by the content
— To consider the use of visual hierarchy to support the clarity of the message

Specifications

1. Size: 7" × 10" with a 1" spine
2. Color: Four-color process (CMYK) or up to four spot colors
3. Title: The Interpretation of Dreams
4. Author: Sigmund Freud

Process

To begin this assignment you should read as much of the book as time allows, to gain insight into the material. You should visit the library and check the Internet to learn more about Sigmund Freud and his work. Once you have completed this portion of the research, visit area bookstores in order to analyze contemporary book cover design. Take notes about what covers attract you, and explain why. Was it the color, image, technique, or message encoded in popular visual language? What is the ratio of the size of the typography to the imagery used in the covers that you consider successful? How many of these covers use only typography as the image? How many covers use images or photographs, illustration, or digital art? You will be asked to discuss your findings in class.

Timeline

Week One

Read the book, research Freud, and be prepared to report your findings on book cover design in class. Continue the design process by making idea lists or thought maps, looking for key ideas expressed in the text or in Freud's general ideas. Select a few ideas and begin drawing thumbnail sketches. Out of these sketches, create three full-size sketch layouts for critique.

Week Two

Based on the feedback that you received in critique, revise your strongest idea and prepare two full-size color sketch variations for the next critique.

Week Three

Select and refine one of the ideas and create a book cover comp mounted on black or gray board, with a 2" margin on the top and sides and 2.5" on the bottom.

Critiques

The Interpretation of Dreams Book Cover, *Scarlett Bertrand,* Figure 4-2.1

Instructor's Evaluation

In the conservative and tradition-bound world of American book publishing, it is highly unlikely that any marketing department would consider this graphic a candidate for the cover of Freud's *The Interpretation of Dreams.* And that's too bad. I would wager it would be a sellout just for the cover image alone. The meanings evoked by a metaphoric comparison of a human penis to a prickly cactus are rich in possibilities.

Although Scarlett's concept and resulting image are quite striking, her selection of a sans-serif typeface is a puzzling choice. The visual language of sans-serif typography evokes machinelike, static, industrial qualities, not lifelike human qualities, especially in the typography for the title of the book. Perhaps another typeface could be considered here to soften the hardness of the black type sitting on the green-tinted image. Otherwise, it is a sensational response to a sophomore graphic design assignment.

Figure 4-2.1

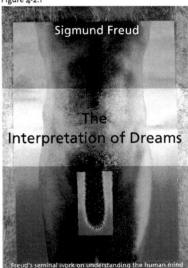

Student Statement

My visual idea for Freud's seminal work was to irreverently play on Freud's own phallic fixation. This became the basic concept—to break a taboo and make the viewer uncomfortable, and possibly elicit an embarrassed gasp, laugh, or some other kind of vocal response.

Figure 4-2.2

Student Statement

The visual concept was to capture the fleeting and starkly layered sensation of a dream. As the focal point, I used a common sleep icon—the sleep mask. By punching the typography out, I created a layer to the white ground underneath.

The Interpretation of Dreams Book Cover, *Anne Baumgardner,* Figure 4-2.2

Instructor's Evaluation

Anne's concept playfully employs a familiar icon for our over-committed and sleep-deprived postmodern society—the sleep mask. Her centered layout is simple, straightforward, and somewhat clinical in feeling, with its stark color palette and sans-serif typography. The integration of the type and image evoke a hospital setting where a sleep experiment is under way. This effect is caused by the successful juxtaposition of subject matter and visual representation that could definitely entice the curious viewer among us.

The Interpretation of Dreams Book Cover, *Michiyo Kato,* Figure 4-2.3

Instructor's Evaluation

Michiyo uses a tunnel metaphor to channel her personal feelings about dreams or being in a dreamlike state. Once she settled on the concept of a tunnel, she spent many hours looking for just the right photo to use. Since Michiyo is from Japan, the tunnel images she found were not what she had pictured in her mind. Finally she contacted a former professor, asking him to photograph the specific kind of tunnel she wanted.

The focal point of the composition is the light at the end of the tunnel; it draws us in. If we raise our gaze northward, there are messages left for us—name of book, author, and so on. The three separate typographic groups are in balance and in harmony with the centeredness of the tunnel.

Student Statement

My concept was to use a tunnel image for the book cover, based on Freud's dream theories. I believe that dreaming is like traveling through a dark, mysterious tunnel without seeing a light at the end. However, Freud's pursuit to understand the meaning of dreams is conveyed in the light at the end. (Tunnel image was taken by Akihiko Kinda, professor of graphic design, Jin-Ai College, Fukui, Japan.)

Figure 4-2.3

Figure 4-2.4

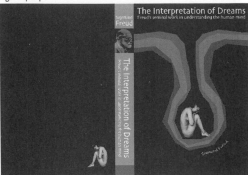

Student Statement
My concept involves one's unconscious sexual desire, which Sigmund Freud discusses in the book The Interpretation of Dreams. The layered colors represent the night, when one is dreaming, as well as deep inside one's mind.

The Interpretation of Dreams Book Cover, *Miho Nishimaniwa,* Figure 4-2.4

Instructor's Evaluation

When I first saw Miho's cover, the dominant form reminded me of an enlarged clogged facial pore in an acne cream advertisement! But Miho is from Japan and has probably never seen such a graphic depiction of a clogged pore. Her colors are like velvet in their richness of value and hue. The blanket layers of sleep surround and cocoon the female figure. She is quietly sleeping and demurely nude, not forthright like Scarlett's male nude. (I wonder if this is a stereotypical gender distinction.)

The female figure commands our attention as the focal point of the composition. However, the author's name is handled in a rather odd way. The handwritten form appears like a signature on a creative work of art. It distracts from the serenity of the sleeping figure.

I would suggest that this element be integrated within the typographic unit at the top.

The Interpretation of Dreams Book Cover, *Kristina Rivers,* Figure 4-2.5

Instructor's Evaluation

Kristina's concept is to present a fragmented portrait of Freud to suggest a duality of thought pervasive within his published opinions and scientific research. She accomplishes this visually by placing the portrait out of focus as the central background form of the composition. Superimposed on it are two jagged fragments, in focus, each bespectacled eye staring out at the viewer.

Like her classmates, Kristina also uses sans-serif typography, but the use of uppercase and lowercase and the weight of type in the book title help to soften the look. It is an engaging cover graphic that successfully integrates the author as the receptacle for the visual concept.

Figure 4-2.5

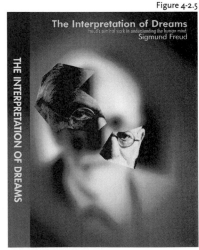

Student Statement
My concept was to focus on Freud's face as an image, as this book is about his interpretation of dreams.

Book Cover Design: Einstein's Dreams *by Alan Lightman*
Massachusetts College of Art, Instructor: Elizabeth Resnick

Assignment Brief

A book cover design requires the creation of an appealing graphic—a mini-poster—that encourages the consumer to pick up the book and look through it. The cover graphic can set a mood or hint at what the reader might experience inside its covers. After reading the book, manuscript, or summary provided by the editorial staff, the designer interprets and translates the work into visual ideas.

Your assignment is to design a book cover for the paperback edition of *Einstein's Dreams: A Novel*, by Alan Lightman.

The following copy was taken from the cover flap of the Warner Books paperback edition, 1993: "It is 1905 in Berne, Switzerland. A young patent clerk has been dreaming marvelous dreams about the nature of time. He is Albert Einstein and he has almost finished his special theory of relativity. What were his dreams like those last pivotal few months? Here, in this extraordinary and highly acclaimed work by physicist Alan Lightman, thirty fables conjure up as many theoretical realms of time, dreamt in as many nights."

Objectives

– To create a conceptual idea based on your own original imagery
– To integrate type and imagery into a cohesive narrative inspired by the content
– To consider the use of visual hierarchy to support the clarity of the message

Specifications

1. Size: 7" x 10" with a 1" spine
2. Color: Four-color process (CMYK) or up to four spot colors
3. Title: Einstein's Dreams
4. Subtitle: A Novel
5. Author: Alan Lightman

Process

To begin this assignment you should read the book to gain insight into the story. The story will inspire you to visit the library and the Internet to learn more about Albert Einstein and his scientific theories. Once you have completed this portion of the research, you should visit area bookstores in order to analyze contemporary book cover design. Take notes about what covers attract you, and explain why. Was it the color, image, technique, or message encoded in popular visual language? What is the ratio of the size of the typography to the imagery used in the covers that you consider successful? How many of these covers use only typography as the image? How many covers use images or photographs, illustration, or digital art? You will be asked to discuss your findings in class.

Timeline

Week One

Read the book, research Einstein, and be prepared to report your findings on book cover design in class. Continue the design process by making idea lists or thought maps, looking for key ideas expressed in the text or in Einstein's scientific ideas. Select a few ideas and begin drawing thumbnail sketches. Out of these sketches, create three full-size sketch layouts for critique.

Week Two

Based on the feedback that you received in critique, revise your strongest idea and prepare two full-size color sketch variations for the next critique.

Week Three

Select and refine one of the ideas and create a book cover comp mounted on black or gray board (2" margin on the top and sides, 2.5" on the bottom).

Figure 4-3.1

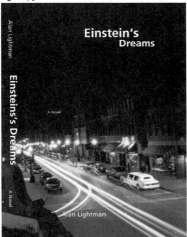

Student Statement

For this assignment, I created an image to display time and space at two different intervals simultaneously. The old buildings, which remain frozen parallel to the passing traffic, symbolize the past and future in one instance. Also, I separated the typographic information to accentuate the perspective of the photograph.

Critiques

Einstein's Dreams Book Cover, *Jaivin Anzalota*, Figure 4-3.1

Instructor's Evaluation

For his visual, Jaivin selected an area of downtown Haverhill, Massachusetts, where he lives, because the buildings evoke an old-style European sensibility with their arch-shaped windows and street-level awnings. He clearly identifies these buildings with the past. The direction of the traffic, on the other hand, moves swiftly through the present and into the future beyond the composition's vanishing point.

This is a structurally dynamic layout built with a dominant diagonal axis forcefully moving from south to west. The viewer enters the scene through the large white letterforms of the book's title and continues to follow the white directional lines of blurred traffic out into the far distance. The viewer is left with the sense of time passing yet everything remaining the same. I find this solution to be a very modern and engaging interpretation of the book.

Figure 4-3.2

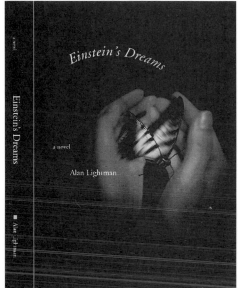

Student Statement
When you read something you can really get a feeling for it. My idea was based on one of the stories in the book—the world where nightingales are captured to stop time, but where unfortunately the captured time eventually fades. To express my idea visually I created a dreamlike image of hands trying to capture an elusive butterfly, to show how our grasp of time is precious and precarious.

Einstein's Dreams Book Cover, *Chikage Imai Cote,* Figure 4-3.2
Instructor's Evaluation
With this incredibly sensitive image, Chikage creates a poetic metaphor for capturing the elusiveness of time. She uses a butterfly as a metaphor for time, both fragile and fleeting— one moment time is at hand, and the next moment it becomes a memory.

The dark background of the composition creates a value contrast with the hands sheltering the butterfly. The image emerges out of the darkness and into the light, focusing the viewer's gaze on the image, while the arched book title typography acts like a halo or crown of protection for the brief moment. The two other typographic elements float from the middle-ground distance around the hands to the foreground to create a sense of dimensionality.

The combined effect of the word and image integration inspires the viewer through its poetic ambiguity—we are left wondering what this book is about.

Einstein's Dreams Book Cover, *Li Xiao,*
Figure 4-3.3
Instructor's Evaluation
As Li expressed in her statement, her idea was to imbue the subject of *time* with a sense of loneliness and mystery. She employs the idea of a dark, empty highway at night as her metaphor. Her blurred image, already a document of movement through time, exudes a mysterious and disquieting feeling—we cannot see beyond the reach of the headlights, we cannot see the future.

The large stacked book title typography formally echoes the double lines of the divided highway. However, its positioning at the very left edge boundary places a strange tension on such an elegant calligraphic typeface. I wonder whether this was the appropriate choice for the image.

Figure 4-3.3

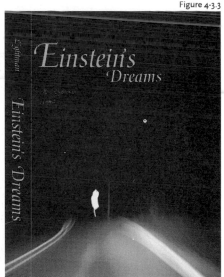

Student Statement
"What is time?" is the idea behind the book. I photographed a highway at night to explore the idea of catching time unaware. For me, the dark, empty road expresses mystery and loneliness, as if I am walking in the dream. The image also expresses my feeling that time is endless and unpredictable.

Einstein's Dreams Book Cover, *Aleksandra Zarkhi,* Figure 4-3.4

Instructor's Evaluation

Aleksandra was fascinated by the many possibilities of time suggested in the text. She felt that time was really an illusion, but the use of inventions to measure time—timepieces such as clocks, watches, or an hourglass—were ways to make the abstract concept concrete. Her idea is to suggest the illusion of time by employing the principle of figure/ground ambiguity. In figure/ground, the viewer identifies the object as the figure and the ground as the area that supports the figure. In figure/ground ambiguity, it is unclear which is the figure and which is the ground, as they alternate equally in commanding the viewer's attention.

Figure 4-3.4

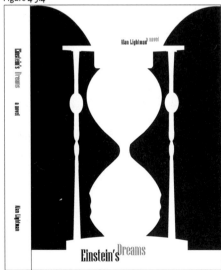

Aleksandra constructs a classic figure/ground scenario using two mirrored human profiles. Instead of the wineglass that is usually seen in as the ground, she manipulates the profiles to suggest an hourglass shape to represent the illusion of time.

Student Statement

In the book there are thirty fantasies about time, and my concept is to express time as an illusion—minutes and hours are an illusion created to serve as measurements of the passage of time. My idea is to suggest the illusion of an hourglass in the negative space by juxtaposing two human profiles. There is no hourglass, but there is an illusion of it.

Postage Stamp Design: A Celebration of Cultural Diversity in America
Massachusetts College of Art, Instructor: Elizabeth Resnick, Glenn Berger

One of the ways a culture defines its national identity is from its use of graphic design for government communications. Most people interact with federally sponsored graphic design daily through currency, transportation signage, and nutrition and health labels, without giving it much thought. However, one form of government-sponsored design that attracts attention is the postage stamp.

The basic purpose of a stamp is to function as currency—a prepaid certificate that can be redeemed for mail delivery services. As a design, it is often an image with a small amount of typography. Stamps are avidly collected and often resemble miniature versions of contemporary posters. Aside from their obvious difference in scale, posters and stamps have much in common. Both are posted or affixed to another surface, and both tend to have an ephemeral existence, although stamp or poster collectors can recycle them. The most effective stamps and posters attract attention by communicating content in a conceptually clear, immediate, and legible manner.

Assignment Brief
Your assignment is to design a series of four postage stamps on the subject "A Celebration of Cultural Diversity in America." Choose one cultural group found in the United States (Irish, Italian, Russian, African, Japanese, Chinese, Indian, etc.) and select four individual aspects of that culture (art, dance, food, drama, sports, politics, religion, etc.) that have been adopted or integrated into the American melting-pot culture.

Objectives
– To develop a design concept as a framework for four separate but equal components
– To communicate the essence of a subject without merely illustrating it
– To design with scale issues in mind

Specifications
1. Size: 1.25" × 1.25".
2. Copy: USA / 34 cents / name of culture (Chinese, Japanese, etc).
3. Configuration: Block of four (grouped as four in a box configuration or in a sequential row).
4. Media: Photography, illustration, collage, and digital illustration.

Process

Make your selection based on a culture you wish to explore in depth. Begin researching your culture through various library and Internet sources. Look around at your classmates. Many of them are from different cultures. If possible, visit areas in the city that are populated by individuals belonging to the culture, and informally interview people that you meet.

The design process begins by reviewing your collected materials and making word lists and thought maps to develop your ideas beyond the obvious that come to mind. Your first ideas may be cultural stereotypes and should be avoided. Once you have identified what aspects you will focus on, begin making thumbnail sketches for each. You must create original imagery using shape, movement, texture, positive/negative, value, and color to reinforce the meaning of each of the aspects chosen. It is important conceptually to push yourself beyond expressing a literal narrative—for example, showing a known painting or sculpture to represent the subject of art.

In order to create a design series, your stamps must share a consistent visual vocabulary (in terms of form, shape, color, and typography) when imaging the different aspects found in the culture. Consider designing on two levels: first, the design of the individual stamp, and second, how the four stamps come together in a block or row as an integrated whole design. This is a *gestalt principle*, where the whole is more than the sum of its parts; each individual stamp has a meaning, but when all four stamps come together they embody a collective meaning.

Use any medium that you feel is appropriate for your concept; consider photography, illustration, collage, and so on. Use the computer to create layouts only after you have selected from your multiple thumbnail sketch ideas.

Timeline

Week One

Research your culture. Present both your research and conceptual idea(s) in the form of color sketches, each 6.25" × 7.5", for class critique.

Week Two

Based on your critique, choose the most successful direction and create four related designs in the form of tight color layout, with scale reductions to the actual postage stamp size to evaluate legibility.

Week Three

Based on the feedback that you received in the last critique, create comprehensive layouts of the four stamps and mount both the full-size designs plus the reduction on a black (or gray) mount board with spacing at least 2" on the top and the sides and 3" on the bottom for class presentation.

Figure 4-4.1

Student Statement
I chose to research and celebrate Japanese culture in America. My concept was to convey a Japanese feeling, which I achieved through my drawings, although it was a challenge to visually connect the four different drawings. I used a similar blue background in each drawing in order to help them flow together as a group. I am still not satisfied with the positioning of the typographic elements in each stamp.

Critiques

Japanese, *Scarlett Bertrand*, Figure 4-4.1

Instructor's Evaluation

For her choice to celebrate Japanese culture in America, Scarlett created colorful Japanese-inspired illustrations for cherry blossoms, fashion, koi (fish), and religion. The challenge for Scarlett, as she mentions in her statement, was to first respond to each of the four different aspects she chose, and then to plan a visual connecting device to group the four illustrations together. The link was made through the color palette—pink, red, blue, green, and black. Although the look of the four illustrations appears very similar, there are two distinct drawing styles: one style for the flowers and fish and another for the fashion and religion. Herein lies the challenge of this assignment. The different drawing style detracts from the cohesiveness of the stamp block. At this stage of development, it is difficult for sophomore students to comprehend the need for visual consistency.

Also challenging for Scarlett was the integration of the typographic forms with her illustrations and finding the right proportional balance of type to image. She probably created the illustrations without planning for placement of typography, especially as a sequential design element. Her typeface choice, of Garamond Bold and Bold italic, is good. The form of the italic mixes well with the style of the drawings, although the letter spacing in the word Japanese needs much kerning for readability. The typographic unit made from USA and 34 seems off balance and unreadable. The dark color is too heavy for the lightness of the illustration.

Scarlett may well choose to enlarge the typographic elements significantly, but she will still find it difficult to integrate typography into the illustrations without reworking the illustrations. The lesson is to develop both word and image within a design environment simultaneously to achieve harmony and balance among disparate elements.

Figure 4-4.2

Student Statement
My concept was inspired by the Chinese New Year festival held in San Francisco's Chinatown every year. A festival scene was my solution to the challenge of creating a single scene merging four distinct elements of the Chinese culture in America. I wanted the stamps to be interesting individually as well as in a group. Extensively researching Chinese propaganda posters helped me to convey an authentic Chinese feeling in my illustration.

Chinese, *Michiyo Kato*, Figure 4-4.2

Instructor's Evaluation

The most challenging design concept for a block of four stamps is to create one overall image that equally separates into four distinct quadrants, and have each one of the quadrants stand alone when separated from the block. Michiyo's illustration of San Francisco's Chinatown is successful on both of these levels. She crafts an illustration that includes her four selected aspects—festivals, food, dress, and architecture—in a balanced composition. She positions her drawing of a festival dragon at the center, where all four stamps connect. This becomes the focal point of the composition and the coordinating element for the stamps.

The sans-serif typeface Michiyo picks is an odd choice, since it is devoid of any visual cultural connections. Much to her credit, she manages to integrate the typeface with the illustration, adding color and value to warm up the font.

Mexican, *Kristina Rivers,* Figure 4-4.3

Instructor's Evaluation

Kristina's idea is to incorporate some of the Mexican cultural symbols associated with celebration: the drink margarita, tacos, piñatas (candy placed inside of a colorful papier-mâché donkey or other animal), and the symbol for the Day of the Dead (a celebration of ancestors). She maintains a consistency within the stamp block by using only one photographic image for each of the stamps. Each large image bleeds off two outside edges, which creates large background areas of solid color—alternating gold and green offer the viewer a colorful, bold patterning, which also serves as the coordinating element for all four stamps.

To continue on her alternating color concept, Kristina successfully integrates a bold block-serif typeface, which also alternates with the background color of the neighboring stamp—the effect is light on dark and dark on light. The combined effect evokes a Mexican flavor with its active, colorful, and festive presentation.

Figure 4-4.3

Student Statement

My idea was to show the fun aspects of Mexican-American culture through symbols of celebration. The margarita, Day of the Dead figure, piñata, and tacos are all recognizable ways in which the Mexican culture has been incorporated into American culture. I also wanted the color to appear as rich as the culture.

Postage Stamp Design: A Celebration of American Primary Education: Reading, Writing, Mathematics, and Science
Massachusetts College of Art, Instructor: Elizabeth Resnick

One of the ways a culture defines its national identity is from its use of graphic design for government communications. Most people interact with federally sponsored graphic design daily through currency, transportation signage, and nutrition and health labels, without giving it much thought. But one form of government-sponsored design that attracts attention is the postage stamp.

The basic purpose of a stamp is to function as currency—a prepaid certificate that can be redeemed for mail delivery services. As a design, it is often an image with a small amount of typography.

Stamps are avidly collected and often resemble miniature versions of contemporary posters. Aside from their obvious difference in scale, posters and stamps have much in common. Both are posted or affixed to another surface, and both tend to have an ephemeral existence, although stamp or poster collectors can recycle them. The most effective stamps and posters attract attention by communicating content in a conceptually clear, immediate, and legible manner.

Assignment Brief
Your assignment is to design a series of four postage stamps on the subject "A Celebration of American Primary Education: Reading, Writing, Mathematics, and Science." Primary education is considered to be kindergarten through sixth grade (K-6) or kindergarten through eighth grade (K-8), depending on the town or city in which you reside. High school is considered secondary education

Objectives
– To develop a design concept as a framework for four separate but equal components
– To communicate the essence of a subject without merely illustrating it
– To design with scale issues in mind

Specifications
1. Size: 1.25" × 1.5"
2. Copy: USA / 34 cents / Reading, Writing, Mathematics, Science
3. Configuration: Block of four (grouped as four in a box configuration or in a sequential row)
4. Media: Photography, illustration, collage, and digital illustration

Process

Begin researching your subject through various library and Internet sources. If possible, visit a primary-school classroom in the city or town in which you live. Perhaps you can make a visit to the primary school you attended as a child. If you have younger brothers or sisters attending primary school, ask to visit their classrooms, or interview them on what they are learning in school.

The design process begins by reviewing your collected materials and making word lists and thought maps to develop your ideas beyond the obvious that come to mind. Your first ideas may be stereotypical responses and should be avoided. Once you have identified what aspects you will focus on, begin making thumbnail sketches for each of the academic topics. You must create original imagery using shape, movement, texture, positive/negative, value, and color to reinforce the meaning of each of the academic topics. It is important conceptually to push yourself beyond expressing a literal narrative—for example, showing a known painting or sculpture to represent the subject of art.

In order to create a design series, your stamps must share a consistent visual vocabulary (in terms of form, shape, color, and typography) when imaging the different characteristics of reading, writing, mathematics, and science. Consider designing on two levels: first, the design of the individual stamp, and second, how the four stamps come together in a block or row as an integrated whole design. This is a gestalt principle, where the whole is more than the sum of its parts; each individual stamp has a meaning, but when all four stamps come together they embody a collective meaning.

Use any medium that you feel is appropriate for your concept; consider photography, illustration, collage, and so on. Use the computer to create layouts only after you have selected from your multiple thumbnail sketch ideas.

Timeline

Week One

Research American primary education and the academic subjects of reading, writing, mathematics, and science. How are these subjects presented in the American school environment? What metaphors can you use to represent a school environment for young children? Present both your research and conceptual ideas in the form of color sketches, each 6.25" × 7.5", for class critique.

Week Two

Based on your critique, choose the most successful direction and create four related designs in the form of tight color layout with scale reductions to actual postage stamp size to evaluate legibility.

Week Three

Based on the feedback you received in the last critique, create comprehensive layouts of the four stamps and mount both the full-size designs plus the reduction on a black (or gray) mount board with spacing at least 2" on the top and sides and 3" on the bottom for class presentation.

Critiques

This assignment challenged my students to create a series of four related stamps that could hold up individually and also come together as a group. At the beginning of the assignment, I emphasized the need for each student to identify a conceptual thread as a framework to construct and stitch together the individual designs into a group identity.

Figure 4-5.1

Student Statement

Through my research on early childhood education, I discovered that in early stages of learning, touching is an integral part of development. My concept was to draw each child touching and interacting with an object related to the four primary subjects.

As the years go by, each different student group brings with it different skill levels and talents. This particular group of sophomore graphic design students (they were all in the same class) was not intimidated by drawing their own illustrations. They were very successful at articulating their ideas in a most engaging manner.

Primary Education Postage Stamp, *Jaivin Anzalota,* Figure 4-5.1

Instructor's Evaluation

After completing much research on elementary education, Jaivin identified that touch was used as an important learning strategy in early childhood education, as children first explore the world through their senses: smell, touch, sight, sound, and taste. Jaivin pictures each child touching an object related to each of the topics assigned for this series. For *writing*, the child plays with an alphabet puzzle, matching the shapes of the letters with actual letters; for *math*, the child plays with the sliding beads of an abacus, an ancient counting device; for science, the child hold a leaf as he ponders the wonders of the natural world; and for *reading*, a child uses her fingers to follow the lines in a book she is reading to another child to her right.

The inspiration for this stylish use of flat color illustration came from Lance Hidy's *Mentoring a Child* stamp design, which had just been released by the Postal Service at the time of this assignment. Jaivin employs the basic design elements of value and color to suggest that children represent different ethnic backgrounds, thus celebrating cultural diversity in American society when the stamps are grouped together in a block of four.

Figure 4-5.2

Student Statement
My concept was to use a tree growing as a metaphor for children learning. I chose a beanstalk to refer to the story "Jack and the Beanstalk," which allowed me to separate the composition into four distinct panels, each panel showing one aspect of learning.

Primary Education Postage Stamp, *Chikage Imai Cote,* Figure 4-5.2

Instructor's Evaluation

Chikage's concept came in the form of a tree metaphor: Children learn and grow just as a tree grows. Her tree (actually a very large beanstalk) serves as the framework for children engaged in learning the assigned topics—for *reading*, a standing child reads from his alphabet book; for *writing*, the sitting child thoughtfully writes a letter; for *math*, a standing child is engaged in counting the hanging beans in front of her; and for *science*, a kneeling child playfully examines his hand.

Chikage exhibits great sensitivity in drawing these children. They appear quite delicate, yet they are actively engaged. In her first sketches, all of her children had Asian features. She was encouraged to be more diverse in depicting the children's ethnic backgrounds. Her choice of a serif typeface exquisitely matches the quality of the illustration with its muted, pastel color palette. She skillfully creates a typographic unit from the three information elements and finds a consistent placement for each unit in the outside corner of each stamp. The resulting symmetrical effect is one of balance, harmony, and great beauty.

Primary Education Postage Stamp, *Alisa Kocharyan,* Figure 4-5.3

Instructor's Evaluation

Alisa presents us with a clever concept that is both humorous and charming: She plays with the idea of the bee, taken from a *spelling bee*, a learning strategy found in elementary education. First the swarm of bees writes the ABCs with their buzzing movements; they fly by a book to read the word bee on the way to an encounter with math as they count themselves ($1 + 2 = 3$ bees), then enjoy the rewards of science by pollinating a flower. Although each of the individual stamps can stand on its own merits, the effect is far more engaging when the stamps are placed in a linear sequence.

Figure 4-5.3

Student Statement
The concept of a spelling bee came to me while I was browsing through children's books at a bookstore. I thought, "What could be more fun and energetic than using colorful bees flying and spelling throughout the stamps?" This project was both challenging and fun.

The palette of primary colors support this children's book lesson with rich blue, red, green, yellow, and black. One challenge Alisa faced was to design and group the informational typography to complement the narrative. Her choice of Meta, an informal sans-serif typeface, is appropriate. But she reduces it to fit within the grassy area, and the result makes it difficult to read when it is reduced to the postage stamp scale. Had she enlarged the height of the grass, the point size of typographic information could have been enlarged as well. This is easy to correct on the original illustrations.

Primary Education Postage Stamp, *Aleksandra Zarkhi,* Figure 4-5.4

Instructor's Evaluation

Aleksandra creates a very playful construct when she envisions her stamp objects taking human or animal characteristics. For *reading,* her book walks down the road as the word curious tumbles off its pages. For *writing,* her very tall pencil bends over to write the s in curious; for *math,* the protractor/ruler takes on the persona of a large bug and the numbers get to ride on its back; and for *science,* the dancing thermometer basks in the heat of the sun. Although each stamp is a self-contained design, when the four are placed side by side, the stamp group becomes more than the sum of it parts—it becomes a visual narrative.

Student Statement
My concept was that primary education is a way to the future, life, and knowledge. To create the sequence, I thought of a road and what things a child might find while studying the four primary subjects.

Figure 4-5.4

Stamp Design

Fachhochschule Schwäbisch Gmünd, Germany, Instructor: Michael Burke

Assignment Brief

Stamp design has an iconographic problem similar to that of a book jacket, but its advantage as an exercise is its reduced format, which enables students to generate alternative models quickly, thus intensifying the learning process.

Process

Week One

Choose from a list of subjects that relate to German cultural, scientific, or political themes or individuals in history. After selection, work alone or in pairs to research and develop three alternative conceptual models in text form. After this presentation, one of the models will be selected for the next design phase.

Week Two

As in the first phase, develop three conceptual models and select one to refine. Here great emphasis is made of thumbnail sketch techniques, storyboard, and so on. The choice of typeface and color is yours to make, as they are largely dependent on the content and relevance to the subject.

Week Three

After the selection, develop one of the models on the computer for the final presentation, which should also include full documentation of the project.

Figure 4-6.1

Critiques

European Transportation Stamps, *Sigrid Lorenz and Vera Zinnecker,* Figure 4-6.1

Student Statement

As a motif, we chose the four main vehicles used in Europe. The nice thing about this theme was creating movement on paper. We utilized horizontal lines as design elements, showing movement through blurriness.

Figure 4-6.2

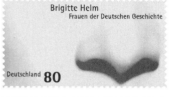

Women of German History Stamps, *Thomas Müller and Stephanie Niewienz,* Figure 4-6.2

Student Statement

The idea was to characterize three totally different personalities who lived in three decisive epochs of film history. Silent film is represented by Brigitte Helm, a very emancipated woman. Marlene Dietrich was the star during the Second World War. In the years following the war, Romy Schneider was seen as a symbol of the modern and self-confident woman.

Our idea was to design one face out of the three women. Each stamp works well on its own as well as part of the series. When the stamps are put together, a new face appears comprised of the eyes of Marlene Dietrich, the nose of Brigitte Helm and the mouth of Romy Schneider. It was important to us to present the three women as a union but, at the same time, to define their personality by means of color and the parts of the picture they make up.

HFG ULM (College of Art and Design) Stamp, *Christian Reissmüller and Klara Plaskov,* Figure 4-6.3

Figure 4-6.3

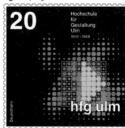

Student Statement

Sketch: As the main topic for the motif of the stamp series, the four main areas of the studies at Hochschule für Gestaltung (College of Art and Design) were used: basic studies, product design, architecture, and visual design/communication. We mostly stylized known images such as the Hochschule für Gestaltung (HFG) chair or the Otl Aichers pictograms.

Final version: The stamp series consists of the typical HFG basic design elements (dot, line, shape). Because there are an infinite number of design possibilities to make the stamps recognizable as a series, we chose the design elements arrow and screen. The screen doesn't change, but the arrow changes to increase the optical appearance. The varying shades of gray in the background emphasize the characteristic HFG style.

Figure 4-6.4

Modern Architecture Stamp, *Erika Usselmann and Jennifer Wiefel*, Figure 4-6.4

Student Statement
The challenging part of this project was the combination of the big dimension of the buildings and the very limited, small format of the stamp. The reduced, illustrative visuals of the chosen architectural objects are intended to mirror the lightness and transparency of our high tech time. The color was consciously chosen from each building.

Sculpture Poster
Massachusetts College of Art, Instructor: Tom Briggs

Assignment Brief
The objective of this exercise is to design a poster that depicts a large-scale public sculpture by a major twentieth-century artist that can be seen in the Boston area, which provides the viewer with an introduction to the artist and to some biographical background about his or her work. The project requires that you work with a partner in the production of text and image content, including both library research and original photography. A simple, disposable 35 mm camera will be provided, together with information about a variety of sculptural examples, which can be chosen as subjects for the project.

Objectives
– To communicate a complex hierarchy of information, both text and image, on a single large surface
– To utilize scanning and image editing software (i.e., Photoshop) as an aspect of design methodology

Specifications
1. Size: 16" × 30" (vertical).
2. Media: Black-and-white media appropriate for various phases of design development, as described below (marker or colored pencil on layout paper for roughs; black-and-white laser Postscript prints composed by tiling three 11" × 17" sheets, mounted on bristol board and/or mount board for comps).

Process
Week One
Visit the site of the sculpture that you and your partner chose as the subject for your poster and make simple, descriptive photos of it using the 35 mm disposable camera provided. You can have this film processed at any standard processing service. Although scanning the negative film will probably be necessary for clarity in the larger image sizes you are likely to want in your final design, positive photo prints will be useful as a reference during the design process.

Using library resources (art history books, monographs about the artist, etc.), develop approximately 1,500 characters of copy, including a one-paragraph biography of the artist and a brief description (optionally including images) of the work for which he or she is best known. Type the text and, including optional images, provide a copy for discussion in class next week. The main title of the poster will be the name of the artist and/or the featured artwork.

Sketch thumbnails of poster design concepts, experimenting with the expression of the main subject in relation to the secondary and text information. Use grids to subdivide the space and organize the information hierarchy. Develop two half-size sketches on layout paper for class discussion.

Week Two

Develop one full-size rough comprehensive mockup of your poster design incorporating ideas discussed in the critique. Scan all images (in grayscale) for use in the poster and adjust and/or retouch details using Photoshop editing. Produce a Quark file, at full size, incorporating all content, and proof it in horizontal, tiled tabloid format on the laser printer.

Week Three

Further refine the design relationships of the poster and produce a finished, comprehensive mock-up. Proof it on the laser printer and mount it for class discussion.

Critiques

Sculpture Poster, *Kate Wheeler*, Figure 4-7.1

Instructor's Evaluation

There are aspects of this design project that received less attention in our critical discussions than the more straightforward formal and technical issues challenging many of the sophomore students in this course. Among the design issues less extensively served were those regarding communication of the physical description and of the aesthetic nature of the sculptural subject.

The example shown is, I believe, quite successful in the visual strategies through which it communicates both the physical and aesthetic representations of the subject. The designer's use of close-up photography and skillful framing (despite limitations imposed by the required use of a disposable 35 mm camera) provides a vivid depiction of the surface texture of the work as well as an indication of the complex geometry and beauty of its shape. The addition of a small photo in the lower left quadrant also provides a description of the sculpture's complete form, although neither that nor the enlarged image occupying the center portion of the poster very successfully conveys information about its position relative to the ground plane or about its size in relation to a human figure. The designer, seemingly aware of this, has included the size of the sculpture at the beginning of her self-authored, descriptive text.

Figure 4-7.1

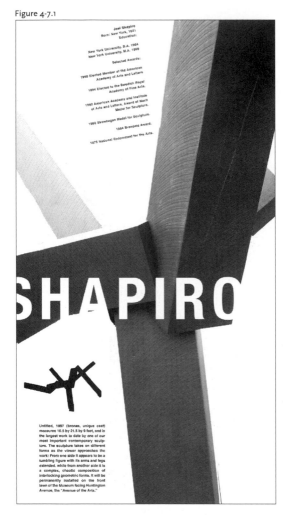

Joel Shapiro
Born: New York, 1941
Education:

New York University, B.A. 1964
New York University, M.A. 1969

Selected Awards:

1998 Elected Member of the American
Academy of Arts and Letters

1994 Elected to the Swedish Royal
Academy of Fine Arts.

1990 American Academy and Institute
of Arts and Letters. Award of Merit
Medal for Sculpture.

1986 Skowhegan Medal for Sculpture.

1984 Brandeis Award.

1975 National Endowment for the Arts.

Untitled, 1997 (bronze, unique cast)
measures 10.5 by 21.5 by 9 feet, and is
the largest work to date by one of our
most important contemporary sculp-
tors. The sculpture takes on different
forms as the viewer approaches the
work: From one side it appears to be a
tumbling figure with its arms and legs
extended, while from another side it is
a complex, chaotic composition of
interlocking geometric forms. It will be
permanently installed on the front
lawn of the Museum facing Huntington
Avenue, the "Avenue of the Arts."

Student Statement
*Seeing Shapiro's sculpture up close, it is
a massive, looming form with pieces
jutting out at playful angles. I wanted to
capture the experience of standing near
it and being consumed by one of these
angles. However, I also thought it
important to show somewhere what the
full sculpture looked like—thus the small
silhouette above the descriptive text. I
wanted a constructivist look to match
the simple, jutting forms, and it was also
important to me that the piece look
intentionally black and white instead of
seeming limited by the assignment. I
hope that the final composition captures
the size, movement, and energy of
Shapiro's work.*

Another design strategy that contributes to the success of this example is the compositional interplay of the typography and the imagery. The designer has clearly stated the required text information in three subject categories and, by using the résumé form for the artist's biography, the prose form in the sculpture's description, and only the artist's surname, has provided a basis in content for a triad of typographic form variations. The typography of the name/title and the biography are both more heavily (and successfully) inflected to the image, whereas the body of text in the lower left seems a little heavy and static—perhaps it would have benefited from more leading, with smaller type, and/or from the angling of one of its justified edges.

Gardening Poster

Carnegie Mellon University, Instructor: Karen Berntsen

Assignment Brief

Students became familiar with the subject matter though an earlier project to design a table of contents for a book about gardening. The goal behind designing the table of contents is for the students to organize their books in a unique way that reflects their point of view about the subject. Their solutions covered a broad range of thinking about gardening, from regional to seasonal gardening, gardening for children, gardening as a spiritual process, humorous gardening, or gardening as physical exercise, to name a few.

The gardening poster is intended to promote the book I've just described. Since the concepts were already in the students' minds, the real challenge with this project is for the students to integrate type and image in order to communicate their unique point of view about gardening. Students write their own titles, plus any additional copy to appear on the poster. They either select or generate their own images.

Figure 4-8.1

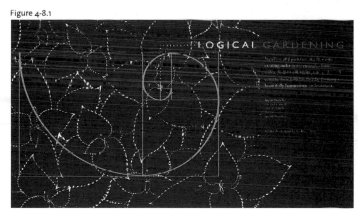

Student Statement
When creating this poster, my intent was to target those who are unfamiliar with gardening and who generally approach things in an organized, methodical manner. The image simultaneously portrays the natural world and also references the mathematics and systems within it. I reference the golden section to further emphasize that, deeper than we imagine, a profound order exists within nature.

Critiques

Gardening Poster, *Mickey Mayo,* Figure 4-8.1

Instructor's Evaluation

Mickey was initially a bit daunted by the prospect of gardening and admitted that he had no heartfelt attraction to the subject matter. To overcome his discomfort, I encouraged him to embrace his genuine responses, as they constituted his unique point of view. Relieved, Mickey gave up trying to connect to gardening emotionally and instead took an intellectual approach. He began to look for logic and order in nature, and found exactly what he was looking for in the spiral growth pattern of the leaves in the photo he found.

Mickey then found a mathematical diagram, also demonstrating the growth of a spiral, and began to experiment with integrating the two images. By overlapping the two images he makes them appear interlocked, thus supporting the somewhat paradoxical notion that something as organic and free-form as plant life is, in fact, ordered and logical.

Figure 4-8.2

Student Statement

This poster is a bookstore advertisement for a gardening book whose concept is a comprehensive collection of information about plants and gardening practices. I set out to convey the dignity owed to such an impressive collection of knowledge. The illustrations of the tools and the plants are meant to create this sense of dignity through their line quality. The arrangement of the illustrations in a line that bleeds off either side suggests that only a small portion of the collection is represented.

The type treatment, reserved and low-contrast, exists in deference to the two enmeshed images. The white dotted perpendicular rules that lead us from the center of the spiral to the word logical are Mickey's human effort to mimic the edges of the leaves themselves. The single leaf in the lower right-hand corner breaks out of the photo and onto the black field, helping us see the plant in three dimensions. Almost in spite of himself, Mickey's final poster strikes an emotional chord because of the bridge he makes between mathematical theory and natural beauty.

Gardening Poster, *Jordan Offut,* Figure 4-8.2

Instructor's Evaluation

Jordan approached gardening with great respect and guarded emotions. He created a practical and comprehensive guide for gardeners. At a glance the vertical orientation, with central axis and symmetrical composition, makes a formal presentation. It is restrained, and some students initially criticized it as static and "traditional."

Jordan's poster stands up to close scrutiny. In fact, it invites us to take a very close look. The handcrafted illustrations are highly detailed, and the typography is sensitive and intimate. By adding extra letter spacing, Jordan activates the white space around the type and slows us down as we read the words. The silhouetted illustrations also bring liveliness to the white page. The black illustrations draw us in close, allowing us to discover an enlarged pale gray drawing that almost covers the entire height of the page. This scale change is a nice surprise, as is our perceptual shift from ambiguity to clarity as we recognize the contour of the gray drawing as a flower (a pansy) with its root system.

This scale change plus the brightly colored type and the illustrations bleeding off the edges are all ways that Jordan gently surprises us. The white space on this poster is luxurious and confident, creating a perfect environment for the delicate components that Jordan so sensitively places in our view.

Gardening Poster, *Andrea Stephany,* Figure 4-8.3

Instructor's Evaluation

Andrea was very relaxed about the idea of gardening. Having just taken photography, she used her poster project to experiment with her new medium. Andrea's decision to print the photograph as a negative produced some strong responses from other students. While the freshness of her original white background was also perceived as sterile, some students responded to the negative image as dark and menacing. Emotions aside, I appreciate the ambiguity that emerged when Andrea reversed the image to the negative. This ambiguity motivates me to read the words, looking for an explanation, which is precisely the integration between type and image that I had set as a goal for the project.

Figure 4-8.3

Setting the title, "Personalized Gardening," in all lowercase is consistent with Andrea's casual approach. Another visual/verbal connection are the quotes, bringing personal voices to the page. These quotes are doing what the title is saying. The quotes are set in typographic clusters, forming organic shapes that are nestled loosely around the edges of the natural objects in the photograph. The color changes between letters in the typography gives the effect of dappled light, which also helps integrate the type with the fluctuations of light and shadow that exist within the photo.

Student Statement

The concept behind my gardening poster is that individuals choose to garden for different reasons. The poster illustrates this idea visually by pairing type with the related item within the image. I photographed the items together, coated in baby powder, to make the objects a similar tone. The resulting photograph was stark white, which felt too clinical. When I reversed the image, the poster began to evoke the feeling of gardening for one's self.

The Kitchen of Meaning Exhibition Poster

North Carolina State University, Instructor: Kermit Bailey

Assignment Brief

Research and define each word below. Bring three examples of the communication concept (word) used in print to the next class.

Through a random selection process each student will be assigned one word. Based on that word, design a poster that thematically translates (interprets, makes a connection of meaning with) the word.

bricolage	isomorphic	mnemonics	parataxis	vernacular
denotation	kitsch	morphology	pastiche	zeitgeist
dialectical	lexicon	nascent	polysemy	
dissonance	mélange	nonlinearity	simulacrum	
hyperbole	metonymy	panache	tautology	

Objectives
– To develop critical thinking skills as a means of analysis, talking about, and making design
– To understand the relationship of audience, design choices, and communication performance goals
– To understand meaning in context (cultural, social, technical, temporal, etc.)
– To expand design vocabulary
– To design in a large-scale format, considering how a poster functions in the public domain

Specifications
Communication components to include:
1. Title of the series: "The Kitchen of Meaning"
2. Place, time, date of the exhibition
3. Names of the twenty-three exhibitors (students)
4. Other text information of relevancy and meaning (added value that intensifies the word or context of the image). The added text or information of relevancy may be words, text phrases, ideas, teasers, and so on. For example: repositioning ideas from Roland Barthes's essays "Semantics of the Object" and "The Kitchen of Meaning" or other sources.

Process
Thematic and conceptual criteria:
– Emphasize the meaning of the concept (word). The title of the exhibition ("The Kitchen of Meaning") is secondary in the hierarchy but still is the thematic umbrella for all the word-image expressions.

— Give equal attention to type and image as a visual reading experience.

— Use words effectively to intensify the image and message in addition to being a vital part of the compositional whole. Consider the type as having photogenic or image qualities (woven into the surface, having levels of spatial depth, a narrative, or perceptual immediateness). Consider the image message as having a typographic flavor (i.e., variation in formal tone, rhythm, and the ability to facilitate dialogue).

Figure 4-9.1

Student Statement

To illustrate the idea of dialectics I chose to focus on the most simple and powerful dialectics: those of childhood (mine). The design process allowed me to understand myself by seeing and understanding through the innocence of objects. I created all the photography, painting, and illustrations in the poster.

Critiques

The Kitchen of Meaning "Dialectical" Poster, *Emmet Byrne,* Figure 4-9.1

Instructor's Evaluation

In a broad discourse sense, the term *dialectical* may be any idea or event (thesis) that generates its opposite (antithesis), leading to a resolution of opposites (synthesis). For the purpose of the poster study, Emmet has effectively visualized this principle of logic as both a visual and verbal phenomenon in communication, and a personal narrative based on his childhood. His design positions elements of opposition or contrasts from his childhood, such as ketchup/mustard, teepee/igloo, Velcro/laces, cowboy/Indians, and so on.

The poster is particularly effective in articulating the intended hierarchy of primary conceptual idea (dialectical) first, and various required pragmatic components (title of exhibition, student participants, etc.) subordinate. He uses color effectively and has good sensitivity to scale in his typographic choices. The integrity of the information is not compromised at any level. Emmet's formal decisions embody the spirit of play, perhaps consistent with the theme of childhood narrative. His surface treatment of the compositional area is both full and open, creating a well-balanced, interesting arrangement.

Emmet's poster solution invites multiple layers of understanding, perhaps reflective of the texts on meaning (Roland Barthes) being read in the class at the time. He effectively uses wordplay (and image play) as visual and verbal codes are deciphered and others discovered. The poster reads at multiple viewing distances, reinforcing further ideas of how the dialectical might function as a communication principle. In improving the work, I might suggest being more meticulous in giving credit of authorship for any quotes used, however embedded or fragmented in an otherwise beautiful, highly conceptual design.

The Kitchen of Meaning "Hyperbole" Poster, *Charlie Earp,* Figure 4-9.2

Instructor's Evaluation

To hyperbolize a subject is to exaggerate it. Historically, hyperbole has been an effective strategy in graphic design communication. This strategy may lend itself to the exaggeration of form and/or concept in effective communication. In translating the problem of hyperbole, Charlie exaggerates the form within the word hyperbole. His design creates an interesting contrast and focal point of entry, immediately teasing a viewer toward its possible meaning.

At the formal level, the poster speaks with a degree of clarity and simplicity, almost literally inviting and challenging us to see less as more. The typographic arrangement is simple but mostly effective. The distribution of color in the arrangement, using hits of yellow as accentuating moments, effectively signifies content or text. The defamiliarized state (recolored, cropped, filtered, etc.) of appropriated imagery offers a design setting of open meaning, thus directing the viewer toward the certainty of the verbal message as the primary site for excavating meaning.

Figure 4-9.2

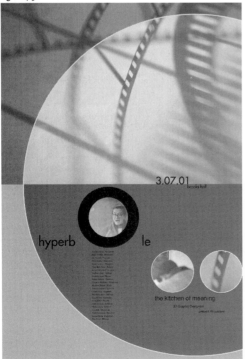

Charlie's poster is a successful design for all the aforementioned acts of restraint and tease. In improving the work, I might suggest refining the typographic codes, focusing on font and style (bold, italic, etc.) contrast. The addition of other pragmatic components via text would also serve to reinforce its success as communication. Overall the piece is striking and immediate in its ability to be read, seen, and understood.

Student Statement
My solution refers to the student/teacher relationship. The word that I was assigned, hyperbole, played well with this idea. I made the o in hyperbole extraordinarily large. The idea of the filmstrip is a personal reference to how I was taught many subjects in elementary school.

The Kitchen of Meaning "Kitsch" Poster, *J. Matthew Pelland,* Figure 4-9.3

Instructor's Evaluation

The term *kitsch* has been historically applied to cultural objects (design or visual arts), music, or writing. It may be best understood as a value judgment applied to these categories of expression, usually signifying work of a cheap, garish, sentimental nature. Kitsch embodies production values (mass-produced versus custom) and social values (high art versus low art). Its social meaning often considers the design object over time (new, retro, old, antique). Kitsch elements are usually calculated to have popular appeal. Matthew's poster visualizes perfectly this last aspect of kitsch through the use of a TV dinner as the primary visual signifier of kitsch.

The use of the verbal pun kitsch/kitchen is fortuitous, since each student was randomly assigned a word and not every student would find this possibility. Matthew seizes this in an effective, integrated way with the typographic reference to the exhibition title. As a form, the poster successfully negotiates the desire for a well-designed arrangement in contemporary graphic design terms and an intended referral to a past advertising or commercial aesthetic (through the use of process colors, heavy headlines, and the vernacular symbols of commerce).

At the final presentation poster scale of 18" × 24", the pragmatic information on the poster (dates, times, place, etc.) would be readable by its intended audience. In general it works and honors the spirit of the no-frills aesthetic approach. Its lack of prominence on the page does leave room for some reconsideration of arrangement. How else might the typographic problem have been solved? The martini glass illustration is an interesting, intended contradiction to the TV dinner, situating conceptual tension and contrast. However, it too leaves room for other formal possibilities (in scale, position, maybe even necessity). In general, my review of this work is a highly favorable one. The work is honest in that it finds a solution to the problem from within the question of what is kitsch.

Figure 4-9.3

Student Statement

My solution was to incorporate my word, kitsch, into the title of the show, thus creating a play on words. The image of the TV dinner and martini together serve to reinforce the definition of kitsch. The bright colors, sharp diagonals, and dashed lines work to create the feel of a retro product advertisement.

GRID AND VISUAL HIERARCHY

A work of communication design carries its meaning through the arrangement and ordering of the design elements, as discussed in section 1 of this book. In order to achieve and communicate its meaning, a design needs visual unity, and a grid is a useful tool for this purpose. A *grid* provides a compositional framework through its network of horizontal and vertical intersecting lines that subdivide the page into field and interval, therefore creating a guide to establish proportional relationships between the design elements. The concept of subdividing space is commonplace in our culture: our houses and apartments are divided into rooms, our drawers are designed with divided compartments to separate our things, the post office sorts mail into divided rows of boxes. Subdividing space is a traditional organizing principle.

"The primary purpose of the grid is to create order out of chaos."
– Andre Jute

The structure of a grid should emerge from the analysis of the visual material that has been gathered or generated to use in the design. The grid will allow considerable flexibility in arranging many disparate elements within any given two-dimensional environment. The grid can sit behind the design and be invisible in the finished design, or it can be visible to use as a design element. The grid is an absolute necessity when there are multiple pages, such as publications where each page or spread requires a different layout due to its content. If the grid is well conceived, it provides a fast and easy way to create multiple layouts that maintain a constant visual unity.

Another organizing principle that supports unity in a design is visual hierarchy, as mentioned in section 4. The term *visual hierarchy* refers to the arrangement of visual elements according to their order of importance within the message or information being delivered. It is especially needed when handling complex information containing a mix of text and images to establish a hierarchy of the information and ensure the readability of the message. Hierarchy in type can be suggested by emphasizing its size, weight, or color. Viewers will always be attracted to the most emphasized type first. When this structure is provided, even the most passive viewer can gain some knowledge by quickly glancing over the text.

The assignments in this section explore the organizing principles of grids, visual hierarchy, and sequence within multiple-page documents and poster series.

Typographic History Spread
Massachusetts College of Art, Instructor: Elizabeth Resnick

Assignment Brief

Designing spreads (two facing pages) for a magazine article or any multipage publication requires you to work with both the written content (information) and images (supporting pictorial information). With so many different elements to coordinate, you will need to employ the two design principles of the grid and visual hierarchy to help organize and group the visual elements into a cohesive and recognizable pattern that any reader can understand.

Your assignment is to choose a topic from the list below, research it through various sources, write a short descriptive text of 300–600 words, select appropriate imagery, and assemble all the elements into a visually arresting page layout *that is influenced by the period itself* for a tabloid-sized international typographic design journal.

Subjects (choose one of the four):

Movable typography in Europe. With the availability of paper, relief printing from woodblocks, and a growing demand for books, the mechanization of book production by such means as movable type was sought by printers in Germany, the Netherlands, France, and Italy. In 1454, Johann Gutenberg (1387–1468), a goldsmith, perfected a system of casting individual metal letters from a mold. These predesigned and reusable letters allowed for greater freedom in printing typographic books.

William Morris and the Kelmscott Press. The Arts and Crafts movement was inspired by the writings of English philosopher and critic John Ruskin in the late 1800s. William Morris (1834–1896) translated Ruskin's utopian ideals into practice. Morris called for a fitness of purpose—being true to the nature of materials and methods of production of industrialized goods, emphasizing the role of hand workmanship, as in his own book design for the Kelmscott Press.

Futurism and the visual word. Italian poet Filippo Marinetti (1876–1944) published his "Manifesto of Futurism" in the Paris newspaper *Le Figaro* in 1909, launching the modern art movement Futurism. Marinetti and his followers produced an explosive and emotionally charged poetry that defied correct syntax and grammar. Having freed themselves from typographic tradition, the Futurists visually animated their work with dynamic, nonlinear compositions created by collaging words and letters in place for reproduction from photoengraved printing plates.

The International Typographic Style. A few years after World War II, a design style emerged from Switzerland and Germany that has been referred to as the International Typographic Style. The style incorporates object photography, sans-serif typography, no ornamentation, and strict adherence to a modular grid system. This style has

Figure 1-7.1: **Emma Ekblad**

Figure 1-7.2: **Susie Halim**

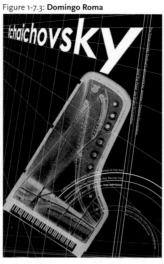

Figure 1-7.3: **Domingo Roma**

Figure 1-7.4: **Samuel Yap**

Figure 2-6.1: **Lindsay Crissman**

Figure 2-6.2: **Charles DiSantis**

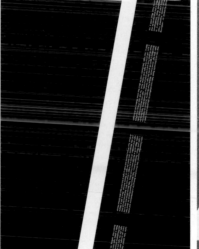

Figure 2-6.3: **Chris Holub**

Figure 2-6.4: **David Reed Monroe**

Figure 1-8.1: **Meg Dreyer**

Figure 2-7.1: **Michael Koid**

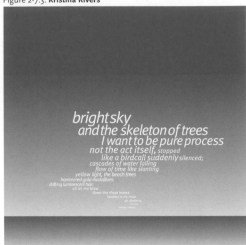

Figure 2-7.3: **Kristina Rivers**

Figure 2-7.2: **Sam Montague**

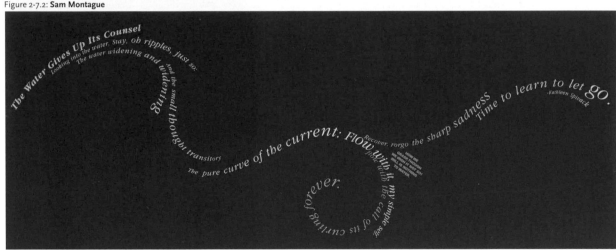

Figure 3-2.2: **Hyun Kim**

Figure 3-2.3B: **Kynchang Shin**

Figure 3-5.3: **Casey Krimmel**

Figure 3-5.4: **David Kroll**

Figure 3-5.5: **Ellen Sitkln**

Figure 4-2.1: **Scarlett Bertrand**

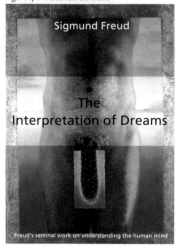

Figure 4-2.4: **Miho Nishimaniwa**

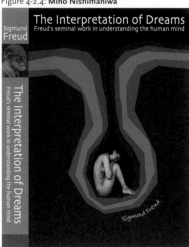

Figure 4-2.5: **Kristina Rivers**

Figure 4-1.1: **Jaivin Anzalota**

Figure 4-1.2: **Chikage Imai Cote**

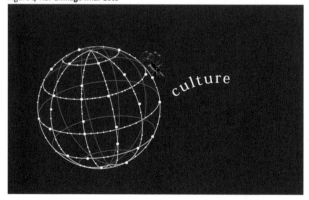

Figure 4-1.3: **John Dennis**

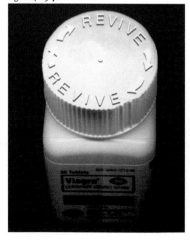

Figure 4-1.4: **Timothy J. Welch**

Figure 4-3.1: **Jaivin Anzalota**

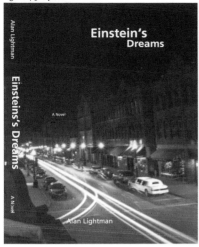

Figure 4-3.2: **Chikage Imai Cote**

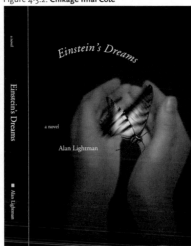

Figure 4-3.3: **Li Xiao**

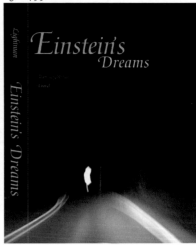

Figure 4-4.1: **Scarlett Bertrand**

Figure 4-4.2: **Michiyo Kato**

Figure 4-4.3: **Kristina Rivers**

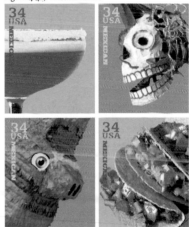

Figure 4-5.1: **Jaivin Anzalota**

Figure 4-5.2: **Chikage Imai Cote**

Figure 4-5.4. **Aleksandra Zarkhi**

Figure 4-6.1: Sigrid Lorenz and Vera Zinnecker

Figure 4-6.2: Thomas Müller and Stephanie Niewienz

Figure 4-6.3: Christian Reissmüller and Klara Plaskov

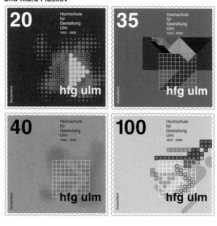

Figure 4-6.4: Erika Usselmann and Jennifer Wiefel

Figure 4-9.1: Emmet Byrne

Figure 4-9.2: Charlie Earp

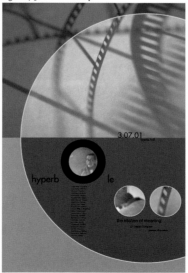

Figure 4-9.3: J. Matthew Pelland

Figure 5-3.3: **Terri Watkins**

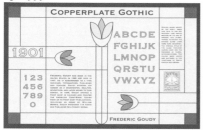

Figure 5-4.1: **Andrew Dunmire**

Figure 6-1.2: **Christina Beck**

Figure 6-1.5: **Michelle Georgilas**

Figure 6-2.2: **Nelson Couto**

Figure 5-5.1: **Jennifer Lopardo**

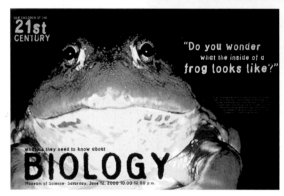

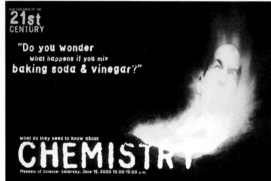

Figure 6-6.2: **Garrett Jones**

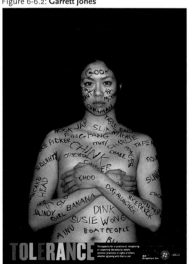

Figure 6-6.3: **David Reed Monroe**

Figure 6-6.5: **Colleen Tomlinson**

remained a major force for many decades because it is suitable to the requirements of international business. Early examples of this style can be seen in issues of the Swiss magazine *Graphis* from the 1950s to the 1970s.*

Objectives
– To research a specific historical period and design from its influence
– To construct an appropriate modular grid system given the content gathered
– To explore visual hierarchy through arranging different-sized elements in a composition

Specifications
1. 17" × 11" (facing pages 17" × 22"), one or two sequential spreads.
2. Four-color process (illustrations can be scanned and output as color laser prints or done as color photocopies).
3. Copy that must appear in the spread:

   Title of article and subtitle if necessary
   by (your name)
   Article (300–600 words)
   One or two callouts (sometimes known as *pull quotes*)
   Captions for photos/illustrations

Process
Begin your design process by researching all four typographic time periods. Select the one that you are most interested in pursuing. Gather as much information from books, periodicals, and the Internet on your subject as you can in the given time frame.

Read the materials, select what is most important, and weave your narrative together in 600–1,000 words. Type your copy into Microsoft Word. Select and scan your images (do not download Web images; they are too low-res for use in this project).

Once you have all the elements, think about how you wish to present them. At this point establish a grid that can accommodate all the elements and allow for flexibility in creating alternative layouts. Do as many thumbnail sketch ideas as you need until you find the one that you wish to draw at full size.

* Note: *"A History of Graphic Design,"* Third Edition by Phillip B. Meggs was used as a source for the above descriptions.

Timeline

Week One

From your thumbnail sketch ideas, draw one at full size. Bring for class critique along with your research.

Week Two

Based on the feedback that you received, make revisions as discussed in critique and present the finished spread for the next class meeting.

Figure 5-1.1

Student Statement

I wanted to utilize the design language of the International Style to express the context of Adrian Frutiger's development of the Univers typeface. The content provided some obvious design choices, including type selection, the strong linear division of space, and red as the accent color. While my composition borders on becoming a Swiss style cliché, it was a good visual exercise in expressing the design philosophy that influenced Frutiger's work.

Critiques

International Style, *Sam Montague,* Figure 5-1.1

Instructor's Evaluation

Working within the confines of a Swiss-inspired grid structure is far more difficult than it may appear. The asymmetrical nature of this style challenges the designer to create a sense of balance, harmony, and stability using only contrast and hierarchy as tools. Sam takes up this challenge when he focuses on the type design work of Swiss-born Adrian Frutiger. On the first spread, the large portrait of Adrian Frutiger at work serves as an entry point and commands our attention before our gaze moves left and right to the smaller typographic elements on either side of the picture. The three text columns appear to support the large photograph as if they are steel beams holding up the floor of a building. The second spread is a more symmetrical composition, and as such it has less movement or variation.

Although Sam is successful in conveying the spirit of the style, in the second spread he needs to create more visual interest by staggering the length of his text columns to create a visual rhythm and to free up much-needed negative space to rest the eyes.

Figure 5-1.2

Student Statement

The concept for this project became very clear to me after discovering that Futurism was such a chaotic and energetic artistic movement. I challenged myself to build a spread in such a way that both the energy of the movement and the hierarchy of information were easily accessible to the reader. Although the project budgeted for four-color process, I chose to use only black and one spot color, as this mirrored what I saw of Marinetti's own work.

Futurism, *Bryant Ross*, Figure 5-1.2

Instructor's Evaluation

Bryant has challenged himself to capture the zeitgeist of the Futurist era by creating a spread inspired by their unique typographic spirit. He is able to maintain a visual hierarchy within an energetic layout that enables the reader to access the information. I think that he does an admirable job at this. The focal point is the large word Futurism dominating the center of the spread with its bold slab-serifed F. The rest of the word dances across the page and takes our gaze with it to the edge. Luckily, this is balanced by the grouping of three typographic poems on the bottom left of the composition, along with a large pull quote from the manifesto itself.

The spot color red is used to distinguish certain kinds of information. It is used for the captions, subhead, and exclamation point. This adds a bit of spice and just enough color, but does not compete with the overall power of the composition. Bryant also playfully shapes his text box, so it too becomes an element that contains shape, movement, and texture.

Figure 5-1.3

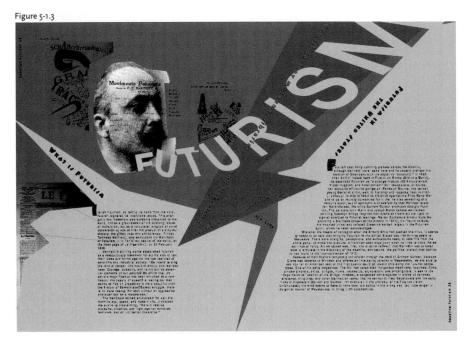

Student Statement

My concept was to express the spirit of Futurism, the style that caused a revolution in the history of typography. I was inspired by this assignment and have since read many articles about Futurism and its founder, Marinetti. The layout was directly influenced by the expressive visual language common to what I saw in Futurist work.

Futurism, *Aleksandra Zarkhi,* Figure 5-1.3

Instructor's Evaluation

Aleksandra's concept is to express the spirit of Futurism. She does so through active, sharp, and colliding design elements and bright, rich hues of red, blue, and yellow. She also shapes her text boxes in recognition that they are elements as well.

Her focal point is a large blue lightning bolt that zooms down from the right-hand corner of the composition and brings the word Futurism sweeping down with it. The word curves and directly connects with a portrait of Marinetti, the movement's chief architect. Surrounding Marinetti's portrait are two "word in freedom" poems, there to illustrate the typographic essence of the movement's political ideas. The viewer is left with a sense of positive and enthusiastic energy and a willingness to read on.

Two-Sided Typeface Poster

Simmons College, Instructor: Judith Aronson

Assignment Brief

Using your assigned typeface, write a short essay, then design a two-sided poster (one side conceptual, one side informational) to inform people about the nature, history, or qualities of your typeface.*

There are three parts to this project:

1. Essay Text (approximately 4,000 characters)

– A short biography of the type designer
– An essay about the history, technical details, and characteristics of the typeface, and any anecdotes that are worth mentioning

Include two or three headings within the text, as appropriate. By now you should have carried out your research, so you should need only to write it up. You must have three or more sources, and not all should be from the Internet. Use books and magazines from outside libraries as well as those on our reserve shelves and any other printed matter you can find. Attribute all of your sources, either within your essay or at the end. If you need to find more information, look at old issues of U&lc (Upper & lowercase), a magazine full of type information. If you have chosen a very new typeface (developed in the last ten years or so) with almost no written information, you may need to phone the designer's office and work your way through the system until you find an informed person or, better yet, the designer. If you cannot put together 4,000 characters, you may be allowed to use dummy copy.

2. Conceptual Side

Illustrate the specific or some specific characteristics or qualities of the typeface. Here you will be showing how your typeface is unique or differs from other typefaces either historically, structurally, or in overall tone. In other words, what particular characteristics or qualities quickly identify your typeface? What is the essence of the typeface? Include the name of the typeface (title) somewhere on this side of the poster; you may include an alphabet or not, as you see fit. Instead of describing in words and illustrations the important features of your typeface, you will demonstrate its individuality with your concept. What you present and how you do it is entirely up to you; all elements on this side should contribute to your idea (again your concept). You can use images, type, or both.

---

* A selected list of approximately thirty typefaces (some classical, some existing only in digital format, some nonalphabetic) was presented to the class seven weeks prior to the assignment's official start date. Each student initially chose two faces, which were narrowed down to one during the following two weeks. Students researched the selected face over the remaining five weeks, so that when time came to begin the assignment most information had been collected. Many, however, found it necessary to carry out further research after they began creating their poster.

Specifications

1. 15.5" × 20", vertical or horizontal (can be tiled or printed as two single pages and mounted together).
2. Title—name of typeface.
3. Other type and/or images representing your concept.
4. Four-color process or PMS colors (can also have specific paper color, but must match informational side).

3. Informational Side (Using a Grid)

With the text describing the history, development, and/or important stylistic features of your typeface, plus a few images (photographs, illustrations, drawings, etc.), develop a simple hierarchical structure to convey the information while remaining sympathetic to your overall poster concept. In addition, incorporate the designer's bio and a photograph or illustration of him or her as one of your images (preferably a real one; if unavailable, use a dummy one, but see the instructor first).

Specifications

1. 15.5" × 20", vertical or horizontal (can be tiled or printed as two pages and mounted together).
2. Title—name of typeface.
3. Whole alphabet and most characters (punctuation and numbers).
4. Designer bio and image or illustration.
5. Typeface essay, including at least two headings.
6. Two or three images or graphics.
7. No dingbats or extra elements unless they are part of the typeface.
8. Bleeds are allowed (place the images ⅛" beyond the poster edge).
9. One or two colors (you can print on colored paper if you wish, but then use the same for both sides of poster).
10. Typefaces: The one you have researched. If you have a typeface that can't be used for text—one with only caps, for example—you are permitted to use a second face for the body copy. All display type must be your typeface.
11. This side of the poster should also reflect, through the design, grid, and layout, an understanding of your concept for the front side of the poster and the typeface's qualities. Remember, the grid should come from your concept and sketches, not the other way round.
12. Use a simple one-page grid created in QuarkXpress. Be sure to create your grid on the master page. With Quark's guidelines (not automatic columns), create multiple columns and intervals to suit your concept. Use the text's leading to measure the

depth of your columns. Link your text boxes. Try to keep subheads in the same box as the text, using Paragraph Formatting (space before and after) to position them correctly and to create a strong informational hierarchy.

13. Employ the rules for fine typography (typesetting), including kerning display type, adjusting rags, base-aligning text, using em and en dashes, and so on.

Process

It is best to begin by reading over your research. Make lists of concepts, ideas, and some characteristics of your typeface. Brainstorm as discussed in class. Decide how much of this information you want to include. Try to determine if you need more information, photographs, or illustrations. Then start sketching. Remember that you do not need a grid at first, but make use of the information you learned from the grid discussions. You need to go back and forth between your typeface information and your sketches to see how it will all fit in and together. Make adjustments and do more sketches. Some students have found it very useful to cut out gray shapes (text areas), black, white, or color boxes (pictures or illustrations), and some large black or gray rectangles (display type), and move them around on a piece of paper or board as if you were designing a collage. Through this technique you will get a structure and overall composition; later you can fit in the specific text or images. This collage technique might apply more to the conceptual side but can be used for both.

When you have selected your final idea for each side, develop a grid structure on tracing paper for the informational side (you may develop one for both sides, but this is not required); annotate it with the dimensions you have used and try it out on the computer.

Timeline

Week One

– Essay draft—turn in (instructor will return corrections the next week)

Conceptual side:

– Quarter-size sketches (six to eight different concepts) in correct proportion
– Select one to comp at half size, with colored markers or as collaged layout with dummy images
– Next class we will meet in small groups (three or four students) so that each person has plenty of time to discuss concepts and receive feedback before moving on to the next stage

Informational side:
– Quarter-size sketches (six to eight concepts)
– Practice dummy grid on computer

Week Two
Conceptual side:
– Half-size computer roughs

Informational side:
– Half-size hand comp
– Three possible grids that you have developed from the half-size comp
– Select the best comp and grid; develop on the computer at full size; make accurate tracing paper grid

Week Three
Conceptual side:
– Revised full-size layout, printed (preferably in color)

Informational side:
– Revised computer layout on grid including final graphics, printed

Week Four
– Final critique for both sides

Week Five
– Final review; turn in your assignment

Critiques
Wiesbaden Swing, *Alex Brannon,* Figure 5-2.1
Instructor's Evaluation
Conceptual side: The image Alex chose has the essential qualities needed for a poster plus a clear connection to the typeface, a requirement of this assignment. The photograph works in several simple ways: first, it is striking, and direct with an unmistakable focal point emphasized by the position of the typeface title, which appears to be flying into the air by the kick of the woman's foot; second, the high-contrast image (manipulated in Photoshop by Alex to look this way) of a couple swing dancing reinforces the nightclub atmosphere and further attracts our attention. Alex was able to take this image straight from the Internet, something one is rarely able to do because of resolution problems, but here the low resolution

Figure 5-2.1

Student Statement
On the front of the poster, I wanted to accentuate the movement at the focal point. I eliminated irrelevant details by increasing the contrast and darkening the background. To make it more playful, I put the title at an angle. Using the grid on the back of the poster, I focused on hierarchy and negative space, as well as readability. This was the more tedious side to design. After many weeks, however, I finished, and it turned out exactly how I had envisioned.

serves to enhance her concept. Alex rightly decided to gray in the background figures to make them recede, causing the swing dancers to be more prominent. The title gets its force not only by appearing to be kicked, but also by repeating the angle of the highlighted floorboards. The combination of factors in this poster has created a simple but strong poster.

Informational side: I like this side of Alex's poster for its airiness, nice use of negative space, and the original way Alex has set off the quote. By substituting an extra-large pair of brackets for quotation marks, she has cleverly illustrated their unique qualities without having resorted to the traditional format of putting them in a separate box with a caption. The balance created by the strong title at the top with the whole character set at the bottom works well here, while the image of the designer is well contrasted with the unusual dingbats. Originally Alex had the dingbats two or three times the size we see here; this detracted enormously from the quality and lightness of the typeface. It seemed the dingbats would have to be eliminated, but Alex realized she could reduce them so that they became just another part of the typeface. Making the dingbat text red emphasizes the separate nature of these little creatures, while the fact that the column width and type size are the same as the main text gives a sense of repeatability and coherence to the information side of the poster. Alex could have improved the kerning in her subheads; she probably could have made the baseline of the text align, and it would have been more internally consistent to make both subheads either flush left or centered, though I must admit that I don't think what she has done is incorrect or unnatural. Alex was right in not adhering to the grid all the time and in thinking that overall composition and hierarchy of her information must be more important than sticking to the grid.

Futura, *Jennifer Gray,* Figure 5-2.2

Instructor's Evaluation

Conceptual side: There is nothing in itself very unusual about this poster concept; however, it is clear, to the point (Futura was created with drawing tools on graph paper and is classified as a geometric sans-serif font), and has a strong focal

Figure 5-2.2

Student Statement

This project was my introduction to working conceptually as well as with a grid. The front underwent several conceptual changes, ranging from substituting the letters with various tools, such as a T-square and compass, to placing Renner's rendering of Futura onto graph paper. For the backside, I feel that a rigid grid structure helps define the strength of Futura. Overall, I feel that the project is a success because it illustrates the effectiveness of a grid.

point plus nice dynamic tension created by the angle of the compass. These features coupled with the asymmetry, the slight bleed of the compass on the left, which helps to bring our eye into the poster, and the strong use of negative space all make this a thoroughly satisfying poster. Jennifer met all the assignment objectives and used many of the design principles in the conceptual side of her poster.

Informational side: The informational side of Jennifer's poster shows a strong command of the principles of design and composition as well as a sound understanding of the grid structure. There are numerous examples of good contrast—color, size, and position of elements. Jennifer has effectively balanced the positive and negative spaces while making them varied. Several features might benefit from some subtle changes. For example, use of the half-column grid lines by extending the title to the right so that it ends at the half column position might break up the grid's rigidity and give more interest. Creating a stronger sense of hierarchy by making it obvious where one should visually enter the poster (either with the information at the top or at the bottom) would also contribute to making the focal point clearer. Jennifer has mastered many of the fine points of typesetting, as witnessed by her use of hung punctuation, em dashes, correct style and position for the author attribution under the quote, and minimal use of hyphens in the text. Three things—a little more work on the rag, removal of the one widow, and base-aligning the text—would bring this project to the level of a more advanced typography class. Jennifer, however, excelled beyond my expectations for a student taking a first course in the field, and I was very pleased with her poster.

Bauhaus, *Christine Kromer,* Figure 5-2.3

Instructor's Evaluation

Conceptual side: This is, in my judgment, near perfect for a student in Type I. Christine struggled with many ideas prior to this one—using images of a right angle and T-square was a promising start that I've often seen work for this assignment when Bauhaus was the chosen typeface. Finally Christine abandoned that idea. She never really had a concept, but rather only elements she was forcing into a composition. The next week she came to class with this poster, which has

Figure 5-2.3

Student Statement

*For this two-sided typeface poster
assignment, I wanted the concept of my
design to incorporate the ideas of
both the Bauhaus and Herbert Bayer. I
deliberately chose to use red and black as
my color scheme, write all the headline
text in lowercase letters, and use three
long vertical columns as my grid, as
these are all in the Bauhaus style. I also
included an image of circles, angles,
and horizontal and vertical lines, all of
which Bayer used to create the universal
typeface upon which Bauhaus ITC
is based. For the conceptual side of my
poster, I chose to use László Moholy-
Nagy's photograph "From the
Radio Tower" because it evokes the
circles, angles, and straight edges that
were used in creating Bauhaus ITC.*

everything the other one was missing: good composition, contrast, asymmetry, and a clear sense of where and how the title should be placed. It was virtually as you see it, except the type was a bit smaller and the progression of the letters reducing in size wasn't as apparent. The use of one of Moholy-Nagy's photos, which, more than usual, emphasizes the basic elements in design and the Bauhaus (the circle or half circle, the diagonal, and three-dimensional architectural construction), is just right for a Bauhaus poster. Christine's decision to place the type vertically within the architectural construction refers to one of the most recognized Bauhaus signs positioned on the outside of one of its buildings, and her choice of red for the title is apt, as the three primary colors are widely associated with the Bauhaus.

Informational side: Here Christine has accomplished what I had hoped that every student could with this assignment. She's made an asymmetric composition using a grid with a very clear sense of hierarchy. She has employed many of the principles of design that were emphasized in this course. There is a strong focal point near the top, where the title plus the typographic characters and image of Herbert Bayer all come together; we are led into the poster and the focal point by the bleed on the left edge. She's also used repetition in a thoughtful way, as the red color in different intensities (repetition) carries the eye through the poster, but is varied enough in structure not to be repetitious. Contrast is also well used, as we see in the elements' sizes and shapes, type sizes, and column widths and lengths. Probably the most important and most difficult principle for beginning typographers to achieve is a sense of hierarchy through grouping smaller items into a few larger ones while keeping the flow of information clear. Christine has managed this, having created either two or three large elements (depending on how you look at it) by overlapping (the red circle and the quote) and by positioning other parts relatively close to each other (the two images and text). Within each group she's established hierarchy by subgrouping.

Christine's command of the typesetting rules taught in the course is appropriate to the course level—sound but not complete yet. She has achieved a good rag with no hyphens (nice to see in a poster), she's used em dashes where appropriate, the baselines of the text blocks align, and the large quote has, appropriately, hung punctuation. There are, as often, some details that could still be fixed: remove the widow in the first column, kern the title, and arrange more evenly the text wrap around the small image on the left and the typeface characters within the red frame. However, considering this is a first-level type course, I am pleased if my students achieve a certain basic level of typesetting in this poster project. Christine is certainly well on her way to understanding the importance of the rules.

Figure 5-2.4

Student Statement

In choosing Meta, I did not think I would encounter so many problems. Coming up with a concept that can be recognized not only in Germany (where the typeface was originally created for the Deutsche Post) but also elsewhere was almost impossible to do. In the four-week time frame that was given, it was not until the end of the third week that I came up with anything that is simple and still shows the great qualities of Meta and its origin.

Meta, *Jocelyne Tjandra,* Figure 5-2.4

Instructor's Evaluation

Conceptual side: Like most of the students, Jocelyne found this project difficult at first because it requires understanding how to apply a concept to a typographic layout. And this requires an ability to use type expressively as well as an appreciation of the fine points of type, which in turn involves typesetting skills. Yet after two or three unsuccessful approaches, Jocelyne came in one day with this almost airtight concept. This often happens with students on the typeface poster project; because it is their first attempt at combining all they have learned in Type I (mostly exercises prior to this assignment) in a "real" project, they need pushing and coaxing to find an idea that both evolves from their typeface and makes a striking poster. Meta, Jocelyne knew, had originally been designed for the German post office. (It might be considered a small flaw that Jocelyne's poster implies it was to be used for stamps rather than for a stationery system and marketing material.) Although it was eventually rejected by the post office for internal reasons and Spiekermann went on to develop it for himself, she was right to think that the connection between the postal service and the typeface was central to its design. She was also right to notice how many different fonts within the family had been developed so that it could be used in numerous ways and with great subtlety of hierarchy. In addition, the cropped blowups show the extremely important and quirky details that Spiekermann employed in his design to make the typeface easily readable on low-quality paper with rough-and-ready printing. Jocelyne managed to get all this information into her conceptual side and create an arresting poster at the same time— a triumph! The two-color approach helped to simplify and accentuate the subtle differences in the numerous Meta fonts that might not have been so clear in four-color process. The Berlin postmark allowed her to incorporate with ease the date and original site for the typeface.

Informational side: Structurally the informational side of the poster is well conceived, with a strong hierarchy of information, contrast of typographic color (the left heavy and dense, the right lighter), and a nice asymmetric (though pleasingly balanced by a more or less central axis) and varied use of her grid. Internally one can see the subcategories of type hierarchy in the use of narrow columns for the biographical information and the smaller size, change of color and off-center use (some to the right and some to the left of the main alphabet) of smaller alphabets and numbers (different fonts) to illustrate the breadth of the Meta typeface family. I question Jocelyne's use of all capital letters for the text (she stood firm when I mentioned this, as she thought the texture and quirks of the face were particularly apparent with Meta caps, which manifest themselves automatically as small caps, rare in a sans-serif face), and I believe the poster needs some additional attention to typesetting rules (missing em dashes, awkward rags within narrow columns, and kerning display type in the title, to name a few instances). On the whole, however, this poster—front and back—shows a strong relationship and an excellent internal consistency that is very pleasing to the viewer; it has drawn praise from other students and faculty for its professional look and strong concept.

Three Type Specimens
University of Utah, Instructor: Carol Sogard

Assignment Brief

In this assignment, you will research three different time periods in relationship to what was occurring in type design during those years. Use the research as a starting point for further, more comprehensive research about a specific typeface. You will create three different type specimens that fall within the three time periods listed.

Period 1 (1450–1890): movable type. William Morris. Gutenberg Bible, Italian Renaissance, Rococo, Industrial Revolution, Arts and Crafts movement, wood type posters, editorial and advertising design, Kelmscott Press, Art Nouveau.

Period 2 (1920–1960): the modernist era. Poster art, Constructivism, De Stijl, the Bauhaus, Swiss design, International Typographic Style.

Period 3 (1980–1999): the information era. Postmodernism, global dialogue, New Wave typography, Memphis School, retro design (1940s–1950s), digital revolution, digital type foundry, digital imaging, interactive media, Internet.

Keep in mind that there are many different influences and movements within each of the time periods I have listed. It is up to the student to explore these time periods in more depth.

Objectives

– To learn about the beginnings of typographic design, its development, and its evolution to where it is today

Specifications

1. Size: 11" × 17", full bleed centered on black museum board with 3" border, flapped with tracing paper.
2. Colors: Two colors, your choice (black is a color).
3. Photos: Include only one photo or illustration that relates to the topic. (A typographic illustration could be considered an illustration.)
4. Fonts: Obviously it is important to use the fonts that you are researching; however, if necessary, you may use a different font for text type.

Process

You will research three types from each period. Choose one typeface from each of the time periods. Create one type specimen for each. The type specimen must include the following information:

1. Background information about the type designer or type foundry—what the purpose was for designing this particular typeface, anything that influenced the designer.

2. Information about the period or movement that influenced the development of the typeface.

3. A sample of some of the letters of the alphabet that make this typeface unique or different from similar typefaces. You may or may not include the whole alphabet.

4. Any other information that you think is pertinent.

It is important that each of the three type specimens be uniquely different but relate to the others as a whole. Imagine that these three layouts will be included in a book of type specimens. Therefore, consider your grid and how it will help to create consistency between the three layouts.

Critiques

Three Type Specimens, *Kyle Iman*, Figure 5-3.1

Figure 5-3.1

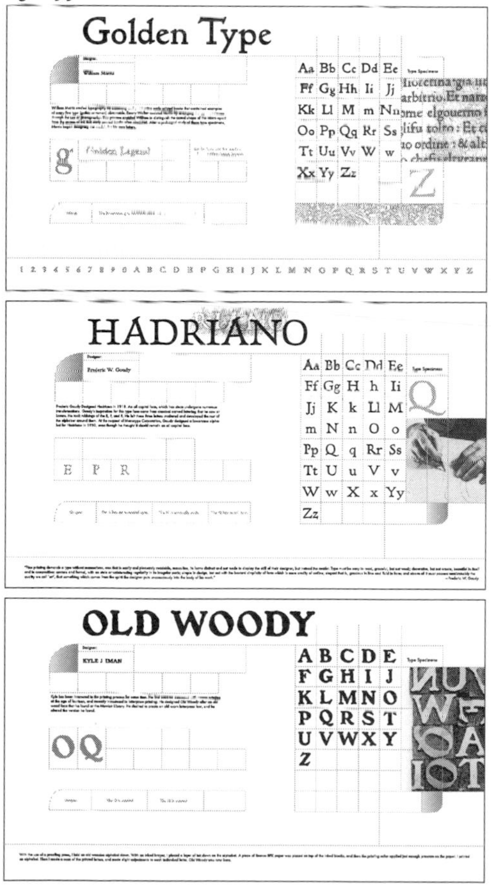

Instructor's Evaluation

For this particular project, students had the liberty to select any typeface they were interested in, as long as it fell into the correct time period specified for each of the three eras. As a class, it was decided that there would be no duplications of a particular typeface so that the group could be exposed to a wide variety of typefaces. This also aided in a better understanding of typographic history. Students were given the option to use a typeface that they had designed earlier in the semester as the typeface for period three. In this case, Old Woody was the typeface that Kyle designed. Kyle made an appropriate choice by selecting his own typeface. The three typefaces work well together. They all have traditional characteristics that relate well. Kyle's grid for the layout is pushed to the foreground of the design and is an appropriate way to unify the three layouts.

The grid could also be seen as a weakness in this scenario. Since the grid does not vary at all between the three layouts, it becomes too restraining. It is difficult to create variety between the three layouts when the grid is delegating the placement of each element in the same spot through each layout. Perhaps this could be resolved if the grid allowed more flexibility for intuitive design decisions directed at each layout.

Student Statement

The purpose of the project was to gain an appreciation for the history and purpose of typography. Through extensive research, I created a binder filled with information on several fonts and their creators. I chose three typefaces (including Old Woody, a typeface that I re-created) that exemplified unique characteristics and qualities. This process gave me new insight into the choice of type and usage of good typography skills.

Figure 5-3.2

Student Statement
For this type specimen project, I wanted to show the display characteristics of each of my chosen typefaces. I came up with a fairly straightforward direction that I hoped would accomplish that: movie posters. Each poster reflects visual characteristics of a movie that would have been either created or set during the same time period as the creation of the particular typeface.

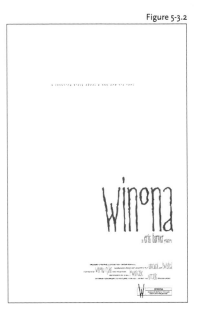

Three Type Specimens, *Eric Turner,* Figure 5-3.2

Instructor's Evaluation

One of the unique components of this project is to create unity between the three type specimens while maintaining a sense of individual character to each layout that exemplifies the unique qualities of the typeface. This challenge can be achieved through the development of a grid and/or concept.

Eric has addressed these challenges with his solution to the problem. He has a concept that helps unify the three layouts by playing off the style of old movie posters. Each specimen becomes a character in a different movie. The development of the copy helps add to this idea. Through the process I encouraged Eric to push the development of this idea.

This project uses each typeface in a creative conceptual way; however, there could be better differentiation between the three specimens—they are possibly too similar.

Figure 5-3.3

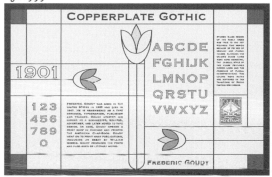

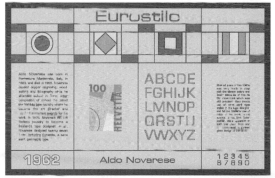

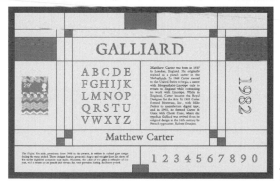

Three Type Specimens, *Terri Watkins*, Figure 5-3.3

Instructor's Evaluation

Terri achieves a good balance of unity and variety in a unique way. Grid and concept work together to create unity and variety among the three specimens. The grid plays a dominant visual role in the design. Terri's investigation of the grid structure of different stained-glass windows and the implementation of this pattern into a grid is what makes this project so unique. Each window pattern relates directly back to the time period in which the particular typeface was created. The selection and application of the color was also done very effectively. One improvement I might suggest would be to integrate the graphic of the stamp with the rest of the layout. The design of a stamp addresses a different concept and does not receive much explanation about its relationship to the rest of the layout.

Student Statement

I focused on fonts established during the twentieth century, one from early in the century, one from midcentury, and one from the end. The two colors, olive and rose, in their varying shades also give the pieces individuality: pastel early in the century, loud and vivid color in the '60s, and somewhere in between for the '80s. I enjoy studying geometric patterning and working in the garden, and both are reflected in these pieces.

Visual Poetry Calendar
University of Maryland, Baltimore County, Instructor: Peggy Re
(developed in conjunction with Beth Hay)

Assignment Brief

This assignment introduces the integration of word and image through basic information design, expressive typography, and the use of found or created images.

This is a four-person group project, in which the group will create a calendar for the year. Each member will design three posters that use both words and images to convey a season. You will use the four-part process outlined below in order to achieve your final design for each month. Together, the group will design the calendar and create a formatting system that unites all twelve pages.

Each group is responsible for designing a typographic system for the calendar (days, weeks, months) area of the page. There should be a consideration of conceptual element(s) from calendar page to calendar page within each group. The system that each group develops must be flexible enough for individual designers to work with it as they develop their image area. The entire composition must be unified.

Why a group assignment?
– The group nature of this project reflects the operating system of most professional design practices.
– Designers are often required to work within given formats to create a unified whole from individual parts.

Objectives
– To enable you to develop a richer use of rhetorical imagery
– To further the understanding and exploration of:

> *Image generation:* the derivation and development of appropriate, interpretive imagery through simple means
> *Expressive typography:* to understand and explore the possibilities of typographic elements as expressive imagery
> *System unification:* to understand how to develop a system that unifies individual elements within a series
> *Sequencing:* to understand the implications of progression within imagery and text and between parts
> *Hierarchy of information*

Specifications
1. Quark, Illustrator, and Photoshop are to be used as production tools. All type should be set in Quark and/or Illustrator. Images originally created using cut and

torn paper, gestural drawings, or brushwork may be re-created using Illustrator and/or Photoshop.

2. Size: 16" × 10" (from a 17" × 11" sheet, to allow for bleeds).

3. Orientation: vertical.

4. For parts 1 and 2, the poster's image area must be at least two-thirds of the entire format area. The actual calendar is restricted to the remaining third of the format area.

5. For parts 3 and 4, the size and composition of the image and calendar areas may be modified so that the composition is unified.

6. Color is limited to black and white for parts 1 and 2. Part 3 is limited to black and one PMS, one screen of each color. Part 4 must use four-color process.

7. Typographic elements such as rules may be used.

8. Letterforms may not be distorted or altered without approval from the instructor.

9. Type does not have to maintain a straight baseline.

10. You may choose your own typeface, weight, slope, size, and so on. You may combine your choices in any way you deem appropriate.

Process

Each person will select one season. Find a quote, lyric, poem, literary passage, or other text (three to four lines in length) that relates to your months. This selection will serve as the text and as a base for image development.

Compile a written list and a scrapbook of images that relate to your text. From this compilation develop a simplified image or group of images that suggest essential qualities. Consider the implicit as well as the explicit.

Develop your own imagery: gestural drawings, brushwork, cut and torn paper, photographs, photocopies, scans, rubbings, and so on, or use found imagery and/or a combination of the two.

Explore how you can work with typeface selection, weight, slope, scale, leading, and other features to suggest the expressive qualities of your text.

Analyze and develop both the typographic and object based imagery with regard to basic design principles. Edit both text and image. Consider how text and image can be joined.

Develop a composition that evokes the expressive qualities of your chosen text with the most evocative and formally rich solutions possible.

As a group, devise a formatting and calendar system that indicates the passing of time. Consider how information such as day, month, week versus weekend, and so on can be revealed.

In what ways can sequence be suggested at all levels within the poster series?

Timeline
Develop the final calendar for each month using the four-part process outlined below.

> Part 1: Image only and calendar, black and white.
> Part 2: Typography only and calendar, black and white.
> Part 3: Combines both type and image developed in parts 1 and 2. Image and text may be edited. Black and one PMS color, one screen of each color.
> Part 4: Combines both type and image developed in parts 1 and 2. Image and text may be edited. Four-color process.

Critiques
These solutions were successful because the designers understood the conceptual difference between creative interpretation and literal depiction. Each designer created a three-month series (three-part sequences) that unified the type and image so that each calendar read as a whole. The designers were deeply involved in researching, exploring, and interpreting the nature of a calendar and their chosen text before entering the design process.

In part 1, success was achieved by exploring the wide variety of processes that can be used for creating images, as well as scale and placement.

In part 2, success was achieved by visually editing the text and creating meaning by exploring structure, proportion, weight, stylistic differences, and placement between words and letterforms.

In parts 3 and 4, the designers succeeded because they further explored how the formal visual qualities introduced in parts 1 and 2 enhanced the understanding of a message. The designers edited and combined words, letterforms, and/or images to create a visual statement that revealed meaning. The most difficult step was the final one, when students were asked to explore the impact of color on meaning and were given freedom to use four-color process.

January, February, March, *Andrew Dunmire,* Figure 5-4.1
Instructor's Evaluation
In part 1, the designer combined heavily edited stock photographs silhouetted into shapes that gave the photographs new meaning with cut-paper illustrations that gave the silhouettes further detail. While in some ways not as successful as it could have been because of the difficulty in reading the photograph (see January), it was

Figure 5-4.1

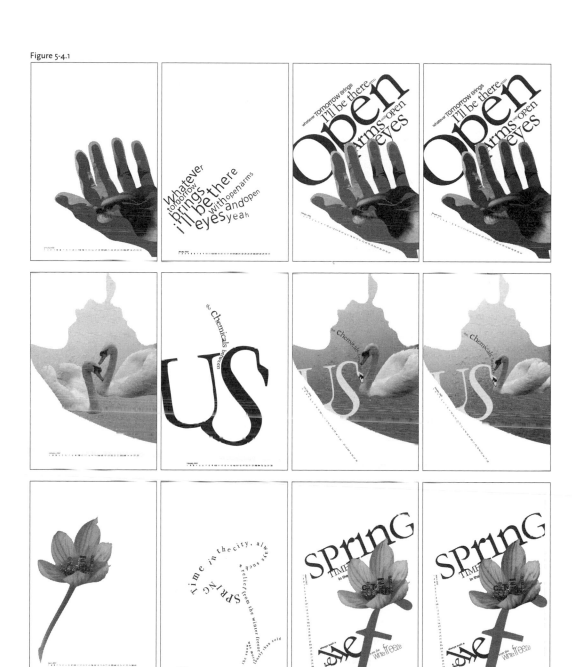

Student Statement

Lyrics from several songs combined with appropriate images express the emotions of the winter months, January, February, and March. This includes lyrics from "Drive" by Incubus, "Chemicals Between Us" by Bush, and "I Don't Know You Anymore" by Savage Garden. The project progressed in steps, from black-and-white imagery to black-and-white text, two-color image and text, and finally four-color image and text, each depending upon modifications to create separate compositions. Size, scale, balance, and seeing typography as an image are key elements of this project.

bold, daring, and inventive. The results were striking especially in February and March—the designer used negative space and scale to provide detail.

In part 2, the text relies too heavily on the image created in part 1 as the inspiration for the typography. Nevertheless, there are very interesting things occurring with the typography that could have been explored further. For example, in January, the text is arranged so that it mimics the form of an outstretched hand. If differences in type weight and slope had been considered, the designer might have discovered that the strokes of the various letterforms could suggest palm lines and fingerprints. The text in February explores dramatic changes in scale and the actual structure of the letterforms. The spine of the s suggests a swan. The calendar begins to subtly twist within the area to which it is confined.

In parts 3 and 4, type and image were richly and simply combined. The daring use of image introduced in part 1 and the typographic scale introduced in part 2 were pushed and combined. There is a further consideration of typeface selection; a serif face is introduced. February is the most successful solution. The word US is treated so that it too becomes a silhouette like the faces. The faces are not silhouetted equally—there is a concern for scale, and one face is closer to the viewer. This shift in space is echoed in the dynamic relationship created by the s, which is combined in part with the neck of a swan. This image is offset so that when combined with the photographic swan, it subtly suggests a twisted or broken heart. In all three months, the calendar breaks free of its confined space. While very simple in its presentation, the concept is very rich. The placement of the calendar is a representation of the position of the sun's rays in relation to the earth as the earth revolves around the sun. In parts 3 and 4, color is used very conservatively.

September, October, November, *Teri Fleshman,* Figure 5-4.2

Instructor's Evaluation

In part 1, the designer borrowed the metaphor of a dragonfly. In this case, it suggests the end of summer. (Each member of this group used one element used in the previous group of three posters for sequencing the twelve months.) The designer used drawing and photography to create her images. Extreme changes in scale and cropped images are used to give energy to the three compositions.

In part 2, a variety of typefaces evoke the mood created by the three haikus. In September, scale, letter spacing, and a curved baseline are used to create a sense of emerging into space for coming. The flourishes of a script face are used to suggest the path of a dragon. Dragon becomes the crossbar of the lowercase f. In September, the letters in flying maintain a straight baseline, but each sits on its own. Scale and

Figure 5-4.2

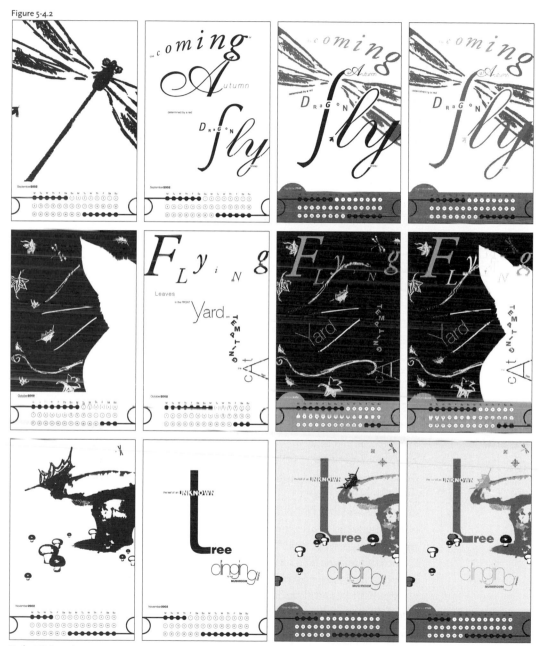

Student Statement

The purpose of this project was to incorporate word and image. We were required to find text and illustrate it with our own images. I drew some elements, photocopied leaves to make the cat, and took photographs of mushrooms with a digital camera to make up the images for each month. I enjoyed experimenting with the type to make it expressive of the meaning of the words. Overall the project was very labor-intensive, but it surpassed my expectations and resulted in a beautiful piece. (Poems are from A Haiku Garden: The Four Seasons in Poems and Prints, *edited by Stephen Addies, Fumiko Yamamoto, and Akira Yamamoto.)*

the structure of the different letterforms are used to suggest the motion of flying. Cat is spelled with a capital A and is turned on its side to suggest whiskers. The stem of the lowercase t in November's haiku is used to suggest a tree trunk. Unknown is reversed out of the t's crossbar and bleeds off on all four sides. The u and the n are "unknown"—parts of these letters are not revealed. The letterforms in clinging are tightly kerned and cling to each other—the final g clutches the right foot of the n.

In the latter part of this assignment, the designer was reluctant to edit both part 1 and 2 and—while the use of scale was still explored—layered the two parts together. September was the most successful solution because the stroke of the italic lowercase f became the body of the dragonfly. Red was used as the text suggests for the second color. In October and November, the designer was able to reposition the text so that its placement responded to the images in some cases.

June, July, August, *Jennifer Woodward*, Figure 5-4.3

Instructor's Evaluation

In part 1, the metaphor of a firefly was developed to suggest the qualities of dusk. The designer struggled to find a means of creating an image that conveyed the lightness and translucency of a firefly. An image of a firefly was created by scanning Saran Wrap. Actual scans of grasses were used to create the firefly's environment. In all three months for part 1, the designer explored scale and combined dramatically different means of image making. The calendar revealed an understanding of time through the use of a half circle on both the left- and right-hand sides.

In part 2, the designer used scale and carefully selected her typefaces, paying attention to the structure of the letterforms, placement, and kerning. In June, the manner in which night and light were integrated was particularly strong. July presented the sound of grown-up shoes passing; the designer set type in semicircular shapes to suggest the sound of heels on pavement. Letterforms with tall ascenders bounced up and down to suggest a flock of birds. August presented the act of playing by letting the l juggle a smaller text passage on the edge of one serif. The designer weakened the powerful and intriguing typographic images she created by making all of her type illustrative and literally depicting a bed. The outside margins created by the calendar as well as the calendar itself might have been better used as a grid for the top composition.

In parts 3 and 4, the designer edited parts 1 and 2 into a whole. June used both image and a passage of type to create an image that can be read as moon and sun. The designer thoughtfully considered the relationship between text and image. The

Figure 5-4.3

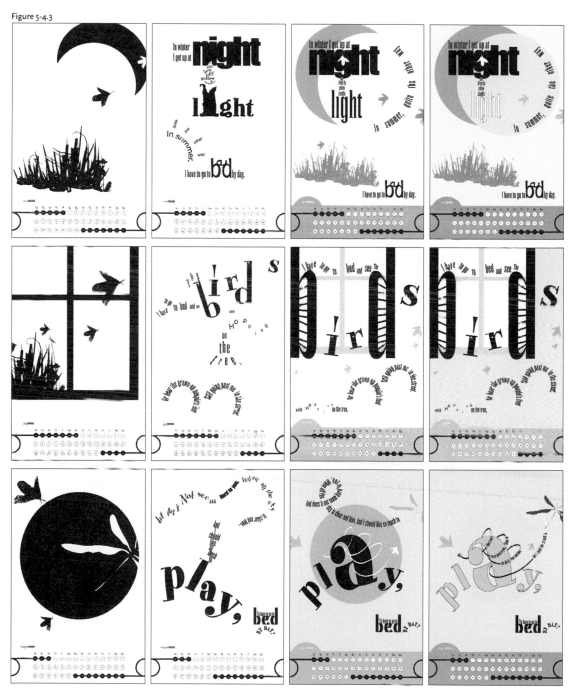

Student Statement

The poem "Bed in Summer" by Robert Louis Stevenson conjures up memories of childhood summers. In keeping with that theme, my goal was to create an expressive and playful design for the summer months of a calendar. The steps progressed from black-and-white image only to black-and-white text only, two-color word and image, and finally four-color word and image, with editing and redesigning to achieve a finished product at each step. This process taught me to use typography in a new and expanded realm as well as the value of continually developing and working through many ideas.

text began with a reference to night and then referred to light; the image, in its duality, can first be read as moon and then as sun. The passage that referred to summer and was set to complete the sun runs counter to reading order, as its content suggests it should. A firefly is reversed to become the counter of the g in night. In July, the b and d, the strongest members of the cheerful flock of birds developed in part 2, are forced to serve as shutters, and the flock is lost. While there are fireflies in the composition, they serve no real purpose; they are decorative. August, however, uses the firefly to suggest activity and dimension. The path of a firefly loops around the stroke and through the counter of the a in play. The path of a second firefly is traced by text that refers to the sky and the color blue. Color is not well explored.

The Science Lecture Series Posters
Massachusetts College of Art, Instructor: Elizabeth Resnick

Assignment Brief

Your assignment is to design and produce a series of three posters for a lecture series entitled "Children of the 21st Century: What Do They Need to Know About _____?"

This three-part lecture series is aimed at middle-school children, who are encouraged to attend the lectures as part of an educational outreach program sponsored by the Museum of Science in Boston and the City of Boston. The lectures will take place over a three-week period on Saturday mornings in June.

Each poster will advertise one of the following topics: astronomy, biology, and chemistry.

The posters will be distributed through a direct-mail campaign to parents of middle-school-age children and through postings at area schools and libraries.

Objectives

– To announce the lecture series to the children of Boston and their parents
– To create an appropriate visual to attract and excite schoolchildren ages eleven to fourteen
– To design three posters that have a visual relationship but different content

Specifications

1. Size: 15" × 22", vertical or horizontal.
2. Media and color: Any.
3. Title: "Children of the 21st Century: What Do They Need to Know About _____?"
4. When:

    Saturday, June 5 10:00 A.M.–12:00 P.M. Astronomy
    Saturday, June 12 10:00 A.M.–12:00 P.M. Biology
    Saturday, June 19 10:00 A.M.–12:00 P.M. Chemistry

5. Copy:

    Astronomy. The Earth is a tiny speck in space. If you imagine it shrunk down to a diameter of a twenty-fifth of an inch (1 mm), the Sun's nearest neighboring star would be 1,800 miles (3000 km) away. The remotest visible galaxies are so distant that the light they send out takes about 10 billion years to reach us, even though light can travel to the Moon in just over a second. Astronomers survey this huge volume of space. Our nearest star, the Sun, sends out light and heat to make life on Earth possible.

Biology. The word *biology* is derived from Greek and means "knowledge of life." Originally biologists studied the structure or anatomy of animals and plants, and tried to describe their relationships with each other. The study of anatomy of animals and humans led quickly to the development of surgery and to medicine becoming a science in its own right. Some of the most important work in biology is directed toward finding out how cells work. This type of study could lead to prevention or cure of many diseases.

Chemistry. Ever since our earliest ancestors began using fire one-and-a half million years ago, we have been able to produce and control chemical reactions to help us observe, investigate, and change the properties of substances. Today, chemical substances of all kinds are mined and manufactured, used for research, and for the production of detergents, dyes, cosmetics, drugs, food additives, glass, paints, paper, and plastics.

6. Where: Museum of Science.
7. Credits: This lecture series is co-sponsored by the Museum of Science and the City of Boston.

Process

Begin your design process by researching all three subjects. Think about how you would attract and excite kids ages eleven to fourteen with these subjects. Look at Nickelodeon (both the TV channel and the associated magazine), MTV, and advertising directed to young teenagers. Try to remember when you were thirteen and what interested you. Consider interviewing teenagers to find out what they like and what interests them. Once you have gathered enough information, begin doing thumbnail sketches. Whatever concept you decide on, remember you will need to unify the three posters through a visual language system, format, or structure. They must be seen as a series of three related visuals.

Timeline

Week One

Concept sketches of all three posters (at least half size) due for class critique.

Week Two

Large roughs for each poster due for critique.

Week Three

Finished posters due for critique.

Figure 5-5.1

Student Statement

For this series of science lectures aimed at young teenagers, my concept was to create colorful, bright posters exuding a semisophisticated style. I organized the typography so that the viewer could easily process the hierarchy of information. Staying consistent with my grid, my use of bold, playful, and powerful imagery, and the organized typography visually connect the three posters as a series.

Critiques

The Science Lecture Series Posters, *Jennifer Lopardo,* Figure 5-5.1

Instructor's Evaluation

I have assigned this challenging poster project to three different classes of students over the past three years. Jennifer has been the only student to really capture and address the target audience for this lecture series event. No matter how many times I've reminded my students that these posters have to appeal to children eleven to fourteen, most of the design solutions they've created reflected a visual sophistication appealing to the student who is college-age or beyond.

My suspicion was that most of my students did not do extensive research focused on the younger age group. Many students lived at home with younger siblings, so the inability to connect to this younger audience visually and conceptually was disappointing.

Preteens and young teens could be characterized as straddling the fence between adult ideas and childish playground behaviors. Why would they want to give up a Saturday in June (or three consecutive Saturdays) to attend a lecture on astronomy, biology, or chemistry when they could be playing sports or hanging out at the mall? In this case it falls to the graphic designer to make the images so appealing that they could sway such a fun-craving audience.

After researching many magazines and printed materials directed at this age group, watching enough MTV and other television programming aimed at preteens, and checking out their Web sites, Jennifer realized she needed to think of common curiosities this group has experienced collectively, and then create big, bold, and bright images to illustrate them.

She selects easily recognizable concepts and images that are fun to view. For her astronomy lecture poster, her headline copy reads: "Do you wonder if there is really a man on the moon?" to spark an interest in thinking beyond our own planet. She presents a bold yellow photo collage of an animated man-moon combination. Her color palette of orange, black, white, and yellow suggests a pleasurable Halloween connotation.

For her biology lecture poster, she asks her viewer: "Do you wonder what the inside of a frog looks like?" It's a gross idea, and gross appeals to this age group; many of them will have to dissect a frog in class before their high school years. The full frontal eye confrontation with a very large, almost monsterlike bullfrog is hard for any viewer to ignore. It is a strong focal point in this poster composition. For her chemistry lecture poster, Jennifer plays with the ideas of chemical explosions, asking: "Do you wonder what happens if you mix baking soda and vinegar?" Here the image is an erupting volcano with a contorted, screaming human face roaring out from its fire. It's a powerful presence, and even I'm hooked.

By staying within the confines of the grid, the consistent placement of the repetitive information—name of the lecture series in the top left corner, subject of the lecture with place, date, and time in the lower left corner—Jennifer easily creates the visual relationship that holds the series together.

Book: Lewis and Clark

Washington University, Instructor: Heather Corcoran

Assignment Brief

In May 1804, Lewis, Clark, and crew departed by boat from Wood River, Illinois (Camp DuBois), at the confluence of the Mississippi and Missouri Rivers. This was an important moment, the expedition's first step into unknown territory.

Your assignment is to create a typographic book that integrates three texts and a map from this moment in history. The texts have been provided; they include a short overview, a series of journal entries by Clark, and a collection of letters by various people involved in the journey.

Your book should be based on a specific idea about the subject matter. Your goal is to find a clear and interesting visual form for your idea.

Objectives

– To explore type hierarchy
– To make type as clear as possible through a process of stripping away unnecessary variation and information
– To work on typographic details and refinements
– To explore type as a texture
– To communicate a conceptual idea through set type
– To refine skills in Quark

Process

– Your book must include a cover, title page, colophon, and folios.
– No images may be used.
– You may use black and one secondary hue.
– You may use a maximum of two type families. Vary the style and weight as you like.
– The order and arrangement of texts is up to you.
– Page size will be of your choosing.
– Books must be bound.
– All work must be generated in Quark. Work only in spreads and trim all work.

Figure 5-6.1

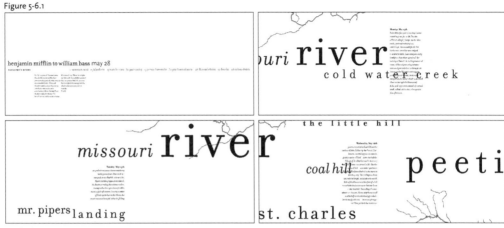

Student Statement

This book illustrates the journey of Lewis and Clark through the integration of various texts—journal entries, letters, lists, other documents, and running narrative. I attempted to create a feeling of distance and travel through a double-sided book (horizontal format) that can be read continuously from side to side. I placed the more structured texts in running columns across the front sides of the spreads. The journal entries appear across the back spreads, typeset and positioned erratically to reference the quality of the writing.

Critiques

Lewis and Clark Book, *Lauren Hartstone*, Figure 5-6.1

Instructor's Evaluation

The idea of a double-sided folding book is a strong one for this content, as it allows the viewer to understand Lewis and Clark's journey from two perspectives—rigid and organized, on the one hand, and organic and unpredictable, on the other. The book's horizontal format suggests travel, especially with the long lines of type that march across it. The palette seems appropriate, and the blue is thoughtfully applied to the details. The typography is well sized, set, and ragged. Lauren's attention to detail and refinement, an important part of her process, is evident here.

On the front side of the book, she might consider slightly larger margins on all sides. On the back, I recommend left-justifying all of the text. I think that Lauren also could explore pushing the scale and drama of some of those back spreads even more. Perhaps the scale of the river could be less constant. At the moment, its drawing seems neither light and elegant nor strong and graphic.

Lewis and Clark Book, *Anna Kardaleva*, Figure 5-6.2

Instructor's Evaluation

What is strongest about this book is its sense of typographic exploration, which serves as a metaphor for Lewis and Clark's study of the landscape. The spreads that

Figure 5-6.2

Student Statement
The aim of my Lewis and Clark book was to depict a visual journey. I tried to link the events of Lewis and Clark's geographic or topographic journey, which was an exploration of vast expanses of land, with my own typographic journey, which was a broad personal exploration of several different forms of typography, new and old.

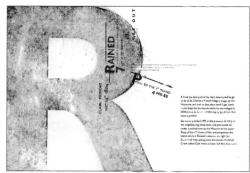

contain the large letterforms are perhaps the strongest, both in form and in communication. Anna makes bold graphic decisions on these spreads, and she supports them with details. On the R spread, for example, the viewer can connect the rainy weather that is described in the text with the dripping quality of the large R. She also has a nice sense of contrast in her type—in scale and weight. This book might benefit from a stronger title to make the typographic metaphor more clear. It might also be interesting to see some of the cleaner spreads (earlier in the book) contain small references to the visual drama to come.

Figure 5-6.3

Student Statement

The Lewis and Clark typographic book combines lists, maps, and journal entries. I positioned letterforms organically on the spreads to portray the flow of the journey along the Missouri River. The sense of movement was essential to the thematic continuity. The book can be viewed either spread by spread or as a whole because of its accordion binding.

Lewis and Clark Book, *Danielle Rifkin,* Figure 5-6.3

Instructor Evaluation

The idea of re-creating the flow of a river through typography works especially well in the linear form of a book. Danielle's visual investigation of letterforms and texture over the course of the project was impressive. It was only in the later stages that she found a solution that combined italic serif forms with sans-serif all caps; this allowed her to show the river as both calm and tumultuous, and also reflects Danielle's sensitivity to type as form. The shift in scale and orientation of the italic letterforms, juxtaposed with the quieter sans-serif type, creates particularly strong spread compositions.

My recommendations for change are minor. The text block that appears on every spread could be positioned even more consistently so that the organic quality of the river gets the attention it deserves. With that goal in mind, I would set those text blocks with as little variation as possible, perhaps minimizing the shift between text and subhead (and keeping the subheads within the text block).

Journey Journal

London College of Printing, Instructors/Tutors: Gülizar Çepoğlu, Bob Britten, Robin Dodd, Pete Green, Sarah Mansell, Vanessa Price, Angela Jones

Assignment Brief

Students are given four different circular routes for a journey beginning and ending at the Elephant and Castle, by the College entrance. These routes were distinguished by their most significant features: the Banker's Route, the Printer's Route, the Archbishop's Route, and the Politician's Route.

Students are then asked to choose one of the routes and make their way around this route, utilizing whatever mode of transport, or combination of modes of transport, they consider most appropriate, and to document their journey.

Objectives

– To identify and apply appropriate research methodologies and to research and provide a body of supporting material through group discussion and self-directed study

– To demonstrate an understanding of organizational, time-management, and presentation skills within project work.

– To understand the importance of visual research to the design process, and apply this to the design solution. (Visual research findings should be expressed in a variety of ways. Evaluate, select, and apply them in a way that enhances the project work.)

– To develop an understanding of the employment of structure and knowledge of language in relation to the project.

– To demonstrate through project work an understanding of structure, form, harmony, balance, and proportion, and to explore implicit meaning. Using letterform, analyze hierarchies within the text, applying hierarchical typographic treatments to exemplify meaning.

Process

You will be assigned a circular route for a journey beginning and ending at the Elephant and Castle. You are required to make your way around this route, utilizing whatever mode of transport you may choose, and to document your journey. It is preferable that you make the journey on more than one occasion, and that you walk the route at least once, enabling you to stop and view more points of interest along the way. The document of your travels should include visual examples, photographs, records of the journey in relation to time and space, notes, and sketches. You might choose to record the changing physical environment, activity observed, personal thoughts and actions, light, temperature, sound, movement, variations in perspective, and viewpoints. You are free to use any medium you feel necessary, though all your ideas, proposals, experiments, reflections, and critique of your working processes must be documented in a hardbound sketchbook. This will form the basis of the visual research element of the project.

For the letterform element, you are required to keep notes from studio seminars, together with an analysis of a range of examples of typography encountered on your journey. This analysis seeks to relate the subject matter from the seminars relating to type history and classification into observed real-life situations. Consider how your typographic examples can evoke the atmosphere or feeling of your progression through a changing urban environment.

You are required to choose one example of a typeface observed and recorded on your journey, and to produce a thorough dossier on its history, designer, and identifying characteristics. Practical examples of where you have seen this typeface used and a range of experiments and sketchbook layouts must also be included. You should note the places and types of work where you would expect to see this typeface, and where you would envisage using it—for instance, in information systems, in advertising, as a body or display face, and so on.

Timeline

Between weeks one and four, you will be required to attend classes with Visual Research and Letterform staff as timetabled, and in week six you will present your final work at a group critique. You are asked to present as a final outcome two separate visual pieces of work, using any medium you feel appropriate, in response to the themes "urban space" and "urban texture." These pieces must incorporate developments from your Visual Research experiments together with typographic examples from the Letterform classes.

You will be required to present evidence of your research: photocopies, notes, rough developmental visuals, and other items. You will also be required to talk as individuals about your ideas to tutors and the group. The final presentation of work can take any form you require to successfully communicate your solution. The emphasis, however, will be on the research and presentation rather than the quality of finish.

Figure 5-7.1

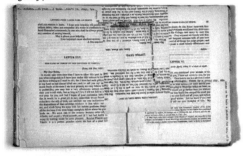 

 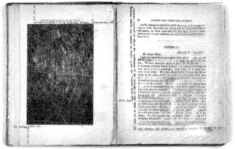

Student Statement

While walking the route I found at a used-book store a volume that contains a collection of letters describing the author's journeys in Europe (Letters from James, Earl of Perth, edited by William Jerdan). The book used to be a library book and so was involved in various journeys itself. By taking the pages out, typing on them, and putting them back, I further involved the book in a series of "journeys." My text, a documentation of my impressions and thoughts from the walk, maneuvers around the original body text, navigating through a city built by descriptions of cities. It explores and redefines the terms "urban space" and "urban texture."

As the piece is very much about the process, it has a very rough, sketchbooklike feeling to it, but at the same time forms a precious, finished piece in its own right. While working on the project, the book, which was supposed to be my sketchbook, gradually turned into the final piece itself.

Critiques

Journey Journal, *Adriana Eylser,* Figure 5-7.1

Instructor's Evaluation (Tutors: Bob Britten, Gülizar Çepoğlu)

In Adriana's case, the most important part of her project was her experience of the journey and her need to put it into a narrative form. Her idea to use a travel book—appropriating a travel book that she bought from a secondhand bookshop on her journey—has been central to her project, which she carried convincingly to the final piece. Her concept of a travel book to house her journey narrative reveals the notion of "book" as well as a particular genre of book while exploring how a book format can affect text and vice versa.

A poetic use of language and the use of typewriter to create a multilinear reading demonstrate her understanding of structure and the use of language and type within the book format. Her interactive idea of removing the pages from the book and then typing the text on the removed pages justifies her potent way of interpreting and conveying the notion of travel metaphorically. The pages undergo the journey she herself has undergone, except this time the journey is transcribed from her memory to the format of the existing layouts.

There is a keen sense of texture and multiple layers. The book reveals itself as a space of inscription, and it returns us to where memories and their manifestations may belong in concrete form. The superimposition of two different texts about different journeys underlines the notion of temporality within the book format.

Journey Journal, *Aman Khanna,* Figure 5-7.2

Instructor's Evaluation (Tutors: Bob Britten, Gülizar Çepoğlu)
Aman's cross-cultural approach to the project is very well realized. Analyzing Western cultural artifacts through an Eastern sensibility is a highly pertinent means of disclosure.

Aman's work progress reveals his editorial skills in organizing and interpreting his ideas. His use of photography in describing his experience of the journey and the tension created between the text and image is very effective. This methodology is positively reinforced in his highly developed sketchbooks.

Aman's very strong personal approach to the project is well conceptualized and well executed. However, the final outcomes for the themes "urban space" and "urban texture" depend on the photographic representation of both cultures. The verbal messages could be more fully evolved. Aman's letterform sketchbook is very well planned and shows the development of his ideas through his walks. His choice of typeface is well researched and is consciously applied. The whole sketchbook sustains personal observations interpreted in a highly skillful presentation.

Aman is a very sensitive observer who is able to express his observations and concepts in intelligent and communicative visual formats.

Figure 5-7.2

Student Statement
The aim of the project was to make a record of the journey route and document it. All kind of ideas were running through my mind, but I decided to stick to my Indian roots and culture. In making a record of the journey route, I took pictures of the Indian-dominated areas in London and then made connections and comparisons between the two cultures. The final outcome was two boards with photographs showing urban space and texture and a book with black-and-white photocopies of the same.

When I look at this book now, it has the feel of a family photo album. Every picture has my experience hidden behind it. I have captured a phase of my life, a phase when I was trying to both accept and gain acceptance in an urban space and as a part of an urban texture.

Figure 5-7.3

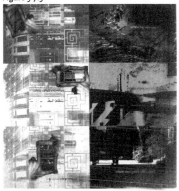

Student Statement

One day, I was hunting for images in a concrete jungle, just close to the River Thames. Every building was similar to each other, showing the dominance of the grid structure. "They are all depressingly flat, rigid, and inorganic. Choking, isn't it?" I thought. But then I found wild ivy spread on the pavement, and a subtle reflection of the water on the wall. No matter how cold the module may be, the city cannot exist without an organic space. Why? Because its contents (human beings) are already a part of nature. Through this project, I looked at different motifs between organic space and inorganic texture, and it was quite enjoyable, as it helped me broaden my method of expression.

Journey Journal, *Kumiko Nasuno,* Figure 5-7.3

Instructor's Evaluation (Tutors: Bob Britten, Gülizar Çepoğlu)

From the beginning of her journey, Kumiko started to ask the appropriate questions, and she intelligently pursued the answers. Her sketchbooks are a delight, with intriguing concepts and a sensitive use of excellent imagery. They show the development of her thinking effectively. This is a very strong personal response to the project, with strong final outcomes.

We told her to keep the same freshness in the next project but asked her to engage with more typographic investigation and exploration and to concentrate on the text-image relationship. Her visual and verbal representation skills justify her idiosyncratic solutions successfully, while her typographic solutions, format, and scale don't as yet.

Kumiko is a mature student with a critical mind. The city structure does not satisfy her sensibilities, and she has looked for more organic and more sensitive human structures within the concrete patterns and structures of urban space. The use of her hands within the repetitive patterns of the buildings reflects a desire to bring the human element into the brutality of urban structures.

Under her directional discretion, images become fully detailed and juxtaposed to each message; we see a contrasting photograph where more organic imagery and poetic language exemplifies her appreciation of nature.

Figure 5-7.4

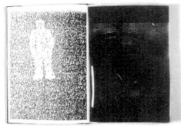

Student Statement

Your brain processes all of the words and bits of conversation that you are unaware of hearing as you walk through the street and other public places. Each word or name is checked against a list of words personally relevant to you. When a match is made, the word explodes into your consciousness and grabs your full attention.

The overlapped, unbroken text contains broken conversations that I taped or wrote down while walking around my route. They are illegible and you do not take in the information, similar to the way that one experiences ambient conversations in public spaces. The overlapped text is symbolic of people mingling in the street, and the projection of a city skyline is to emphasize urban space. The words "excuse me" are the best words to grab someone's attention, as they are on everyone's checklist.

Can I talk to you for 1 min: visual texture

Like our hearing, our sight is selective—we only see the things we look for, like the time of our train or how to get to the exit. I have read and heard about a relationship existing between the viewer and visual information. As viewers, we are very neglectful of this relationship; if the information were a person, he or she would be very worried about the state of the relationship. This final piece is about the visual texture confronting you in the places you can't ignore and trying to discuss the problem of your use and abuse of it. The emptiness of people in each image is to heighten the feeling that the visual texture is talking to just you, the viewer.

Journey Journal, *Liam O'Connor,* Figure 5-7.4

Instructor's Evaluation (Tutors: Bob Britten, Gülizar Çepoğlu)

Liam started with a very dynamic sketchbook where he not only documented type, sign, and image but also developed his concepts and then used the public space— the Underground and train switchboards —to house his messages. They demonstrate high levels of verbal and visual presentation skills. Strong manipulation and editing of photography gives evidence of his visual acuity and his intellectual exploration of encoded meaning. References central in this project were the work of Jenny Holzer, Bruce Nauman, and Barbara Kruger.

The large panorama of type works very well. His final outcomes for the concepts "urban texture" and "urban space" are very effective both conceptually and visually; their format, placement, and scale combine to provide a highly engaging and informative solution. This level of fluency about concepts, both verbal and visual, is highly commendable.

VISUAL ADVOCACY

In professional practice, clients provide the content and designers are hired to create the form in which this content is delivered, be it a book, magazine, Web site, advertisement, or television commercial. A designer's projects can range from the absolutely essential, such as transportation and environmental signage or drug labeling and packaging, to the downright deceitful, as in many advertising campaigns that foster *want* where there is no *need*. But in reality, most client work lies in between.

As a graphic design educator employed by a publicly funded art college, it is my job to train students how to communicate using visual language. It is my responsibility to encourage them to use training responsibly and to think beyond only serving business and commerce. They are citizens participating in a democratic society, and as such, they should be cognizant that their communication skills can be put to use as a powerful tool for social change for any number of issues they personally consider important to the well-being of the society in which they live.

Introducing the Idea of Responsible Activism in the Classroom

I write project assignments that address pertinent societal issues to raise general awareness and have my students reflect on their core values to develop their own content. I show materials created by activist artists and designers who espouse public discourse, and whenever possible I organize lectures and exhibitions at the college to inspire and inform them. When I encourage my students to find and express their own "voice," I empower them to think beyond design as a service to a market-driven economy.

> "Corporations have become the sole arbiters of cultural ideas and taste in America. Our culture is corporate culture."
> —Tibor Kalman

For the past decade, the graphic design press has been a prolific source of critical discourse, encouraging a dialogue to examine the profession's moral and ethical responsibility in light of the backlash against corporate branding and consumption excesses. One such catalyst document is the "First Things First" manifesto:

> *In common with an increasing number of the general public, we have reached a saturation point at which the high pitched scream of consumer selling is no more than sheer noise. We think that there are other things more worth using our skill and experience on. There are signs for streets and buildings, books and periodicals,*

catalogues, instructional manuals... and all the other media through which we pro-mote our trade, our education, our culture and our greater awareness of the world.

"As you create and send messages, you develop your own voice, which is a combination of experience, skill, concern, desire, and spirit. Developing your own voice through critical examination of all you do can enrich your experience and work. Asserting your voice, when appropriate, can further your contribution to others."
– John Bowers

Originally written in 1964 by British graphic designer Ken Garland and signed by twenty-one of his fellow visual communicators, "First Things First" was a call to arms to graphic designers to use their talents for "more useful and lasting forms of communication." It is a bit daunting that a manifesto written four decades ago can still sound fresh, and the manifesto has emerged once more in revised form, including contemporary signatories. Published in several of the world's most respected design journals, "First Things First 2000" challenges designers to look inward ethically and morally, and if they don't like what they see, they should adjust their position in some way. Although "First Things First 2000" opened a huge floodgate of debate in arguments for and against its initial idealism, I believe it provided a great stimulus for students who were actively searching for ways to use their skills more meaningfully.

In this last section, there are six assignments that engage students with current social, political, or cultural issues by encouraging them to develop their own visual messages directed toward specific audiences.

"Instead of doing only commercial work, designers can apply their skill and imagination to contribute to a better society... for me, social responsibility, political and ecological correctness in the design process does not take away from the artistic responsibility of designers... I will never accept a job for something that I disagree with politically."
– Phillippe Apeloig

The Literacy Poster: Learn to Read
Massachusetts College of Art, Instructor: Elizabeth Resnick

Assignment Brief

Merriam-Webster's Collegiate Dictionary defines *literacy* as "the quality or state of being literate," and *literate* as "able to read and write."

The Literacy Volunteers of America, Inc. (www.literacyvolunteers.org) defines adult literacy as the ability to read, write, and speak English proficiently, to compute and solve problems, and to use technology in order to become a lifelong learner and to be effective in the family, in the workplace and in the community.

Very few adults in the United States are truly illiterate. But there are too many adults with low literacy skills who lack the foundation they need to find and keep decent jobs, support their children's education, and participate actively in civic life.

Your assignment is to *voice your opinion* on the subject of adult literacy by creating a visual statement in the form of a poster, directed toward a general or specific audience of your choice, using the integration and/or juxtaposition of type and image, possibly in a new or unexpected way. The power of the media can play a significant role in encouraging people to seek help and thereby improve the quality of their lives. The poster will be placed in public buildings, including libraries and schools.

Specifications
1. Size: 18" × 24", horizontal or vertical.
2. Media: Photography, collage, computer illustration, typography.
3. Suggested copy: "Read," "Learn to Read," "Literacy First."

Process

Begin the design process by researching adult literacy initiatives in this country; use the library and the Internet. What programs are available and what strategies do they offer?

Consider the following:
– In order to promote the importance of early language development in children, parents must play a key role. How do you motivate parents with low literacy skills to realize that literacy is the key to breaking the cycle of undereducation and poverty?
– How can you motivate parents with low literacy skills to enroll in family literacy programs to break the cycle in which they find themselves?
Sometimes serious topics require very simple messages in order to be understood. Do not underestimate the power of visual language to articulate your message. People are often more adept at reading images than they are at reading words. The use of humor in any message can add a layer of meaning and get your point across

in a less threatening manner. Who is your intended audience? If the message is directed at low-literacy adults, how can you create a message that they will easily understand?

Timeline

Week One

Begin the design process: research, gather information, brainstorm ideas, and create thumbnail sketches from the best of your ideas. Choose two of the thumbnail sketches and enlarge them to half-size sketch layouts due for class critique. Be prepared to discuss your research.

Week Two

Based on the feedback you received in critique, determine the direction you will take, and complete the final poster for class critique.

Figure 6-1.1

This is not a book.

Think *differently.* Read.

Student Statement

As a society, we have not forgotten what literacy is; we have developed a much broader generalization of its meaning. My literacy poster is a direct commentary on this by exploiting the identity that Apple Computer has created for its iBook product. By adopting this visual language, I wanted the viewer to question the relationship between the computer and a book and the meaning of using the term book for both. Originally intended as a piece of graphic agitation, it is not as simple as it may appear.

Critiques

Literacy Poster, *Ben Barstrom*, Figure 6-1.1

Instructor's Evaluation

Ben is a good conceptual thinker, as demonstrated by the quality of his concept for this poster addressing teenage and young adult literary. "This is not a book," the copy reads, but it is placed underneath an Apple iBook computer. Ben uses this play on words to tell teens that although computer literacy is important, it is not a substitute for reading books. His poster concept references the Surrealist artist Magritte in his painting "Ceci n'est pas une pipe" (This is not a pipe), where this text sits underneath the image of a pipe. The contradiction makes the viewer look again, and the message is received. The poster also works on another level. The visual style language used is the same style language used by Apple Computer in its advertising. The viewer is drawn in because it looks like an advertisement for the iBook. By the time they realize it is not an ad, they have taken in the message.

Literacy Poster, *Christina Beck*, Figure 6-1.2

Instructor's Evaluation

This poster is such a charming response to the assignment. The metaphor Christina employs in her illustration is to encourage her viewer to cultivate her intellectual garden by reading great poets and authors, whom she pictures as petals that form the two large flowers growing

Figure 6-1.2

from her mind. The white picket fence that surrounds and contains the garden evokes a crown or ornate bonnet. Christina places her focal point on the garden first, as it is the largest element and centered in the middle of the composition. As the viewer's eye moves down to the face, hand, and book, the size of these elements shrinks in proportion.

Christina works with cut-paper collage to create her illustration, and uses the computer only to set white letterforms in a black bar that is then applied to the illustration board to complete the experience. This whimsical and engaging image remains with the viewer for a very long time.

Literacy Poster, *Jasanne Blanchard*, Figure 6-1.3

Instructor's Evaluation

In her poster, Jasanne offers two familiar objects lying on a gray table surface. We recognize the ubiquitous stick-on name tag "Hello my name is" from all the gatherings where we had to be identifiable to others, and the black Sharpie marker used to write our name on the name tag. But what if we can't read the words printed on the name tag or write our name? Here the simplest of tasks becomes an obstacle. This message is not meant for people who can't read or write English, so much as it is meant to sensitize the rest of us to the plight of those who are not functionally literate in our culture, perhaps because they do not read or write English. This message calls for action.

Imagine yourself in a train station in Japan. All of the signs are in Japanese and all of the train information is announced in Japanese. No one speaks English. In this situation, in this culture, you would be considered illiterate. It was a most enlightening experience for me.

Figure 6-1.3

Figure 6-1.4

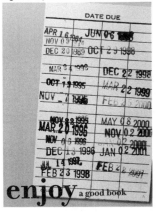

Student Statement
I think of the act of reading as the sharing of ideas and narratives. The inspiration for my concept came from the back of a popular book I was reading at the time. The date stamps document the idea of a book being shared and enjoyed by many over a long period of time. A good book will never go out of fashion.

Literacy Poster, *John Dennis,* Figure 6-1.4

Instructor's Evaluation

John is a very conceptual thinker by nature. Many of his graphic design projects are touched by his light, whimsical approach to expressing ideas in a nonthreatening manner. I recall John trying many humorous and pun-based concepts for this project. But none worked. It's really difficult to make a joke about not being able to read or write English. Finally, as the deadline for the assignment approached, John concentrated his thoughts on the joy of reading, focusing on how one book could offer joy to so many people over an extended period of time.

The typographic textural quality of the different dates stamped over a period of thirty-seven years provides the fascinating content for a viewer to examine. It may not be a "big bang" concept, but it is a pleasant graphic reminder that reading a good book can be a very desirable communal experience.

Figure 6-1.5

Literacy Poster, *Michelle Georgilas,* Figure 6-1.5

Instructor's Evaluation

Michelle enjoys tapping into the humorous side of human nature to articulate her concepts. To do this successfully, she skillfully juxtaposes dissimilar visual elements to create totally unexpected messages. For her literacy poster, her concept is to explore the idea that reading can enlighten the mind. The viewer is probably not expecting to see a nun "enlightening" her mind by reading a sex manual. But this surprise will cause the viewer to look again, and the message is received. The nun's face is the focal point that becomes even further exaggerated by the red and yellow striped background directing the viewer's gaze toward the nun's amazed expression. She is clearly enjoying herself, and as such, the viewer does as well.

Student Statement
In order to draw attention to the subject of literacy, my concept was to shock the viewer with something totally unexpected—a nun reading the Kama Sutra, an ancient text about the art of sex, thus demonstrating that reading can enlighten anyone's mind.

Literacy Poster, *Chris Mitchell,* Figure 6-1.6

Instructor's Evaluation

In his poster, Chris skillfully employs a simple metaphor to advocate for reading and literacy. A metaphor uses a concrete idea to describe an abstract concept. Here, the key conveys the idea that reading can open doors; the outstretched hand of a recessed, shadowy anonymous figure boldly offers the viewer the key to learning and knowing. The viewer needs only to be inspired to reach out and take the advice.

Figure 6-1.6

Student Statement

The key as an object successfully conveys the idea that reading is the first step to accomplishing anything—opening doors and locks, basically enhancing or deepening something that already exists. Not as an object but as a concept (i.e., that an idea or thing can be the key that answers a particular question—almost like a clue is to a mystery, but on a larger scale), the key conveys another powerful message. Having the key being offered to the viewer by this character of contrast and mystique adds an element of wonder and curiosity.

The relationship of word and image is the critical mediator of this message. The key image is understood as a metaphor and not an object only when the word read is placed adjacent to it. Enhancing this interplay of word and image is the strong focal point of the poster's composition; the outstretched hand holding the key. Thrust into the central foreground, the hand and key are illuminated by a strong light source. The viewer's gaze is immediately drawn to this area. From the hand, the viewer's gaze moves to the word *read*, and the brain formulates the message. Although the meaning of the message is reliant on the ability to read the word read, I believe the dramatic power of the image and the metaphor it suggests could possibly be deciphered by those who do not read.

Literacy Poster, *Emily Trescot*, Figure 6-1.7

Instructor's Evaluation

It is important to encourage parents, especially fathers, to take an active role in the nurturing of children. In her poster, Emily supports this initiative by showing us a father and son happily cuddling together reading a Dr. Seuss book. To the viewer, the father is seen as a role model to other men to encourage them to do the same activity with their children. It is a very simple yet very powerful statement.

The tight cropping of the photograph places the focal point of the composition on the book. Emily positions her image to fill the right side of the composition, creating an interesting asymmetrical stress that is balanced on the left with a large white negative space. She places the text message "Read aloud to your child" in the white space. The text acts like an arrow, directing the viewer's eye right to the image. Both the type and image work to create a balanced message.

Figure 6-1.7

Student Statement

For children to become interested in reading, it helps if parents take time to read aloud with them. My concept is to encourage parents to consider reading books as a fun activity to share with their children.

Human Rights Poster
Massachusetts College of Art, Instructor: Elizabeth Resnick

Assignment Brief

This assignment was inspired by the Zimbabwean poster designer Chaz Maviyane-Davies and his *Human Rights* poster series, produced in the mid-1990s. In his *Rights* series, which was influenced by his African heritage, his goal was to fight for human rights in Africa and to remind "authorities of their moral obligations as leaders and human beings." You can see these posters and other work by Maviyane-Davies on the Internet at www.maviyane.co.zw.

Your assignment is to visually articulate one of the thirty-one rights from the "Declaration of the Common Rights of Humanity," written by Jeff Stansbury, given to you as a handout. It is also available on the Amnesty International Web site (www.amnestyusa.org). Read all thirty-one rights and think about what it might mean to be deprived of these most basic human rights.

Specifications
1. Size: 18" × 24" or 20" × 30".
2. Color: Any.
3. Media: Any.
4. Copy: Wording for the "right" you choose. It can be edited for brevity.

Process

Start your design process by doing research on Amnesty International or any other human rights organization to understand the group's mission and motivations. For visual research, look at twentieth-century political propaganda posters (posters that argue or persuade from a political or social point of view). After you have done a sufficient amount of research, review the thirty-one rights again and select a right to focus on. Brainstorm ideas that would enable you to create an engaging, effective, and meaningful message that supports or argues for the right so that the message can be understood by a general audience.

How does the effective poster achieve its aim? By the very nature of its size, a poster can seize the attention of the viewer and then retain it for a brief moment. During that short time a poster can provoke and/or motivate a viewer—it can make the viewer gasp, laugh, reflect, question, assent, protest, recoil, or otherwise react. At its most effective, a poster can sell, promote, encourage, or persuade. It can be employed as a dynamic force for change.

Timeline

Week One

Begin the design process: research, choose the right, brainstorm, and develop thumbnail sketches on possible concept directions. Choose two to make into half-size rough layouts for critique. Bring your thumbnail sketches and your research finding to class.

Week Two

Based on the feedback you received in critique, focus on one concept and revise or rework it into a full-size rough color layout for class critique.

Week Three

Based on the feedback your full-size layout received, create a finished poster comprehensive and bring to class for critique.

Critiques

Human Rights Poster: Right 14, *Christina Beck,* Figure 6-2.1

Instructor's Evaluation

The graphic language Chris employs Is reminiscent of a scene from a concentration camp, prisoner of war camp, or even refugee camp—anguished faces imprisoned by barbed wire become a metaphor for oppression. The right she chose speaks of freedom from denial of basic human necessities or detainment by any army or armed faction.

Figure 6-2.1

Chris reminds her viewer that this scene occurs, and will continue to occur, because the "failure of empathy enables us to hurt one another." Her concept and her graphic articulation are the powerful tools she employs to express her own point of view and, we hope, to encourage others to act on the strengths of their own convictions against injustices they encounter in their lives, whatever they be.

Right 14: All people deserve the Right to be free from execution, torture, denial of basic human necessities, or detainment by any army or armed faction, the Right to be free from indiscriminate or long-lived weapons, including land mines and booby traps, the Right to be free from poisoned or contaminated food, water, air, and the Right to protest such actions without fear of persecution or retaliation.

Student Statement

Failure of empathy enables us to hurt one another. The idea was to encourage the experience of empathy by having the viewer engage in a basic human gesture of emotional acknowledgment as he meets the eyes of the oppressed.

Figure 6-2.2

Right 21: All people deserve the Right to express themselves freely, as long as that expression does not physically hurt others.

Student Statement

My initial concept was to show an individual bringing out exactly what would make him happy: to dress up in his bunny costume for work every day (hey, I've heard of these kinds of things). The idea was to interpret the human rights law: You should be able to express yourself freely, as long as you do not physically harm others.

Human Rights Poster: Right 21, *Nelson Couto,* Figure 6-2.2

Instructor's Evaluation

Nelson possesses considerable illustration skills and often finds visual solutions through this medium. Here his concept and skill set is a perfect match. Rather than take a heavy-handed or dramatic approach, he creates a whimsical and lighthearted celebration of our right of free expression in a democratic society. The scene is an urban setting with tall buildings in the background. This could be any city in America. The street is crowded with pedestrians. One of them is a businessman (he is carrying a black briefcase) dressed in a pink bunny suit. A few heads turn, bemused but unfazed.

Nelson's illustration would make a fabulous cover for the *New Yorker*. It doesn't need any copy to communicate the idea, and it is possibly best seen in close proximity, where the viewer can take in all nuances of expressions and the charming details you cannot see from a distance.

Human Rights Poster: Right 20, *Jennifer Lopardo,* Figure 6-2.3

Figure 6-2.3

Instructor's Evaluation

As the key to her visual interpretation of her right, Jennifer uses a pencil as a metaphor for communication. By binding her hands with rope, she graphically depicts the idea that even though she holds the means of communication (the pencil), she is not free to express herself.

Right 20: All people deserve the Right to form their own opinions, thoughts, and convictions, the Right to express those beliefs, even if those beliefs are considered offensive by others, and the Right to challenge and debate other's beliefs.

Student Statement

In my opinion, the most powerful messages are relayed through strong imagery. I wanted to use an image that had a direct relation to the human rights article, so that it could essentially exist without the text. This article is about the rights of free speech and the ability to express one's ideas and beliefs; therefore the pencil is used as a symbol for communication. The typeface used was chosen to represent handwriting and is placed in the corner of the poster to give more attention to the powerful image.

She employs contradiction to articulate her message—if you are bound, you are not free. Her right speaks of free speech and the ability to express one's ideas.

Her image does not need supporting copy. It can be read as a universal symbol for oppression. But since the assignment called for an integration of text and image, some work still needs to be done. The typeface she uses, although edgy and informal, and the shape of the text block in relationship to the image are weak. The text appears as an afterthought being relegated to the upper left corner of the composition. Jennifer could create a more powerful message if the words of the right could be read and if a visual relationship between the two elements was strengthened.

Human Rights Poster Right 15, *Anna Karin Reihm,* Figure 6-2.4

Instructor's Evaluation

Anna creates a poster that confronts the viewer with a graphic depiction of a consequence related to the right she chose: the right to be free of attack by weapons of mass destruction. The text shapes the missing limb of a man who represents a large population of innocent civilians seriously maimed by land mines left behind by retreating military forces.

Figure 6-2.4

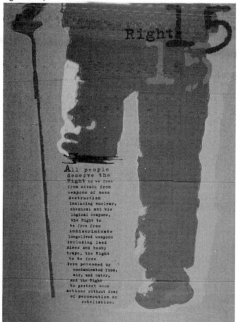

The missing limb is the focal point of the composition. The viewer's attention is drawn there. This is a masterful manipulation of the viewer, who is compelled to read the text to understand why the limb is missing. The message is then delivered and, we hope, processed into thought.

Anna's poster is an excellent example of how word and image integration can support and enhance the meaning of a message.

Right 15: All people deserve the Right to be free from attack weapons of mass destruction, including nuclear, chemical, and biological weapons, the Right to be free from indiscriminate or long-lived weapons, including land mines and booby traps, the Right to be free from poisoned or contaminated food, water, and air, and the Right to protest such actions without fear of persecution or retaliation.

Student Statement

My concept was to visually articulate the horror of mechanical means of continuing destruction, such as land mines and booby traps, left by military forces to injure and maim innocent civilians.

Designing Dissent: Advocacy Poster Series
Massachusetts College of Art, Instructor: Elizabeth Resnick

Assignment Brief

Merriam-Webster's Collegiate Dictionary defines the noun *dissent* as "difference of opinion" and *advocacy* as "the act or process of advocating or supporting a cause or proposal."

Your assignment is to develop a dissenting viewpoint on current political, economic, or cultural causes or issues present within the United States today. You will advocate for your position through a series of three posters that identify and assert your viewpoint to a select or general audience.

There has been a long history of visual propaganda, social protest, and political commentary in the mass media by political and social agitators and activists. Graphic designers, because of their visual training, possess the strategic tools to create memorable messages. They should be encouraged to take on responsibility and use these skills for community and activist purposes, not only to subvert the status quo but also to significantly contribute to public service organizations by conceiving and promoting their awareness campaigns for the good of the society at large.

The posters will be distributed through direct-mail campaigns to a general or specific audience and posted in area institutions, libraries, colleges, public offices, and public transportation and highway systems (billboards).

Objectives
– To provide the opportunity to express your point of view on a critical issue or cause
– To identify what angers you most about contemporary society and what you can do
– To articulate a message in the form of persuasion or information in a simple, straightforward manner to a general audience
– To unify a series of related messages through a visual language system, format, and structure

Specifications
1. Size: Determine the size of the posters by their usage.
2. Media: Any.
3. Color: If you need four-color to get your message across, then use it; otherwise think economically, in terms of one or two colors.
4. Copy: Determined by the cause or issue.

Process

Begin your design process by reading the following essays: "There Is Such a Thing as Society," by Andrew Howard;* "First Things First Manifesto 2000";** "First Things First: A Brief History," by Rick Poynor;** "Can Design Be Socially Responsible," by Michael Rock;* and "Countering the Tradition of the Apolitical Designer," by Katherine McCoy.* After you read each essay, reflect on the author's point of view and note the general thesis of each topic or argument for discussion in class.

Once you have completed the readings, you should feel sufficiently motivated to identify a cause, issue, or crisis where you can "use your voice" through mass-media techniques (the suggested form is a three-poster series). Your messages need to bring public awareness to the issue.

If a current cause, issue, or crisis does not come immediately to mind, consider the following: globalization and overconsumption (depletion of the world's resources), global warming and environmental issues, the AIDS crisis, health concerns (obesity, drugs, drinking), economics, war, and politics.

When you have identified a general issue or topic, pinpoint a specific aspect by brainstorming, using lists and thought maps to narrow down broad topics into smaller, more directed concepts. After you have completed this listing of ideas, begin your visualization by making thumbnail sketches.

Timeline

Week One

Read the essays, choose your issue or cause, and begin the design process by brainstorming and developing thumbnail sketches on possible concept directions. Choose two idea directions to work into half-size rough layouts for critique. Bring your thumbnail sketches and your essay notes to class.

Week Two

Based on the feedback you received in critique, focus on one concept and develop each of the three posters into full-size rough color layouts for class critique.

Week Three

Based on the feedback you received, rework or revise the poster layouts into finished comprehensives and bring to class for critique.

---

* Michael Bierut et al., eds., *Looking Closer 2: Critical Writings on Graphic Design*, Allworth Press, 1997.
** Michael Bierut et al., eds., *Looking Closer 4: Critical Writings on Graphic Design*, Allworth Press, 2002.

Figure 6-3.1

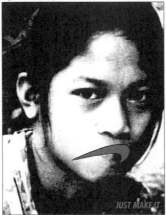

Student Statement

Nike: *The goal of this poster is to suggest that buying Nike products is essentially supporting child labor, poor working conditions, and human rights abuses in third world countries. Nike's shoes are manufactured in Indonesia, a country notorious for human rights abuses and poor working conditions. The entry-level wage for Indonesian girls and young women who sew shoes is about $2.00 a day. The young Indonesian girl pictured makes eye contact with the viewer and provokes an uneasy connection between the person and the product she helps to make.*

Starbucks: *Every city and town has the same stores, the same fast-food places, and the same coffee shops, and there is no longer any distinction between one city and town and all the others—we have become a homogenized society. Our choices as consumers narrow as corporate giants take over small businesses. As citizens and as consumers, we need to just say no to these corporate monopolies.*

McDonald's: *Large global corporations such as McDonald's may provide the world with quick, easy, and cheap meals, but they also cause immense cruelty to animals. The animals that are raised to provide meat for McDonald's hamburgers are kept in congested, filthy environments where overcrowding causes disease, suffocation, and heart attacks. The image that I used for this poster may be considered very disturbing, but my intention is to provoke feelings of rage and disgust with corporations such as McDonald's.*

Critiques
Anticorporate Poster, *Jennifer Lopardo,*
Figure 6-3.1
Instructor's Evaluation
Jennifer did extensive research on the antiglobalization movement. Besides the essays assigned, she read both Kalle Lasn's *Culture Jam** and Naomi Klein's *No Logo*** and supplemented this with visits to the *Adbusters* Web site (www.adbusters.org) and other activist-oriented Web sites.

Jennifer is as inspired by the ideas introduced by Lasn and Klein—that the ubiquity and power of brand advertising, especially in globally active corporations, curtail consumer choice by displacing local businesses and enforcing a bland homogeneity upon cities and towns—as she is disgusted by the notion that companies such as Nike, McDonald's, and Starbucks enrich themselves through sweatshop abuses, animal abuse, and carnivorous takeover business practices.

Nike: In her poster to protest Nike's use of cheap labor from third world countries, Jennifer pictures a young Indonesian girl who stares warily out at her viewer. Her lips are replaced by a grimacing, downturned Nike swoosh logo. The copy encourages her to "Just make it"—just make the shoes and accept the conditions.

Starbucks: Conceptually this is the least successful of the series because it lacks a big visual idea to put the message across. Jennifer's use of the word *monopolize* and the Starbucks logo with a coffee-ring-inspired international symbol for "no" convey that this corporate monopoly needs to be stopped. She wants us to stop patronizing Starbucks, but she doesn't offer the viewer a good reason why.

* Kalle Lasn, *Culture Jam: How to Reverse America's Suicidal Consumer Binge—And Why We Must*, Quill, 2000.
** Naomi Klein, *No Logo: Taking Aim at Brand Bullies*, Picador USA, 2000.

Figure 6-3.2

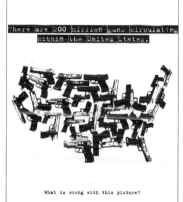

McDonald's: Much of McDonald's advertising centers on enticing viewers with visually enhanced hamburger products. Jennifer's concept is to subvert McDonald's advertising strategy by showing a skinned calf ready for slaughter with the copy line "Mmm (yummy)." Contrary to the usual appetite enhancement of food advertising, this poster encourages viewers to lose their appetite. It is an excellent example of using a contradiction to get the message across dramatically. Could you ever eat a McDonald's hamburger again without this image popping up in your mind?

Gun Control, *Martin O'Loughlin*, Figure 6-3.2

Instructor's Evaluation

The tragedy at Colorado's Columbine High School had a dramatic effect on Martin. Every day our newspapers detail the tragic loss of life from handguns. Martin chose to advocate for gun control in the United States through a series of posters designed to provoke disgust and spur action.

Caution tape: Martin employs the visual language associated with yellow caution tape to convey his text message: "This country has watched the loopholes in gun control become bullet holes. Stop the violence." Blurred in the background is yet another black body bag being carried away from yet another anonymous crime scene. It doesn't matter which one—don't they all look the same?

Two hundred million guns: A handgun possesses a very distinctive shape. In his poster, Martin employs a multitude of different types and sizes of guns to form the shape of the United States. His copy states, "There are 200 million guns circulating within the United States." This startling statistic is reinforced with a simple visual depiction and supported by the follow-up statement asking the viewer, "What is wrong with this picture?"

Student Statement

My poster series project advocates for gun control in the United States.

Caution tape: I used a picture from the Columbine aftermath to show people that anyone can purchase a gun illegally. I find this fact as horrifying as the Columbine shooting and want my viewers to understand that there are very serious loopholes in the gun control laws, which need to be amended.

Two hundred million guns: Every state in the United States has a gun problem. Shootings happen every day, and it's because there are over two hundred million guns in circulation.

Crayons: The broken crayons represent the more than three hundred children under the age of ten who die from gunshot wounds each year in the United States.

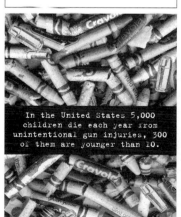

There is no room for debate in this graphically explicit poster—there are just too many handguns in the United States.

Crayons: "In the United States 5,000 children die each year from unintentional gun injuries, 300 of them are younger than 10." Here Martin employs the metaphor of broken crayons to evoke the loss of children's lives to violence. The metaphor is further enhanced by the choice of black and white over color. When crayons have no color, they are lifeless, like the dead children. Conceptually and visually, this is the most powerful poster of this series because it makes such a strong visual statement and offers a poignant reason why there should be stricter restrictions on handgun possession.

Turn Off TV Week, *Emily Ortmans,* Figure 6-3.3

Instructor's Evaluation

Also inspired by reading *Adbusters* and researching its Web site, Emily turned her attention to promoting the benefits of "Turn Off TV Week," an *Adbusters* campaign to get people to not watch TV for one week in April. Emily feels that "Americans watch far too much television."

Her concept involved the design of three subway posters presenting statistical data about the ill effects of television and commercials on children. This, she figured, would force her captive subway viewers to consider how bad TV is for children.

It was easy for her to choose three relevant statistics among the hundreds of terrifying statistics she encountered, but what she most struggled with was how she would visually represent this information. Her early sketches explored the use of images to illustrate the information. But, for the most part, the images lessened the impact of the words. Suggesting to Emily that her content was the message and did not need any window dressing to make it palpable, I encouraged her to present the statistics in a direct and straightforward typographical manner. This idea went over like a lead balloon. "What do you mean, no graphics?" she countered. The idea of text with no images does not appeal to graphic design students in general. After much spirited back-and-forth discussion, the idea of presenting the statistics on a television screen came up. Here was the right visual context, and Emily designed three strong, cohesive posters that she posted at midnight in a subway car to complete the "jamming" experience (see photo).

Figure 6-3.3

Number of ads aired for "junk food" during four hours of Saturday morning cartoons:

202

Percentage of American children ages 6 to 11 who are seriously overweight:

17%

Average number of hours per week that American one-year old children watch television:

6

Number of hours per week recommended by the American Pediatric Association for children two and under: **zero**

Number of violent acts the average American child sees on TV by age 18:

200,000

Percentage of youth violence directly attributable to TV viewing:

10%

Student Statement

I have come to the conclusion that Americans watch far too much television. To get my message out, I designed a set of three subway posters promoting "Turn Off the TV Week." My concept was to post mind-numbing statistics about children and television, in hopes that parents will unplug their children from TV and encourage them to do something creative or educational with their minds.

People complain that their kids are too violent or they aren't doing well in school, and what do they blame? Television. They should be blaming themselves for letting their children sit in front of the TV for hours at a time!

Project Poster Statistics

1. Average number of hours per week that American one-year-old children watch television: 6
   Number of hours per week recommended by the American Pediatric Association for children two and under: 0

2. Number of ads aired for junk food during four hours of Saturday morning cartoons: 202
   Percentage of American children 6–11 who are seriously overweight: 17%

3. Number of violent acts the average American child sees on TV by age 18: 200,000
   Percentage of youth violence directly attributable to TV viewing: 10%

Happy Deutschland
Fachhochschule Augsburg, Germany, Instructor: Jürgen Hefele

Assignment Brief
Anyone returning to Germany after holidaying abroad or visiting Germany for the first time is struck by the same scene: streets that seem empty and people that are in desperate need of cheering up. What is wrong with Germans? Why are they so serious? Why does everything have to be so perfect? Is this a fair picture of Germany or just a preconception? Can designers do anything to promote a more easygoing Germany?

Design a series of posters that will add some cheer to everyday German life. Analyze the topic and develop your communication strategy using a conceptual problem-solving approach. Work on the project should be done in a team.

Objectives
– To encourage students to find intelligent solutions to a complex design problem
– To work on a project aimed at developing a conceptual communication strategy

Process
– Gather information
– Brainstorm
– Develop a concept
– Outline ideas
– Select the best idea to apply to the poster series
– Present your work

Critiques
While all the teams working on the project dealt with it successfully, some were better than others. The team gathered information on the subject (newspaper articles, personal experience, surveys, etc.) and discussed it together in a classroom environment. All the teams experienced initial difficulties with the brief and with developing a conceptual strategy. My own feeling was that the students had been expecting a more "realistic" project brief. Having failed to put enough thought into a proper communications aim and strategy, some of the teams got bogged down by the sheer number of ideas. Other teams experienced difficulties applying their ideas to a design that would work on posters. Having managed to develop their communications strategies during extensive discussions, however, the teams achieved some excellent and unusual design solutions.

Happy Deutschland, Design Team: *Karen Irmer, Christian Rother, Tina Strobel, Ludwig Uebele,* Figure 6-4.1

Instructor's Evaluation

The work presented here is from a team of four students and represents an accomplished and intelligent solution to the brief. The subject is communicated in an ironic way. Each with its own color code and designed to stick in the mind, these posters are clear and unmistakably part of a series. Famous Germans from history and art have been depicted in modern, everyday situations. The effect is to transform these famous personalities into everyday people and to force a smile at the thought of Albert Einstein in the bath. The headlines and text offer a contrast to the pictures. The ironic slant is reinforced by the low-tech typewriter typography, the use of adhesive tape for the collages and images discovered by the students. The teams managed to create individual posters and to avoid imitating current graphic design trends. Unusual designs, simple typography, and witty captions make this project a successful one.

Figure 6-4.1A

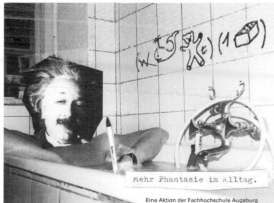

Albert Einstein
"For more imagination in everyday life"

Student Statement

The concept behind the series shows famous persons of German history in contemporary scenes of everyday life. Thus the painter Dürer might be washing dishes or Beethoven might be in a café reading the newspaper. Depicting these famous people (who are usually shown in a quiet, serious manner) in scenes from everyday life is humorous, and we feel closer to them for it. This series encourages the viewer to lighten up and not take things so seriously, thus enhancing the quality of our everyday life.

Albrecht Dürer
Top: "I hope nobody is painting me looking like this"
Below: "For more calmness in everyday life"

Figure 6-4.1B

Ludwig van Beethoven
"For more creativity in everyday life"

Anette von Droste Hülshoff
Top: "Berta, Anette and Amelie couldn't care less if Hermann B. is mowing the lawn again in the nude"
Below: "For a more easygoing everyday life"

Ludwig van Beethoven, Albert Einstein, Albrecht Dürer,
Anette von Droste Hülshoff
Top: "We can do it the other way also; we can be different also"
Below: "For more togetherness in daily life"

Three-dimensional Direct Response (Mail) Solicitation
Massachusetts College of Art, Instructor: Elizabeth Resnick
(assignment written by Elizabeth Resnick and Glenn Berger)

Assignment Brief

In today's society, it is important for graphic designers to balance the work they do for corporate and advertising sectors with work for nonprofit organizations. Why? Because graphic design is an art of purpose, and as such, it should be put to good use in support of groups whose ideals have meaning and purpose, whether they can afford design services or not.

There are many nonprofit organizations that have not been sufficiently addressed by mainstream media in our region of the country. Your assignment is to choose a nonprofit organization and create a design for a three-dimensional direct response solicitation to promote a better understanding of their mission and to ask for support from recipients.

Objectives

This piece may promote either a specific existing fund-raising event or an immediate current need, such as winter coats for the homeless. Your design will become the channel to engage recipients and to elicit some type of response from them that is measurable by the organization: How much money did they collect in support? How many volunteers signed up? How many people attended the event? How many families were assisted? How many coats were collected?

The specific nature of your assignment will be defined in part by the particular organization you choose as your client. Your choice of client will define your project's specific objective, its target audience, and to some degree the nature of your message.

It is important to choose an organization whose mission is something you feel strongly in favor of. Your personal involvement will make the learning process more exciting and stimulating.

This project involves a significant research component:
- Contacting the organization's local or national headquarters.
- Studying its current print material, annual reports, news clippings, and so on.
- Interviewing a representative from the organization in person, or by e-mail or telephone. Prepare your questions in advance and act in a professional manner.
- Interviewing a member or segment of the constituency serviced by the nonprofit if possible.

Specifications

The name of the organization and its current logo must be present. A headline and, possibly, subheads breaking up the copy should also be used in order to establish a logical hierarchy for the flow of information. Additionally, you should write several sentences of body copy that support the idea you are promoting. Your copy should elucidate the conceptual direction you are taking. If you are promoting a specific event (danceathon, fund-raising walk, performance, etc.), make sure you include all the critical information necessary: dates, location, directions, parking, access for the disabled, and RSVP if required by the organizers of the event.

Process

Do the research as stated above. Collect materials, save correspondence, and take notes. Brainstorm ideas for your concept by making lists and a thought map. Once a concept has been identified, write a design brief. It should include the following information:

1. Clarify the project's objective (what you want recipients to do). This is referred to as a *call for action.*
2. Summarize the key points you want to communicate (no more than three).
3. Briefly define the organization's mission (ask for the mission statement), its target audience (limit yourself to one demographic group), and its market position (ask who their competitors are).
4. Define the current goals or identity of the organization. What image does your client need to present in order to accomplish their goals? You need to consider how the organization wishes to be perceived or, after having spoken to the group's representatives, how you think they should be perceived. Are they on top of things? Relaxed and friendly? Accessible and approachable? What subliminal message do you want to convey? Write down a short list of adjectives describing the image you want to convey and another describing messages you wish to avoid.
5. Find a unique selling point: What makes this organization special or unique? Include any pertinent historical highlights that might help focus your thinking. However, you do not need to conform to your client's current graphic standards, especially if they are poorly designed!
6. Design considerations: What form and size will your direct mail be? What shape will it be? How much will your piece weigh? This will be sent through the mail. Therefore it is important that you factor in size and weight as you consider form. It's not that you can't send a brick through the mail, but do consider that at $10 (and that's just postage) the piece might be perceived as wasteful by a potential donor.

Nonetheless, if your audience consists of people such as Donald Trump, Ted Turner, or Bill Gates and you really think a brick would get their attention (and indeed into their hands), such a project could be justified.

Your brief should be concise—one or two pages are fine. The purpose is to provide information. It should also help you assess the assignment and, later on, critique your own proposed solution as to whether it answers the need stated in the brief.

Once your research is complete and the brief has been written, begin concept development and thumbnail sketches. Based on initial in-class critiques, revisit your concepts and design executions. The final step will be the actual execution of the form and the preparation for final presentation to the class.

Timeline
Week One

Start the design process by doing the research. Write and present your design brief to the class. Give your instructor a copy of the brief with any sketch ideas attached after your presentation.

Week Two

Once your instructor has approved your brief, conceptualize several ideas in sketch format and bring for class critique.

Week Three

Based on the feedback you received in critique, choose one direction and develop it into a working prototype.

Week Four

Based on the feedback you received on the working prototype, make the finished mock-up for final presentation.

Critiques
Community Healthlink, *Jaivin Anzalota,* Figure 6-5.1

Instructor's Evaluation

Jaivin is familiar with Community Healthlink (a nonprofit organization affiliated with University of Massachusetts Memorial Health Care, in Worcester) because his sister works for the organization. In these times of strenuous budget cutting

Figure 6-5.1

Student Statement

Most people have encountered a homeless person asking for spare change on the street. My concept in using a paper cup was to evoke an emotional response from the viewer to promote Community Healthlink, a nonprofit community-based provider of services for the homeless in central Massachusetts.

by state government agencies, the search for funding grows more urgent.

Jaivin cares about the plight of the homeless, and that shows in the quality of his thinking. He wants recipients of the funding plea to experience what it would be like to hold a "spare change" cup in their hands.

The plain brown cardboard box arrives in the mail. The copy on the box, printed in a plain black sans-serif typeface, reads: "Imagine if your next meal depended on..." The recipient opens the box and sees a message on the inside bottom of a white paper cup: "Whether or not you can fill this cup." The recipient lifts the cup out of the box. It is a plain white paper cup with a message printed on it in black type. The message reads: "Community Healthlink needs your help in order to continually support Worcester's citizens most in need." The copy continues with how the reader can help, and provides contact information. This is a straightforward, no-nonsense, and direct appeal for money. There is absolutely nothing superficial or decorative about its execution or presentation, which makes it an amazingly powerful visual and emotional experience. I am left in awe at the quality of this young man's thinking.

Massachusetts Citizens for Life, *Elizabeth Barnard,* Figure 6-5.2

Figure 6-5.2

Instructor's Evaluation

Elizabeth feels passionate about and committed to pro-life initiatives. For her project she focused on teenage girls who might want to become members and support the initiatives of the pro-life organization Massachusetts Citizens for Life. She felt she needed to project a fun concept that would appeal to this age group. Teenage girls love to adorn their bodies with brand logos and messages. Elizabeth thought of stick-on temporary tattoos as a way to identify support of the pro-life group. Two of the message tattoos are "Choose life" and "Former fetus."

Student Statement

My concept was to promote the pro-life organization Massachusetts Citizens for Life to teenagers. Although I had the basic inspiration of using stick-on tattoos as message holders and the copy "We need you to help our message stick," I struggled with form until my teacher suggested the notion of a disposable tape dispenser. It not only strengthened the pun, but also allowed me to organize all the information on an accordion-style card backing.

With her idea in place, Elizabeth struggled with how to connect her idea with the form the mailer would take. The notion of a disposable tape dispenser to "dispense" individual message tattoos was suggested during a class critique.

This would be great fun to receive in the mail. The typography has a hand-cut quality, and the feel of the project is playful with the possible exception of her color palette, which is caramel brown and light blue. I think the brown color could be replaced with something brighter. Otherwise, it is a very clever approach and appropriate to her specific audience.

Figure 6-5.3

Student Statement
When I first moved from California to Boston, one of the first things I noticed was the community gardens in the South End. When this assignment was given, I learned that there were more than two hundred gardens in need of community participation. Inspired by the expression "the tree of life," I first thought of a tree as the concept for my mailer, which then progressed to "the seeds of life." This led me to imagine a seed packet as the form for an invitation to attend the annual Open Garden Day, an event sponsored by Garden Futures, whose mission is to secure the long-term viability of all Boston-area community gardens.

Garden Futures, *Scarlett Bertand,* Figure 6-5.3

Instructor's Evaluation

Open Garden Day is a showcase of Boston-area community gardens, sponsored by Garden Futures, which teaches urban gardening and community garden management by sponsoring the City Gardener Certificate education program. This intensive eight-week course trains the "trainer" gardener, who then volunteers time to provide workshops and mentoring programs for community gardeners.

To publicize the event, Scarlett develops her concept around the metaphor of the "seeds of life," and the invitation itself takes the form of a seed packet filled with flower seeds to plant at the event. Scarlett targets women, who she believes will bring along their female friends, husbands, and children. Her intended recipient influences her feminine drawing of a tree illustration, with "many feminine shapes and curves to accentuate warmth; the curls of the branches wait to stretch and extend a connection to all the communities that attend."

It is very appropriate to keep the gardening theme for her outside mailer, which is a burlap bag and leaf-shaped labels for the address block. Everything from the illustration to the sensitive handling of the typography evokes Mother Nature's care.

Figure 6-5.4

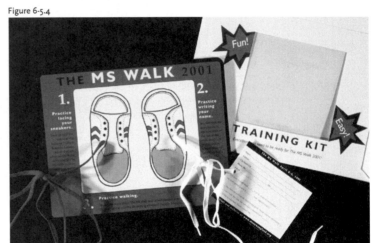

Student Statement
The annual MS Walk is an important fund-raiser for research into a cure for multiple sclerosis. My concept for an invitation to participate in the walk was based on a childhood craft toy, the sewing card. The idea was to provide a training kit to lace up your walking shoes to prepare for the upcoming event.

MS Walk, *Meghan Reilly*, Figure 6-5.4

Instructor's Evaluation

Meghan travels down a nostalgic route to remember the toy sewing cards of her youth. She likes the idea of converting the entry form materials into a manipulable toy object to evoke a fun celebration for the annual fund-raiser for multiple sclerosis, the MS Walk.

Her bright red, black, and white packaging, with a large cellophane window, reveals the shoelace sewing cards. I can't imagine this package going to the trash bin unopened. Together with her informal style of illustration, sans-serif typeface, and clear visual hierarchy in her layout, this is a strong visual concept accessible to a general audience.

MSPCA, *Kristina Rivers*, Figure 6-5.5

Instructor's Evaluation

Of the many programs and activities the MSPCA organizes, Kristina chooses to focus on one of their outreach programs, bringing volunteers and their pets to nursing homes. Animals cannot live in nursing homes with their residents. It is sad to think that many elderly people who move to nursing homes have to leave

Figure 6-5.5

their pets behind with family members or give them away. By bringing pets to visit in a nursing home, it offers the residents an opportunity to give and receive the affection of a pet.

Kristina's concept was to inspire volunteering for this program through the visual form of a memory book. Using photos of the elderly enjoying the company of animals, she felt the potential volunteers would also see the experience as a significant one in their lives as well.

Tolerance Bus Shelter Poster

Philadelphia University, Instructor: Frank Baseman

Assignment Brief

The assignment is to design a bus shelter poster using the theme of tolerance. We encouraged a diversity of expression and opinion. This project was a student poster design competition administered by the Philadelphia chapter of the American Institute of Graphic Arts during the spring semester 2002. The project was open to any student studying graphic design, illustration, or photography in the area served by the chapter. Bus shelters were chosen as a medium because of their accessibility to the general public. Student designs were done at one-quarter scale and entered into the competition, where they were judged by a panel of professional graphic designers. The top ten student poster designs were produced as full-size bus shelter posters and displayed on the streets of Philadelphia.

Objectives

Design a bus shelter poster using the theme of tolerance and submit a full-color comp to the student poster competition. This is a conceptually driven, idea-based project.

Specifications

1. Size: $11\frac{7}{8}$" × $17\frac{1}{8}$"
2. Color: Full color, no limitations.
3. Outcome: Full-size color output, inkjet or fiery, mounted on black board.
4. Copy: Students are not required to use any copy on their poster, although they may use whatever copy they would like.
5. Logo bar: Each designer must use the tolerance logo bar at the bottom of the poster. The typographic elements of this logo bar may not be altered in any way, but students are encouraged to adjust the coloration to complement your design. Students must update the credit information with their name and name of school. The electronic version of this logo bar, in the form of an EPS file, was supplied to a representative of each of the participating schools.

Process

The events of September 11, 2001, touched each and every one of us in deep and profound ways. Perhaps the best way to begin this project is to try to put down in words and/or sketches what our feelings are about these events. Tolerance is a very personal thing, with each of us having our own degree of tolerance. What does tolerance mean to you? What does intolerance mean? Beyond your own soul-searching and reaching for ideas, remember that these posters will be displayed on the streets, in full public view. Is there something about your design that could take advantage of this positioning, either by proximity or by scale?

Keep in mind that a poster design should have some impact and that the viewer may just look at it for just a few seconds. For these reasons, it is advisable to keep your ideas and designs simple and clear.

Timeline

Week One

What does tolerance mean? Even if you think you know, referring to a dictionary and looking up the proper definition could help. How can you possibly convey your thoughts and feelings in a poster design? Based on some of the ideas that you are starting to come up with, is there any research that you might have to do to reinforce an idea? Do a minimum of twenty thumbnail sketches for your tolerance poster. These should be done in pencil, pen, and/or markers before you begin to work on the computer. Make your thumbnail sketches clearly understandable, crisp, and detailed. Do not work on the computer until your thumbnail sketches have been approved for direction. Bring these thumbnail sketches to class for critique.

Week Two

Based on the feedback you received in the last classroom critique, choose two of your idea sketches and develop them further to laser-print sketches printing out at half size. Make variations on a theme if necessary by adjusting the same idea slightly, and then redo by changing something else. Make sure to use the tolerance logo bar at the bottom of your poster designs and update the credit information accordingly. Continue to refine your sketches until you are satisfied that you have some strong results, and bring all of your work to class for critique.

Week Three

Based on the feedback you received in the last classroom critique, continue to refine your laser-print sketches. Make adjustments to your designs, keep refining your ideas, and print out at full size so you can check your work. Print out in color so you can check your colors. Make refinements to the tolerance logo bar if necessary, including adjusting the color to complement your design. Bring all of your work, including your earlier sketches, to class for critique.

Week Four

Based on the feedback you received in the last classroom critique, it's time to go to a finish on your chosen design direction. You may still make further design refinements, adjusting minute details of your design and perfecting it. Once you are pleased with your final design, make sure to load up all of your files (working document, all graphics, all fonts used) and collect for output. Make sure to take along a clean, accurate laser print of your design. Go to a service bureau and request full-size color output, inkjet or fiery, for your tolerance poster, and mount to black board per specifications.

Figure 6-6.1

Student Statement

Tolerance is conveyed and felt through words. Are words just words, or do they mean something different to everyone? This poster asks that same question: "What do these words mean to you?" or, more importantly, "What do they mean to those who hear them?"

Critiques

Tolerance Bus Shelter Poster, *Stephen DeWitt,* Figure 6-6.1

Instructor's Evaluation

Stephen DeWitt's solution to the project was one of the bravest, in the sense that Stephen was willing to use the hateful, vicious words that people will often think about other people—even say to other people—as a large part of his conceptual basis. Stephen created a very effective typographic pattern of hate words: clearly derogatory, awful, vile words. On a technical level, Stephen used an overall black background with the words set in a version of Garamond, in all caps, floating and hovering, all tinted in different shades of gray, so as to be there but almost not be there. But of course they are there, and we can read them. I find it disturbing to read them, but this is his point, isn't it? He then poses the simple question "Just words?" set in the same Garamond, all lowercase, but this time dropping out to white so we don't miss it for a minute. Are these words just words? Or, as I suspect, does the designer want us to think about the fact that they are much more than that?

Tolerance Bus Shelter Poster, *Garrett Jones,* Figure 6-6.2

Instructor's Evaluation

The strength of Garrett Jones' project is the use of language, which to me is interesting because he uses a striking full-color photograph (his own photography), full bleed and with plenty of impact. But what grabs me (and I take it this was Garrett's intent) is not so much the visual message but the verbal one. Handwritten words cover practically every inch of the young woman in the photograph: racial slurs such as dink, chink, nook, rice picker, slant eyes, gook, and so on, which have an enormous impact and are, unfortunately, words that we may have heard before to describe an Asian-American person. Garrett takes this idea one step further, cementing his concept by using the copy line "I believe the term is Asian-American." He wisely set this type in a small-size serif font, centered in a sea of black space above the woman's

Figure 6-6.2

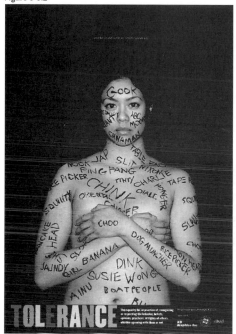

Student Statement

My concept for this project was to express the idea of tolerance by juxtaposing its antonym in the face of the viewer. My hope is that the viewer won't be able to avoid the realization of bigotry that some people are forced to endure on a daily basis.

head, to contrast with the impact of the photograph, making this, in my opinion, a very effective solution. Garrett's poster was selected as a second-place winner in the student poster design competition.

Tolerance Bus Shelter Poster, *David Reed Monroe,*
Figure 6-6.3

Instructor's Evaluation

In his project David Reed Monroe looked at the word tolerance and tried to figure out what other words could come out of this one word. He intelligently saw that one could find the word *learn* within, and better yet the phrase "to learn." But this is only part of the way to a strong solution; a designer still has to do something with this. What David did was wonderful. Beginning with the idea of learning, David first set the scene well by choosing to use a blackboard as his backdrop. Then, using a projector to project the type onto a real blackboard, he took his own photograph of the scene. Further enhancing his already strong foundation, David worked on the image in Photoshop to create a dramatic lighting effect, to create shadows, and to enhance the typographic and color treatments of his poster. Lastly, he added the clever copy line "Erase your ignorance" in small type just above the blackboard eraser at the bottom of his poster, for what is overall a very strong solution. David's poster was selected as a finalist in the student poster design competition and was produced as a full-size bus shelter poster.

Figure 6-6.3

Student Statement

My poster developed entirely from my initial design query: "What I can spell from the letters t o l e r a n c e ?" Immediately the word learn jumped out at me from the characters, perfectly preceded by the word to. From then on, the poster practically finished itself, as the classroom blackboard and hand-chalked type (created using an overhead projector) were photographed and composed in Photoshop.

Tolerance Bus Shelter Poster, *Heather Robertson,* Figure 6-6.4

Instructor's Evaluation

Conceptually, Heather Robertson's solution to the project is subtle—at first. But when you put the whole package together, her solution hits you like a ton of bricks. Utilizing effective research at the outset of the project, Heather came across an interesting statistic regarding the number of hate crimes committed in the city of Philadelphia. She found that fifty-four people in Philadelphia fell victim to hate crimes in 2000 because of their race, religion, or sexual orientation. Heather then asks, "Are we really the City of Brotherly Love?" She effectively created an overall pattern of alternating graphic men and women (the figures bleed off the edges of the page, making it seem as though they go on forever). But the beautiful part of her solution lies in the center of the poster, where she has cleverly ghosted back exactly fifty-four of the figures to give the viewer the sense of the number of victims. The type is handled in a delicate, tasteful, and straightforward way, and because of its position on the poster it is inviting to read. The use of the gray color in the logo bar at the bottom of the poster complements her overall design and harks back to the grayed-back figures that are such an important part of her solution.

Tolerance Bus Shelter Poster, *Colleen Tomlinson,* Figure 6-6.5

Instructor's Evaluation

The strength of Colleen Tomlinson's poster is its sheer simplicity: a black-and-white image of a shadow cast on what looks like blacktop. And then in the dark of the shadow, set in aggressively small serif type, is the copy line "A shadow knows no color." Colleen seems to be telling us that, just as we shouldn't judge a book by its cover, we shouldn't judge others by the color of their skin. What a powerful message, presented with such efficiency. There aren't too many bells and whistles with this one—just a strong visual and a clever line to bring home the concept.

Figure 6-6.4

Student Statement
After contemplating and researching the notion of tolerance, I decided to focus on hate crimes. By patterning the figures across the entire poster, I created a sense of the city's population. In the center, fifty-four figures are ghosted back to parallel the hate crime statistic. Finally, a simple question was added to quantify the poster.

Figure 6-6.5

Using her own photography, Colleen photographed many variations of shadows cast on different kinds of surfaces and at many different angles. In the end she chose to use black-and-white photography in a composition where the shadow comes in from the right edge off the page and continues across the surface at an angle to the left. The figure is (wisely) nondescript: It could be anyone, which is precisely the idea. The shadow does represent everyone, as everyone has a shadow. And one thing about a shadow is that it "knows no color." Colleen's poster was selected as a finalist in the student poster design competition and was produced as a full-size bus shelter poster.

Student Statement

The first things that occurred to me when challenged to create a poster regarding tolerance were racial and cultural differences, and the human similarities that unite us all. I thought that one way to portray this would be by using shadows, because everyone's shadow is basically the same. "A shadow knows no color" shows the similarities in us all. You can't tell much about a person from their shadow—except that they are a human being.

BIBLIOGRAPHY

I am a passionate consumer of graphic design and typography books. I began my collection thirty-five years ago, when I purchased Armin Hofmann's *Graphic Design Manual;* Alan Fletcher, Colin Forbes, and Bob Gill's *Graphic Design: Visual Comparisons;* and Joseph Albers's *Interaction of Color* at the Rhode Island School of Design bookstore my sophomore year. The following bibliography includes the books that were consulted in the writing of my introductory texts and assignments briefs, and a small fraction of the seminal design texts and monographs that have been influential to me throughout my career as a designer and educator.

Basic Design and Color

Albers, Josef. *Interaction of Color.* New Haven: Yale University Press, 1963.

Berger, Arthur Asa. *Seeing Is Believing: An Introduction to Visual Communication,* 2nd edition. Mountain View, Cal.: Mayfield Publishing Company, 1998.

Bowers, John. *Introduction to Two-Dimensional Design: Understanding Form and Function.* New York: John Wiley & Sons, 1999.

Cheatham, Frank R., Jane Hart Cheatham, and Sheryl Hater Owens. *Design Concepts and Applications.* Englewood Cliffs, N.J.: Prentice Hall, 1983.

De Sausmarez, Maurice. *Basic Design: The Dynamics of Visual Form.* London and New York, Studio Vista and Van Nostrand Reinhold Company, 1974.

Dondis, Donis. *A Primer of Visual Literacy.* Cambridge, Mass.: MIT Press, 1973.

Eiseman, Leatrice. *Pantone Guide to Communicating with Color.* Sarasota, Florida: The Grafix Press, 2000.

Elam, Kimberly. *Geometry of Design: Studies in Proportion and Composition.* New York: Princeton Architectural Press, 2001.

Gerstner, Karl. *The Forms of Color: The Interaction of Visual Elements.* Cambridge, Mass. and London, England: The MIT Press, 1986.

Graham, Lisa. *Basics of Design: Layout and Typography for Beginners*. Albany: Delmar Thompson Learning, 2002.

Itten, Johannes. *The Art of Color*. New York: Van Nostrand Reinhold, 1970.

———. *Design and Form*. New York: Van Nostrand Reinhold, 1975.

———. *The Color Star*. New York: John Wiley & Sons, Inc., 1986.

Kepes, Gyorgy. *Language of Vision*. Chicago: Paul Theobald, 1944.

Lauer, David A., and Stephen Pentak. *Design Basics*, 5th edition. Orlando: Harcourt, Brace & Company, 2000.

Lupton, Ellen, and J. Abbott Miller. *The ABC's of The Bauhaus: The Bauhaus and Design Theory*. New York: Princeton Architectural Press, 2000.

Maier, Manfred. *Basic Principles of Design*. New York: Van Nostrand Reinhold, 1980.

Martinez, Benjamin, and Jacqueline Block. *Visual Forces: An Introduction to Design*, 2nd edition. Upper Saddle River, N.J.: Prentice Hall, Inc., 1995.

Moholy-Nagy, Laslo. *Vision in Motion*. Chicago: Paul Theobald, 1947.

Oei, Loan, and Cecile De Kegel. *The Elements of Design: Rediscovering Colors, Textures, Forms and Shapes*. New York: Thames & Hudson, 2002.

Peterson, Bryan L. *Using Design Basics to Get Creative Results*. Cincinnati: North Light Books, 1996.

Siebert, Lori, and Lisa Ballard. *Making a Good Layout*. Cincinnati: North Light Books, 1992.

Stewart, Mary. *Launching the Imagination: A Comprehensive Guide to Basic Design*. New York: McGraw-Hill, 2002.

Wallschlaeger, Charles, and Cynthia Busic-Snyder. *Basic Visual Concepts and Principles for Artists, Architects and Designers*. Dubuque: William C. Brown, 1992.

Wheeler, Susan, and Gary Wheeler. *The Visual Design Primer*. Upper Saddle River, N.J.: Prentice Hall, 2002.

Wingler, Hans M. *The Bauhaus*. Cambridge, Mass.: MIT Press, 1986.

Wong, Wucius. *Principles of Form and Design*. New York: Van Nostrand Reinhold, 1993.

———. *Principles of Two-Dimensional Design*. New York: Van Nostrand Reinhold, 1972.

———. *Principles of Color Design*, 2nd edition. New York: John Wiley & Sons, 1997.

Wong, Wucius, and Benjamin Wong. *Visual Design on the Computer*, Second Edition. New York and London: W.W. Norton and Company, 2001.

Zelanski, Paul, and Mary Pat Fisher. *Design Principles and Problems*, 2nd edition. Orlando: Harcourt Brace & Company, 1996.

———. *The Art of Seeing*, Fifth Edition. Upper Saddle River, N.J.: Prentice-Hall, 2002.

Graphic Design and Typography

Aldersey-Williams, Hugh, et al. *Cranbrook Design: The New Discourse*. New York: Rizzoli, 1990.

Ades, Dawn, et al. *The 20th Century Poster: Art of the Avant Garde*. New York: Abbeville, 1984.

Baines, Phil, and Andrew Haslam. *Type and Typography*. New York: Watson-Guptill, 2002.

Andrews, Richard, and Kalinovska, Milena. *Art into Life: Russian Constructivism, 1914–1932*. New York: Rizzoli International Publications, 1990.

Arntson, Amy E. *Graphic Design Basics*, 3rd editon. Orlando: Harcourt Brace College Publishers, 1998.

Blackwell, Lewis, and David Carson. *The End of Print: The Graphic Design of David Carson*. San Francisco: Chronicle Books, 1995.

Blackwell, Lewis, and Lorraine Wild. *Edward Fella: Letters on America*. New York: Princeton Architectural Press, 2000.

Bringhurst, Robert. *The Elements of Typographic Style*, version 2.4. Vancouver, BC: Hartley & Marks, 2001.

Burns, Aaron. *Typography*. New York: Reinhold Publishing, 1961.

Carter, Rob, Ben Day, and Philip B. Meggs. *Typographic Design: Form and Communication*, 3rd edition. Hoboken: John Wiley & Sons, 2002.

Clair, Kate. *A Typographic Workbook: A Primer to History, Techniques, and Artistry*. New York: John Wiley & Sons, 1999.

Craig, James. *Designing with Type: A Basic Course in Typography*, Fourth Edition. New York: Watson-Guptill Publications, 1999.

Dickerson, Leah, editor. *Building the Collective: Soviet Graphic Design, 1917–1937: Selections from the Merrill C. Berman Collection.* New York: Princeton Architectural Press, 1996.

Dowding, Geoffrey. *Finer Points in Spacing & Arrangement of Type.* Vancouver, BC: Hartley & Marks Publishers, 1995.

Elam, Kimberly. *Expressive Typography.* New York: Van Nostrand Reinhold, 1990.

Evans, Donald. *John Heartfield, AIZ: Arbeiter-Illustriete Zeitung, 1930–1938.* New York: Kent Fine Art, 1992.

Felici, James. *The Complete Manual of Typography: A Guide to Setting Perfect Type.* Berkeley, Cal.: Adobe Press, 2003.

Fletcher, Alan, Colin Forbes, and Bob Gill. *Graphic Design: Visual Comparisons.* London: Studio Vista, 1966.

Friedman, Dan. *Dan Friedman: Radical Modernism.* New Haven: Yale University Press, 1994.

Friedman, Mildred, editor. *Graphic Design in America: A Visual Language History.* Minneapolis, Minn. and New York: Walker Art Center and Harry N. Abrams, Inc., 1989.

Gerstner, Karl. *Compendium for Literates: A System of Writing.* Cambridge, Mass. and London, England: The MIT Press, 1974.

Gill, Bob. *Graphic Design Made Difficult.* New York: Van Nostrand Reinhold, 1992.

Gottschall, Edward, M. *Typographic Communications Today.* Cambridge, Mass.: MIT Press, 1989.

Glaser, Milton. *Milton Glaser Graphic Design.* Woodstock, N.Y.: Overlook Press, 1972.

———. *Art Is Work.* Woodstock, N.Y.: Overlook Press, 2000.

Grear, Malcolm. *Inside/Outside: From the Basics to the Practice of Design.* New York: Van Nostrand Reinhold, 1993.

Greiman, April. *Hybrid Imagery: The Fusion of Technology and Graphic Design.* New York: Watson-Guptill, 1990.

Grundberg, Andy. *Alexey Brodovitch.* New York: Harry N. Abrams, 1989.

Hall, Peter, and Michael Bierut, editors. *Tibor Kalman: Perverse Optimist.* New York: Princeton Architectural Press, 2000.

Heller, Steven. *Paul Rand*. London: Phaidon Press, Ltd., 1999.

Heller, Steven, and Seymour Chwast. *Graphic Style: From Victorian to Post-Modern*. New York: Harry N. Abrams, 1988.

Heller, Steven, and Louise Fili. *Typology: Type Design from the Victorian Era to the Digital Age*. San Francisco: Chronicle Books, 1999.

Hidy, Lance. *Lance Hidy's Posters*. Natick, Mass.: The Alphabet Press, 1983.

Hiebert, Kenneth J. *Graphic Design Processes: Universal to Unique*. New York: Van Nostrand Reinhold, 1992.

Hinrichs, Kit, and Delphine Hirasuna. *Typewise*. Cincinnati: North Light Books, 1990.

Hofmann, Armin. *Graphic Design Manual: Principles and Practice*. New York: Van Nostrand Reinhold, 1965.

———. *Armin Hofmann: His Work, Quest, and Philosophy*. Basel and Boston: Birkhauser Verlag, 1989.

Hollis, Richard. *Graphic Design: A Concise History*. New York and London: Thames and Hudson, 1994.

Holmes, Nigel. *Designing Pictorial Symbols*. New York: Watson-Guptill Publishers, 1985.

Hurlburt, Allen. *Publication Design*, revised edition. New York: Van Nostrand Reinhold, 1976.

———. *The Design Concept: A Guide to Effective Graphic Communication*. New York: Watson-Guptill, 1981.

Johansson, Kaj, Peter Lundberg, and Robert Ryberg. *A Guide to Graphic Print Production*. Hoboken, N.J.: John Wiley & Sons, Inc., 2003.

Jute, André. *Grids: The Structure of Graphic Design*. Mies, Switzerland: Rotovision, 1996.

Kane, John. *A Type Primer*. Upper Saddle River, N.J.: Prentice-Hall, 2002.

Kince, Eli. *Visual Puns in Design*. New York: Watson-Guptill, 1982.

Kubasiewicz, Jan, and Elizabeth Resnick. *The Art of the Poster: Makoto Saito*. Boston: Massachusetts College of Art, 1999.

Kunz, Willi. *Typography: Macro- + Micro-Aesthetics: Fundamentals of Typographic Design*. Sulgen, Switzerland: Verlag Niggli AG, 1998.

Landa, Robin. *Graphic Design Solutions*, 2nd edition. Albany: Delmar Thompson Learning, 2001.

———. *Thinking Creatively: New Ways to Unlock Visual Imagination*. Cincinnati: North Light, 1998.

Lavin, Maud. *Cut with the Kitchen Knife: The Weimar Photomontages of Hannah Höch*. New Haven and London: Yale University Press, 1993.

LeCoultre, Martijn F., and Alston W. Purvis. *A Century of Posters*. London: Lund Humphries Publishers, Ltd., 2002.

Lissitzky, El. *El Lissitzky: Architect, Painter, Photographer, Typographer*. Einhoven, N.L.: Stedelijk Van Abbemuseum, 1990.

Maeda, John, and Nicholas Negroponte. *Maeda@Media*. New York: Rizzoli, 2000.

Mau, Bruce. *Life Style*. New York: Phaidon Publishers, 2001.

McLean, Ruari. *Jan Tschichold: Typographer*. London: Lund Humphries, 1975.

McQuiston, Liz. *Graphic Agitation: Social and Political Graphics Since the Sixties*. London: Phaidon Press, Ltd., 1995.

Meggs, Philip B. *Type and Image: The Language of Graphic Design*. New York: Van Nostrand Reinhold, 1989.

———. *A History of Graphic Design*, 3rd edition. New York: John Wiley & Sons, 1998.

Mollerup, Per. *Marks of Excellence: The History and Taxonomy of Trademarks*. London: Phaidon Publishers, 1997.

Müller-Brockmann, Josef, and Shizuko Müller-Brockmann. *History of the Poster*. Zürich: ABC Verlag Zürich, 1971.

Müller, Lars, editor. *Josef Müller-Brockmann, Designer: A Pioneer of Swiss Graphic Design*. Baden: Verlag Lars Müller, 1995.

Noordzij, Gerrit. *Letterletter*. Vancouver, BC: Hartley & Marks Publishers, 2000.

Oldach, Mark. *Creativity for Graphic Designers*. Cincinnati: North Light Books, 1995.

Paret, Peter, Beth Irwin Lewis, and Paul Paret. *Persuasive Images: Posters of War and Revolution*. Princeton: Princeton University Press, 1992.

Poynor, Rick, and Edward Booth-Clibborn. *Typography Now: The Next Wave*. London: Internos Books, 1991.

Poynor, Rick. *The Graphic Edge*. London: Booth-Clibborn Editions, 1993.

Purvis, Alston. *Dutch Graphic Design: 1918–1945*. New York: Van Nostrand Reinhold, 1992.

Rand, Paul. *Thoughts on Design*. London: Studio Vista, 1970.

———. *A Designer's Art*. New Haven and London: Yale University Press, 1985.

———. *Design Form and Chaos*. New Haven and London: Yale University Press, 1993.

———. *From Lascaux to Brooklyn*. New Haven and London: Yale University Press, 1996.

Re, Margaret. *Typographically Speaking: The Art of Matthew Carter*. Baltimore, Md.: Albin O. Kuhn Library and Gallery, 2002.

Resnick, Elizabeth. *Graphic Design: A Problem-Solving Approach to Visual Communication*. Englewood Cliffs N.J.: Prentice Hall, 1984.

Ruder, Emil. *Typography: A Manual of Design*. Teufen AR, Switzerland: Verlag Arthur Niggli, 1967.

Scotford, Martha. *Cipe Pineles: A Life of Design*. New Haven and London: Yale University Press 1998.

Snyder, Gertrude, and Alan Peckolick. *Herb Lubalin: Art Director, Graphic Designer, and Typographer*. New York: American Showcase, 1985.

Spencer, Herbert. *Pioneers of Modern Typography*, revised edition. Cambridge, Mass.: MIT Press, 1985.

———, editor. *The Liberated Page*. San Francisco: Bedford Press, 1987.

Spiekermann, Erik, and E. M. Ginger. *Stop Stealing Sheep and Find Out How Type Works*. Mountain View, Cal.: Adobe Press, 1993.

Stuart, David, Beryl McAlhone, and Edward de Bono. *A Smile in the Mind*. New York: Phaidon Press, Inc., 1998.

Swann, Alan. *The New Graphic Design School*. New York: John Wiley & Sons, 2000.

Tanaka, Ikko, editor. *Images for Survival*. Washington, D.C.: Shoshin Society, 1985.

Teitelbaum, Matthew, editor. *Montage and Modern Life, 1919–1942*. Cambridge, Mass., and London: MIT Press, 1992.

Thompson, Bradbury. *The Art of Graphic Design*. New Haven and London: Yale University Press, 1988.

Thornton, Richard S. *The Graphic Spirit of Japan*. New York: Van Nostrand Reinhold, 1991.

Troxler, Niklaus. *Jazz Posters*. Schaftlach, Switzerland: Oreos, 1991.

Tschichold, Jan. *The New Typography*. Berkeley: The University of California Press, 1998.

Tufte, Edward R. *Envisioning Information*. Connecticut: Graphics Press, 1990.

Tufte, Edward R. *Visual Explanations: Images and Quantities, Evidence and Narrative*. Connecticut: Graphics Press, 1997.

Tufte, Edward R. *The Visual Display of Quantitative Information*. Connecticut: Graphics Press, 2001.

VanderLans, Rudi, and Zuzana Licko, with Mary E. Gray. *Émigré: Graphic Design into the Digital Realm*. New York: Van Nostrand Reinhold, 1993.

Weingart, Wolfgang. *Typography: My Way to Typography*. Baden: Verlag Lars Müller, 2000.

Werde, Stuart. *The Modern Poster*. New York: Museum of Modern Art, 1988.

West, Suzanne. *Working with Style: Traditional and Modern Approaches to Layout and Typography*. New York: Watson-Guptill, 1990.

Wheeler, Alina. *Designing Brand Identity: A Complete Guide to Creating, Building, and Maintaining Strong Brands*. Hoboken, New Jersey: John Wiley & Sons, Inc., 2003.

Wheeler, Susan, and Wheeler, Gary. *Typesense: Making Sense of Type on the Computer*. Upper Saddle River, N.J.: Prentice Hall, 2001.

Wilde, Judith, and Richard Wilde. *Visual Literacy: A Conceptual Approach to Graphic Problem Solving*. New York: Watson-Guptill, 1991.

Winkler, Dietmar, editor. *Jacqueline S. Casey: 30 Years of Design at MIT*. Cambridge, Mass.: MIT Museum, 1992.

Wozencroft, Jon. *The Graphic Language of Neville Brody*. London: Thames and Hudson, 1988.

Zapf, Hermann. *Manuale Typographicum*. Cambridge, Mass. and London, England: The MIT Press, 1970.

Other Resources

Albrecht, Donald, Ellen Lupton, and Steven Skov Holt. *Design Culture Now: National Design Triennial.* New York: Princeton Architectural Press, 2000.

Bierut, Michael, William Drenttel, Steven Heller, and D. K. Holland, editors. *Looking Closer: Critical Writings on Graphic Design.* New York: Allworth Press, 1994.

————, editors. *Looking Closer 2: Critical Writings on Graphic Design.* New York: Allworth Press, 1997.

Bierut, Michael, Jessica Helfand, Steven Heller, and Rick Poynor, editors. *Looking Closer 3: Classic Writings on Graphic Design.* New York: Allworth Press, 1999.

Bierut, Michael, William Drenttel, and Steven Heller, editors. *Looking Closer 4: Critical Writings on Graphic Design.* New York: Allworth Press, 2002.

Blauvelt, Andrew, editor. "New Perspectives: Critical Histories of Graphic Design," 3 parts. *Visible Language* 28(3), 28(4), 29(1): 1994–95.

Chappell, Warren, and Robert Bringhurst. *A Short History of the Printed Word,* Revised Edition. Vancouver, BC: Hartley & Marks Publishers, 1999.

Drew, John T., and Ned Drew. *Design Education in Progress: Process and Methodology,* volume 1: *Typography.* Richmond: Center for Design Studies, Virginia Commonwealth University, 1998.

————. *Design Education in Progress: Process and Methodology,* volume 2: *Type and Image.* Richmond: Center for Design Studies, Virginia Commonwealth University, 2001.

Helfand, Jessica. *Paul Rand: American Modernist.* Falls River, Conn.: William Drenttel New York, 1998.

Heller, Steven, editor. *The Education of a Graphic Designer.* New York: Allworth Press, 1998.

Heller, Steven, and Julie Lasky. *Borrowed Design: Use and Abuse of Historical Form.* New York: Van Nostrand Reinhold, 1993.

Heskett, John. *Toothpicks and Logos: Design in Everyday Life.* Oxford: Oxford University Press, 2002.

Holland, D. K., editor. *Design Issues: How Graphic Design Informs Society.* New York: Allworth Press, 2001.

Kinross, Robin. *Modern Typography: An Essay in Critical History*. London: Hypen Press, 1992.

——. *Fellow Readers: Notes on Multiplied Language*. London: Hypen Press, 1994.

Klein, Naomi. *No Logo: Taking Aim at Brand Bullies*. New York: Picador USA, 2000.

Lasn, Kalle. *Culture Jam: How to Reverse America's Suicidal Consumer Binge—and Why We Must*. New York: Quill, 2000.

Lavin, Maud. *Clean New World: Culture, Politics, and Graphic Design*. Cambridge, Mass.: MIT Press, 2001.

Lupton, Ellen. *Mixing Messages: Graphic Design in Contemporary Culture*. New York: Princeton Architectural Press, 1996.

Lupton, Ellen, and J. Abbott Miller. *Design, Writing, Research*. New York: Princeton Architectural Press, 1996.

McLuhan, Marshall, and Quentin Fiore. *The Medium is the Massage: An Inventory of Effects*. San Francisco: HardWired, 1996.

McLuhan, Marshall. *Understanding Media: The Extensions of Man*. Cambridge, Mass. and London, England: The MIT Press, 1995.

Ockerse, Thomas, and el. *Spirals '91*. Providence, R.I.: Rhode Island School of Design, 1991.

Postman, Neil. *Technopoly: The Surrender of Culture to Technology*. New York: Vintage Books, 1993.

Poynor, Rick. *Design Without Boundaries: Visual Communication in Transition*. London: Booth-Clibborn Editions, 1998.

Rothschild, Deborah, Ellen Lupton, and Darra Goldstein. *Graphic Design in the Mechanical Age: Selections from the Merrill C. Berman Collection*. New Haven and London: Yale University Press, 1998.

Thompson, Ellen Mazur. *The Origin of Graphic Design in America, 1870-1920*. New Haven and London: Yale University Press, 1997.

Williams, Theo Stephan. *Creative Utopia: 12 Ways to Realize Total Creativity*. Cincinnati: How Books, 2002.

Wurman, Richard. *Information Anxiety 2*. Indianapolis: QUE, 2001.

Yelavich, Susan. *Design for Life*. New York: Rizzoli, 1997.

Recommended Periodicals

Adbusters, Canada

Baseline, England

Communication Arts, USA

Design Issues, USA

Eye, England

Graphics International, England

Graphis, USA

How, USA

Idea, Japan

Novum, Germany

Print, USA

Step Inside Design, USA

TipoGrafica, Argentina

Visible Language, USA

Zed, USA

"I don't, indeed can't, teach students to be designers, but I can and do teach attitudes and strategies that help them become designers."
– Malcolm Grear

INSTRUCTOR CONTACT INFORMATION

Judith Aronson
Instructor, Graphic Design
Communications Department
Simmons College
300 The Fenway
Boston, Massachusetts 02115

Kermit Bailey
Associate Professor of Graphic Design
North Carolina State University
College of Design
Campus Box 7701/319A, Brooks Hall
Raleigh, North Carolina 27695-7701

Frank Baseman
Assistant Professor, Graphic Design
Philadelphia University
Graphic Design Communication
School of Architecture and Design
School House Lane & Henry Avenue
Philadelphia, Pennsylvania 19144-5497

Karen Kornblum Berntsen
Associate Professor, Graphic Design
Carnegie Mellon University
School of Design
Margaret Morrison 110
Pittsburgh, Pennsylvania 15213-3890

Tom Briggs
Assistant Professor, Graphic Design
Massachusetts College of Art
621 Huntington Avenue
Boston, Massachusetts 02215

Michael Burke
Professor, Viselle Gestaltung
FH Schwäbisch Gmünd
Hochschule für Gestaltung
Rektor-Klaus-Strasse 100
73525 Schwäbisch, Gmünd, Germany

Gülizar Çepoğlu
Instructor
London College of Printing
School of Graphic Design
Elephant and Castle
London SE1 6SB England

Jan Conradi
Associate Professor of Graphic Design
State University of New York at Fredonia
Department of Visual Arts and New Media
Rockefeller Arts Center
Fredonia, New York 14063

Heather Corcoran
Assistant Professor, Graphic Design
Washington University
School of Art
1 Brookings Drive
Box 1031
St. Louis, Missouri 63130

Kenneth FitzGerald
Assistant Professor of Art
Old Dominion University
Visual Arts Building
Norfolk, Virginia 23529

Lisa Fontaine
Associate Professor of Graphic Design
Iowa State University
Department of Art & Design
College of Design
Ames, Iowa 50011-3092

Jürgen Hefele
Instructor
University of Applied Sciences Augsburg
Department of Design
Communication Design
Multimedia
Henisiusstrasse 1
86152 Augsburg
Germany

Arnold A. Holland
Assistant Professor, Graphic Design
California State University, Fullerton
P.O. Box 6850
Fullerton, California 92834-6850

Esen Karol
Associate Professor
Mimar Sinan University
Graphic Design Department
Meclis-i Mebusan Caddesi
Findikli 34430 Istanbul
Turkey

Hyunmee Kim
Assistant Professor
Samsung Art and Design Institute (SADI)
Bojun Bldg. East 70-13
Nonhyun-dong Kangnam-ku
Seoul 135-010 Korea

Susan Merritt
Associate Professor of Graphic Design
San Diego State University
School of Art, Design and Art History
College of Professional Studies and Fine Arts
5500 Campanile Drive
San Diego, California 92182-4805

Peggy Re
Assistant Professor, Visual Arts
University of Maryland, Baltimore County
1000 Hilltop Circle
Baltimore, Maryland 21250

Elizabeth Resnick (author)
Chair, Communication Design
Massachusetts College of Art
621 Huntington Avenue
Boston, Massachusetts 02115

Hank Richardson
President
Portfolio Center
125 Bennett Street
Atlanta, Georgia 30309

Carol Sogard
Assistant Professor, Graphic Design
University of Utah
Department of Art and Art History
375 South 1530 East, Room 161
Salt Lake City, Utah 84112

Richard C. Ybarra
The Art Institute of California
10025 Mesa Rim Road
San Diego, California 92121-2913

INDEX

About the Author

Elizabeth Resnick is currently the Chair of the Communication Design Department at the Massachusetts College of Art, Boston, where she has taught since 1977. She holds both a B.F.A. and M.F.A. in Graphic Design from the Rhode Island School of Design, Providence.

Elizabeth is the principal in Elizabeth Resnick Design, and currently the art co-director for *Art New England* magazine, a regional arts publication. She serves on the Board of Directors of AIGA Boston chapter and has organized numerous graphic design lectures and exhibitions since 1990. She is a design curator and has organized three large exhibitions: Russell Mills: Within/Without (1991) with Teresa Flavin; Dutch Graphic Design: 1918-1945 (1994) with Alston W. Purvis; and Makoto Saito: Art of the Poster (1999) with Jan Kubasiewicz.

Her publications include *"Graphic Design: A Problem-Solving Approach to Visual Communication"*, Prentice-Hall Publications (1984). She writes short critical commentaries and event reviews, and has published full-length interviews with designers and design educators in EYE (England), Graphis (USA), AIGA Journal of Graphic Design (USA), Graphics International (England), TipoGrafica (Argentina) and IDEA Magazine (Japan).